PACEMAKER®

General
Science

Third Edition

GLOBE FEARON

Pearson Learning Group

Reviewers

We thank the following educators, who provided valuable comments and suggestions during the development of this book:

Philip Altshuler, River Ridge Middle/High School, New Port Richey, Florida
Anthony Arbino, Woodward High School, Cincinnati Public Schools, Cincinnati, Ohio
Shirley Johnson-Young, Memorial Middle School, Houston, Texas
Martha Kelly, Belleville Middle School, Belleville, New Jersey
Dorie Knaub, Downey Unified School District, Downey, California

Subject Area Consultants:
Gregory L. Vogt, Ed.D, Aerospace Education Specialist, Oklahoma State University. Dr. Vogt has degrees in General Science, Earth Science, and Aerospace Education. He taught science in the Milwaukee Public Schools, helped design and run the Discovery World Museum of Science, Economics, and Technology in Milwaukee, and is now part of the Teaching from Space Program at NASA's Johnson Space Center in Houston, Texas.
Dr. Lisa K. Wagner, Director of Education/Associate Professor South Carolina Botanical Garden, Clemson University, Clemson, South Carolina

Pacemaker Curriculum Advisor: Stephen C. Larsen, formerly of the University of Texas at Austin

Executive Editor: Eleanor Ripp; *Supervising Editor:* Stephanie Petron Cahill; *Lead Editor:* Maury Solomon; *Editor:* Theresa McCarthy; *Production Editor:* Laura Benford-Sullivan; *Assistant Editor:* Kathy Bentzen; *Designers:* Susan Brorein, Jennifer Visco; *Market Manager:* Katie Kehoe Erezuma; *Research Director:* Angela Darchi; *Cover Design:* Susan Brorein, Jennifer Visco; *Editorial, Design and Production Services:* Navta Associates; *Electronic Composition:* Linda Bierniak, Phyllis Rosinsky, Jeff Wickersty

About the Cover: Science is the study of everything in the universe, from Earth's moon to the farthest galaxies, from the motion of atoms to the forces on a roller coaster. The images on the cover of this book show areas of life science, physical science, and earth science. In life science, you study living things, such as plants and animals. In physical science, you study motion and forces, such as those affecting a roller coaster. In earth science, you study things on the Earth and in space, such as oceans and moons. You also learn about the skills and tools used to carry out scientific investigation, such as the microscope.

ISBN: 0-130-23434-6
Printed in the United States of America
 6 7 8 9 10   05 04

1-800-321-3106
www.pearsonlearning.com

Contents

A Note to the Student

Science is the voice of the past and the language of the future. Science has showed us how to feed millions of people. It has helped us to fight off diseases with medicines and vaccines. It has helped to transport people around the world, to the moon, and beyond. Science will certainly help us meet many of the challenges of the future.

Science has done a lot. However, there is still much more to do. We have cured many diseases, but there are still many left to find cures for. We have been to the moon, yet we still need to learn about other planets in our solar system—perhaps even travel to Mars. We have created fast and powerful computers, yet we are always looking for ways to improve them.

By studying science, you are making a place for yourself in the future. Science creates more and more jobs every day. People are needed to run, fix, and program computers. They are needed to protect our forests. They are needed to work in hospitals and laboratories, to keep the environment clean and safe, and to grow food.

This book teaches about three different areas of science: life science, physical science, and earth science. You will learn about living things, including plants and animals. You will study motion and forces, such as those that affect a thrown baseball and a roller coaster racing along on its track. You will come to better understand the features of the Earth, including its oceans and moon. When you finish this book, you will be prepared to continue studying any field of science you choose. You will be on the road to success in the 21st century.

Throughout the book you will find notes in the margins of the pages. Sometimes they give you information about material that you are learning. Often they provide fascinating science facts. A few will remind you of something you already know.

There are several study aids in the book. The beginning of every chapter contains Learning Objectives. These can help you focus on the important points in the chapter. A Words to Know list gives you a look ahead at some of the science vocabulary you will come across in your reading. The colorful photos, drawings, and diagrams in each chapter will help to bring science and its concepts to life. There are special features in each chapter, such as the Lab Activity, On-the-Job Science, and Science in Your Life. The Lab Activity gives you a chance for hands-on experiences using concepts and information you are studying in the chapter. On-the-Job Science introduces some interesting jobs and careers in the science field. You might consider some of these opportunities when thinking about your future. Science in Your Life relates science to everyday life. On these pages, you will read about such things as wind chill temperature and kitchen tools. These may be things you never thought were related to science in any way. At the end of each lesson and chapter, you will find reviews to help you recall important concepts. Finally, you will find lesson summaries of each chapter.

We hope you enjoy reading and learning about the amazing world of science. Everyone who put this book together has worked hard to make it useful and interesting. The rest is up to you. We wish you well in your studies. Your success is our greatest accomplishment.

Unit 1 ▶ The Wonders of Science

Chapter 1 What Is Science?

Chapter 2 The Process of Discovery

Scientists study tornadoes to learn how to predict their behavior.

Scientists study known facts and try to discover new facts. The basic steps in the science process, which is used by scientists to uncover new facts, are listed in the chart. Scientists perform different activities to carry out those steps.

Use the chart to answer the questions.

1. What are the steps of the science process?

2. Which step has measuring as an activity?

3. What is the last step of the science process?

The Science Process	
Basic Steps	**Examples From a Study on Tornadoes**
1. Describe a problem.	Find highest tornado wind speed.
2. Gather information.	Check science journals.
3. Suggest an answer.	Tornado winds can reach speeds of 200 miles per hour.
4. Perform experiments.	Measure tornado winds, using special instruments.
5. Draw conclusions and report results.	Tornado winds can reach speeds of at least 300 miles per hour.

Chapter 1

What Is Science?

This scientist is looking at stars that are trillions of miles away. Scientists study many things here on Earth and far away. What are some of the things you think scientists study?

Learning Objectives

- Define science and identify what scientists do.
- Describe what the universe consists of.
- Explain the science process.
- Explore the meaning and uses of technology.
- List the three main branches of science.
- Identify two careers in science.
- **LAB ACTIVITY**: Observe and describe common objects.
- **SCIENCE IN YOUR LIFE**: List examples of technology.

Words to Know

science	the study of nature and the universe
universe	all that exists, including the planets, sun, stars, and space
galaxy	a very large group of stars that travel together through space
atom	the smallest part of a substance that can still be recognized as that substance
observation	the careful study of something
experiment	a kind of test that scientists use to discover or prove something
research	to study a subject, usually using books and doing experiments
technology	science discoveries and skills that are put to use
laser	a device that produces a narrow, strong beam of light
life science	the study of living things and how they behave
physical science	the study of matter and energy
earth science	the study of the Earth, including its rocks, oceans, air, and weather; also the study of the sun, moon, planets, and stars
matter	anything that takes up space
energy	the ability of something or someone to do work or produce heat

From Atoms to Galaxies

Words to Know

science	the study of nature and the universe
universe	all that exists, including the planets, sun, stars, and space
galaxy	a very large group of stars that travel together through space
atom	the smallest part of a substance that can still be recognized as that substance
observation	the careful study of something
experiment	a kind of test that scientists use to discover or prove something
research	to study a subject, usually using books and doing experiments

Amazing Facts

Imagine that you are outside on a clear night. You look up. What do you see? Stars, of course. You can see hundreds or even thousands of them. Actually, you are seeing the stars as they were many years ago.

The stars are so far away that it takes years for their light to reach the Earth. In fact, some of the stars you see may not exist anymore! They may have burned themselves out long ago. Yet, the light they once gave off is still traveling through space. This is one of the amazing facts of **science**, the study of nature and the **universe**. The universe is all that exists, including the planets, sun, stars, and space.

Another amazing science fact is that at this moment, you are covered with tiny living creatures. They snack on pieces of dead skin. These eight-legged animals are called *mites*. Some even live on your eyelids. Science is filled with amazing facts.

✓ **What is science?**

Understanding the Universe

Scientists try to make sense of things in the universe. They study very large objects, such as galaxies. A **galaxy** is a very large group of stars that travel together through space.

Scientists also try to understand the smallest objects in the universe. Galaxies and all other objects in the universe are made up of tiny particles called atoms. An **atom** is the smallest part of a substance that can still be recognized as that substance. Atoms are so tiny that you cannot see them with your eyes alone. Scientists must use special instruments to study atoms.

✓ **What do scientists study to make sense of things in the universe?**

Science as Facts and Processes

Science has two parts. The first part is the knowledge that scientists have already gathered. This includes many science facts. An example of a science fact is that plants need sunlight to grow.

The second part of science is the process of discovery. By reading this book, you are taking part in the process of discovery.

The process of discovery is the way people learn new facts. It is a series of steps leading from one discovery to another.

For example, a scientist may make an **observation** and may then perform an **experiment**. An observation is the careful study of something. An experiment is a kind of test that scientists use to discover or prove something. Based on observations and results of experiments, scientists draw *conclusions*. This is how scientists discover new facts.

✓ **What are the two parts of science?**

Science Fact

Scientists once thought that the atom was the tiniest thing in the universe. Now they know that the atom is made up of even smaller parts.

Science Fact

Scientists are expected to report the results of their experiments honestly and accurately. This is part of what is known as science ethics. Science ethics is a set of rules for acting in a responsible and caring way when doing science.

Facts that Change

Many people think science is only facts. They think that once scientists discover a fact, there is little left to learn about the fact. However, in science, facts are always changing. For example, people used to believe that the Earth was flat. They thought that they had good reason to believe this. Of course, now we know that the Earth is round. A new fact was discovered, and an old fact is no longer believed to be true.

Figure 1-1 *At one time, people believed that the Earth was flat. They thought that ships fell off the Earth when they reached its edge.*

The Greek philosopher Aristotle was one of the first people to do scientific **research** on plants and animals. To research a subject is to study it, usually using books and doing experiments. Research is the testing of old facts to discover something new. Aristotle lived more than 2,000 years ago. He made many discoveries. He also made some mistakes. For example, he observed that male horses have more teeth than female horses. So he decided that men have more teeth than women have!

Aristotle was not a bad scientist. Two thousand years ago, science was still very young. Scientists were just beginning to learn how to do research. For his time, Aristotle was a great scientist. His work led to many discoveries by scientists who followed him.

✓ **Why do facts in science change?**

Lesson Review

1. What does the universe contain?

2. What do scientists study?

3. What is an experiment? How do scientists do research?

4. CRITICAL THINKING Suppose you have a houseplant that you want to plant outside. You do not know if it can live outside. How could you find out?

Great Moments in Science

THE FIRST LIQUID-FUELED ROCKET
In 1926, the American scientist Robert H. Goddard launched the first rocket to use liquid fuel. It burned gasoline and liquid oxygen. The rocket reached a height of 41 feet (12.5 meters) and traveled at a speed of 60 miles (96 kilometers) per hour.

Goddard's invention made spaceflight possible. Today, liquid-fueled rockets are used to launch spacecraft that explore the planets. They also launch the space shuttle. Scientists perform experiments in the space shuttle. Other spacecraft gather information about the Earth and other objects in space. They also receive and send signals that are used by televisions and telephones.

The work of Robert H. Goddard led to the space shuttle.

CRITICAL THINKING How was Goddard's invention important to the exploration of space?

Words to Know

technology	science discoveries and skills that are put to use
laser	a device that produces a narrow, strong beam of light
life science	the study of living things and how they behave
physical science	the study of matter and energy
earth science	the study of the Earth, including its rocks, oceans, air, and weather; also the study of the sun, moon, planets, and stars
matter	anything that takes up space
energy	the ability of something or someone to do work or produce heat

Science as Solution

Laser beam

Every day, new scientific discoveries are making life better for the world. **Technology** is science discoveries and skills that are put to use. Technology helps to solve problems or make life better for people. The following paragraphs describe a few problems that technology has solved.

For many years, people used tape cassettes to record music. However, when the music was played, background noise could sometimes be heard. Another problem was that the tape eventually wore out. So scientists and engineers came up with a new technology for recording and playing music. It uses a metal-coated plastic disc instead of tape. It is called a *compact disc* or *CD*. A beam of light inside a CD player plays the music. The beam of light is very narrow and very strong. A device called a **laser** produces a narrow, strong beam of light. Music played from a compact disc is always sharp and clear. There is no background noise, and the discs rarely wear out.

Braille is a system of writing for the blind. It was invented by Louis Braille, a Frenchman who himself was blind. Braille consists of a code of 63 characters. Each character is made up of one to six raised dots. Many books have been translated into Braille. The process, however, takes a lot of time and is expensive. To solve this problem, a new machine was invented called the Kurzweil Personal Reader. This machine uses an electronic device that reads the print on a page. Then a computer voice says the printed words aloud. Blind people can use the Kurzweil Personal Reader to read anything in print.

Cassava is an important food crop in Africa. Several million Africans eat this root. In the early 1970s, mealybugs were brought to Africa by accident from South America. They began attacking the cassava crops. Scientists searched for a way to stop the bugs. They went to South America to look for a natural enemy of the bug. They brought back to Africa a wasp that feeds on the mealybug. In this way, scientists saved the food supply for millions of people.

✓ **How does technology help people?**

The Branches of Science

Science is a large area of study. In this book, you will study the three main branches of science: **life science**, **physical science**, and **earth science**.

Life science is the study of living things and how they behave. Life scientists study plants, animals—including humans—and other living things.

Physical science is the study of **matter** and **energy**. Matter is anything that takes up space. Matter can be in solid, liquid, or gas form. Physical scientists study matter. They also study forms of energy such as light, heat, and electricity. Energy is the ability of something or someone to do work or produce heat. Finally, physical scientists study how machines work.

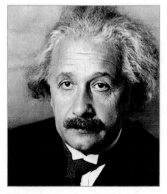

The great physical scientist Albert Einstein (1879–1955) made important discoveries about matter and energy.

Earth science is the study of the Earth, including its rocks, oceans, air, and weather. It is also the study of the sun, moon, planets, and stars.

✓ **What are the three main branches of science?**

Careers in Science

Science is one of the fastest-growing career fields in the world. There are science-related jobs in medicine, farming, computers, forestry, and building, among others.

People with science backgrounds work in zoos, factories, laboratories, hospitals, and parks. In fact, just about every industry uses scientists for at least some of its work.

Not all people who work in science have college degrees. You can work in many science-related jobs with a high school diploma and on-the-job training.

✓ **Where can people with science backgrounds find jobs?**

Modern Leaders in Science

RITA ROSSI COLWELL

In 1998, Rita Rossi Colwell became the director of the National Science Foundation (NSF). NSF is a government agency that gives money for science research. It also supports science museums. NSF helps teachers improve science courses in elementary schools and high schools. Dr. Colwell's job includes deciding what science projects the government should support. She has done research and has written many articles and books.

CRITICAL THINKING Why does Dr. Colwell need to decide which science projects to support?

Rita Rossi Colwell

Making the Right Choices

The technologies you read about earlier in this chapter all helped to solve problems. The solutions took a long time to come up with, however. Millions of dollars were spent. Thousands of people had to make choices about which research to support and how to pay for it.

Science today is practiced mostly by groups of people working together. Once in a while, a brilliant scientist working alone makes a big discovery. More often, though, a lot of people are involved in making the discovery.

This is where you come in. Even if you do not choose a career in science, you can help choose what projects should be supported. Should tax money be spent on new weapons or to grow more food? Should it be spent finding a cure for AIDS or on cancer research?

Now, more than ever, it is important for people to know something about science. As a citizen, you can help make the right choices.

✓ **How are most choices in science made today?**

Lesson Review

1. What are two ways technology has made life better?

2. What kinds of things are studied in life science, earth science, and physical science?

3. Why is it important that people today know about science?

4. **CRITICAL THINKING** You already know many science facts. Name one science fact from each of the three branches of science.

LAB ACTIVITY
Making Observations

BACKGROUND
One of the ways scientists make new discoveries is by observing. Scientists make observations by looking at things closely. They also make observations by listening, feeling, and smelling.

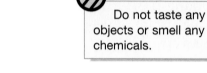

Safety Alert

Do not taste any objects or smell any chemicals.

PURPOSE
You will make careful observations to accurately describe objects.

MATERIALS
paper, pencil, hand lens, 5 classroom objects

WHAT TO DO
1. Copy the chart to the right.
2. Work with a partner. Choose four classroom objects to observe. List the objects in the chart.
3. For each object, observe the characteristics listed in the chart. Use a hand lens to observe the objects close up. Record your observations in the chart.

Object	Size	Shape	Color	Texture	Other Observations
Mystery Object:					

4. Choose a "mystery" object in the classroom to observe. Describe the object, but do not say what the object is. Have your partner record what he or she thinks the object is based on your descriptions. Switch roles and try to guess your partner's mystery object.

DRAW CONCLUSIONS
- How did your observations help you describe each object?

- Did you identify your partner's mystery object? What other observations or descriptions would have made the object easier to identify?

SCIENCE IN YOUR LIFE
Using Technology

Technology can make life easier. For example, it is less work to wash laundry in a washing machine than by hand.

You can save time by using technology. Airplanes transport people across the country in just a few hours. Microwave ovens allow you to make dinner faster.

Today, people are safer because of technology. Smoke alarms help protect you from fires. Air bags in cars help protect you in accidents.

Finally, technology can make your life more fun or more interesting. Think of how video games, CD players, and computers might make your life more fun.

Although technology helps people, it also can do harm. For example, cars and trucks pollute the air. Chemicals from factories are dumped into lakes and rivers. Computers and machines now do some work that people were once paid to do. However, most people feel that technology has made life better.

Make a technology chart.

The chart above shows some examples of technology. In a similar chart, list five other examples. Next to each example, tell how that technology makes your life better. Does it make your life easier, safer, or more fun? Does it save you time?

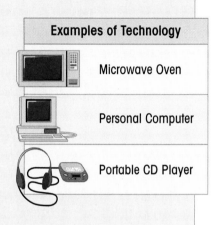

Examples of Technology	
	Microwave Oven
	Personal Computer
	Portable CD Player

Critical Thinking

Choose one of the examples of technology in your chart. How do you think people in the past got along without that technology?

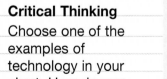

Chapter

1 ▷ Review

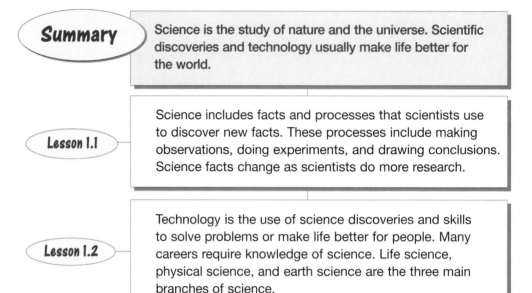

Summary Science is the study of nature and the universe. Scientific discoveries and technology usually make life better for the world.

Lesson 1.1 Science includes facts and processes that scientists use to discover new facts. These processes include making observations, doing experiments, and drawing conclusions. Science facts change as scientists do more research.

Lesson 1.2 Technology is the use of science discoveries and skills to solve problems or make life better for people. Many careers require knowledge of science. Life science, physical science, and earth science are the three main branches of science.

Vocabulary Review

Complete each sentence with a term from the list.

universe

observation

experiment

research

technology

science

galaxy

earth science

1. As part of their _____, scientists may do experiments.

2. A _____ is a very large group of stars that travel together through space.

3. The study of nature and the universe is called _____.

4. The branch of science that studies rocks, weather, and oceans is _____.

5. The sun, planets, and stars are part of the _____.

6. Scientists use a test called an _____ to discover or prove something.

7. When scientists study something carefully, they are making an _____.

8. Using science discoveries and skills to make life better is called _____.

Chapter Quiz

Write your answers on a separate sheet of paper.

1. What makes up the universe?

2. Why must scientists use special instruments to study atoms?

3. What is the process of discovery?

4. How do scientists discover new facts?

5. What are three examples of technology in your home?

6. How does technology help people?

7. What do life scientists study?

8. What do physical scientists study?

9. What are two careers in science?

10. Why is it helpful to know about science?

Test Tip
Make sure you understand what each test question is asking. Read a question twice before you answer it.

Research Project

Do research and write a report on a science-related career. You might gather information by using books from the library and using the Internet. You can also set up interviews. The report should describe the career and tell the skills that a person needs to do the job. Also include the amount of education or training needed. Tell about how much the job pays.

Scientists study practically everything, from rocks to the human body. Can you think of anything that scientists do not study?

Learning Objectives

- Explain the five steps of the scientific method.
- Identify metric units of length, volume, and weight.
- Describe equipment used in a science laboratory.
- Discuss safety rules for work in the laboratory.
- LAB ACTIVITY: Measure the length and volume of objects.
- ON-THE-JOB SCIENCE: Explore the duties of a medical lab technician.

Words to Know

procedure	a plan that is used to complete a task
scientific method	a step-by-step procedure that scientists use to do experiments and make new discoveries
hypothesis	a possible answer to a problem
measurement	the size or the amount of something
unit	an amount that is used by everyone when measuring a particular thing
metric unit	a unit of measurement that is based on the number ten and multiples of ten
meter	the basic metric unit of length
area	the number of square units that is needed to cover a surface
volume	the number of cubic units that is needed to fill a space
liter	a metric unit used to measure volume of a liquid or gas
mass	the amount of matter in something
gram	the basic metric unit of mass
laboratory	a place with equipment that people use to do science
microscope	an instrument used to study very small objects; it makes them appear much larger

The Scientific Method

Words to Know

procedure	a plan that is used to complete a task
scientific method	a step-by-step procedure that scientists use to do experiments and make new discoveries
hypothesis	a possible answer to a problem

The Five Steps

In ancient times, people thought the sun was a god. Somehow they knew that without the sun's light and heat, life on Earth would be impossible. Today we know that the sun is a star. We also know that stars are big, hot balls of glowing gas. We know these things from the work of scientists.

Remember
The process of discovery includes observing, testing, and drawing conclusions.

Scientists have used the process of discovery to learn about stars. They learned that the sun is about 93 million miles (about 150 million kilometers) away. They also found out that the sun is not a very special star. Its size and temperature are about average.

Scientists use a step-by-step **procedure** to do experiments and make new discoveries. A procedure is a plan that is used to complete a task. This step-by-step procedure is often called the **scientific method.** As you saw earlier, it is also called the science process.

The scientific method has five steps. Each step is listed below and explained on the next page.

1. Describe the problem.
2. Gather information.
3. Suggest an answer.
4. Perform experiments.
5. Draw conclusions and report the results.

1. Describe the problem.

There are many, many problems that can be studied in science, from the common cold to exploding stars.

2. Gather information.

Suppose a scientist wants to find a cure for the common cold. He or she might read books and articles on colds, talk to other scientists, and use the Internet to do research.

3. Suggest an answer.

After doing research, the scientist suggests a **hypothesis**, which is a possible answer to the problem. For example, the scientist might suggest that vitamin C will cure the common cold.

4. Perform experiments.

Now, the scientist must set up an experiment to test the hypothesis. To test the effect of vitamin C, he or she might use twenty people with colds. Ten will be given vitamin C. Ten will be given nothing. Then the scientist observes the people for a certain length of time. This test may be repeated several times. Later, other scientists might repeat the test to see if they get the same results.

5. Draw conclusions and report the results.

Finally, the scientist draws conclusions and writes up the results of the tests that were performed. Charts or graphs may be used to report the results.

✓ **What are the five steps of the scientific method?**

Continuing the Process

Usually, the results of one experiment lead to another experiment. In the common-cold experiment, ten people were given vitamin C. Most of them got over their colds more quickly than usual. However, some did not get well faster. The scientist now wants to know why taking vitamin C does not work every time.

Science Fact

Scientists can test how changes in conditions affect an experiment. These changes are called *variables*. To test only certain variables, a *control* group can be set up. For the control group, these variables do not change. Scientists can then compare results of the actual experiment with results from the control group.

Science Fact

Scientists have to make *inferences* from what they observe in an experiment. An inference is how you explain what you observe. Inferences help scientists draw their conclusions.

The scientist repeats the experiment. This time, he or she pays special attention to those people who take vitamin C but do not get better faster. The scientist notices that these people do not sleep much during the experiment. The scientist then performs another experiment to test how sleep affects the common cold.

Figuring out cause and effect is an important part of the scientific method. So are observation, testing, and continuing the process of questioning. There is always more to explore.

✓ **Why does one experiment often lead to another?**

Lesson Review

1. What is the scientific method used for?

2. What step follows making a hypothesis?

3. CRITICAL THINKING Why is it important that scientists gather information about a problem?

On the Cutting Edge

ARTIFICIAL SKIN

Scientists use the scientific method to solve problems. One problem they faced was how to help burn victims. People who get severe burns may need *skin grafts*. A skin graft is a piece of healthy skin that is taken from a person's body and used to cover that person's damaged skin. The grafted skin grows with the healthy skin. However, sometimes the burned area is too large for a graft to work. So scientists made artificial skin.

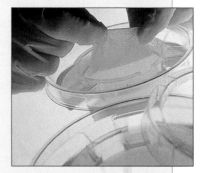

Artificial skin is grown in a dish in a laboratory.

Some artificial skin is made of a protein and human skin cells. When the artificial skin is placed on a wound, it helps the real skin around the wound to grow. Eventually, healthy skin covers the wound, and the artificial skin disappears.

CRITICAL THINKING How is artificial skin better than a skin graft?

Measuring in Science

Words to Know

measurement	the size or the amount of something
unit	an amount that is used by everyone when measuring a particular thing
metric unit	a unit of measurement that is based on the number ten and multiples of ten
meter	the basic metric unit of length
area	the number of square units that is needed to cover a surface
volume	the number of cubic units that is needed to fill a space
liter	a metric unit used to measure volume of a liquid or gas
mass	the amount of matter in something
gram	the basic metric unit of mass

Measurement

Remember
Experiments help scientists to discover new facts.

You need certain skills to perform science experiments. A very important skill is figuring out how big something is or how much it weighs.

Measurement is used to express the size or the amount of something. Your height and weight are measurements of how much of you there is.

A **unit** is an amount that is used by everyone when measuring a particular thing. For example, when people in the United States drive cars, they measure distance in miles. A mile is a unit.

In most countries, however, people do not measure distance in miles. They do not use feet and inches to measure height. They do not use pounds and ounces to measure weight.

Some road signs give speed limits in both miles and kilometers.

Most people in the world use the metric system to measure things. Each **metric unit** is based on the number ten and multiples of ten, such as 100 and 1,000. Scientists all over the world use metric units. This makes it easier for them to share scientific information, even if they speak different languages.

✓ **What are metric units based on?**

Unit of Length

The basic metric unit of length is called a **meter.** It equals 39.4 inches. Most adults are about 1.5 to 2 meters tall.

You know from using money that the word *cent* means $\frac{1}{100}$. A centimeter is $\frac{1}{100}$ of a meter. The prefix *milli-* means $\frac{1}{1,000}$. A millimeter is $\frac{1}{1,000}$ of a meter.

The prefix *kilo-* means 1,000. A kilometer is 1,000 meters. A kilometer is a little more than half a mile.

✓ **What is the basic metric unit of length?**

Units of Area and Volume

Science Fact

To find the area of something, multiply length × width.

To find the volume of a solid, multiply length × width × height.

To find the volume of a liquid, measure using liters.

Area is the number of square units that is needed to cover a surface. This page is about 440 square centimeters, or 68 square inches, in area. The area of the Earth's surface is about 510 million square kilometers. That is about 197 million square miles.

Volume is the number of cubic units that is needed to fill a space. This book is about 870 cubic centimeters, or 53 cubic inches. The **liter** is a metric unit that is used to measure the volume of a liquid or gas. It is a little more than a quart.

Often, scientists work with very small amounts of liquids. They use milliliters to measure small volumes. A milliliter is $\frac{1}{1,000}$ of a liter.

✓ **What metric units are used to measure area and volume?**

Unit of Mass

Mass is the amount of matter in something. An object with more mass is heavier, or weighs more, than an object with less mass. For example, a car has more mass than a bike. The basic metric unit of mass is a **gram.** There are about 28 grams in 1 ounce. A kilogram is equal to 1,000 grams, or about 2.2 pounds. One metric ton is equal to 1,000 kilograms, or about 2,200 pounds.

✓ **What metric unit is used to measure mass?**

Units of Temperature and Time

Most people in the United States use the *Fahrenheit* scale to measure degrees of temperature. However, scientists and most people in the world use the metric unit for temperature, which is degrees *Celsius*.

The metric unit of time is the second. You know that 60 seconds make 1 minute and 60 minutes make 1 hour.

✓ **What are the metric units for temperature and for time?**

Getting a Feel for Metric Measurements

Here are some measurements that may help you become more comfortable using metric units:

- A dime is about one millimeter thick.

- Five city blocks are about one kilometer long.

- The button on a push-button telephone is about one square centimeter in area.

- A little less than three cans of soft drink equal one liter.

- One book from an encyclopedia set weighs about one kilogram.

- Room temperature is about 20 degrees Celsius.

✓ **How can you get more comfortable using metric measurements?**

Most people in the United States use the English system of measurement. This system includes units such as the inch and pound. It was developed in England hundreds of years ago. Today, however, England uses the metric system.

Lesson Review

1. What do measurements tell us?

2. What are meters, liters, and grams?

3. What do the prefixes *centi-*, *milli-*, and *kilo-* mean?

4. CRITICAL THINKING Why would you not measure the thickness of a dime in kilometers?

A Closer Look

THE ATOMIC CLOCK

The clocks and watches that most people use are not always correct, or accurate. Batteries run down. Parts wear out. Even changes in temperature may affect their accuracy. So scientists made a clock that does not use batteries. It is not affected by temperature, either. This clock is an atomic clock.

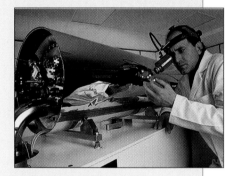

An atomic clock uses atoms to measure time. It does so by measuring the motion of a certain kind of atom. The speed of an atom's motion changes very little over time. For that reason, an atomic clock may gain or lose only one second of time every million years! Since 1958, scientists have used atomic clocks to measure time.

This atomic clock is from the National Institute of Standards and Technology. The long cylinder is the clock.

Today, people can buy wristwatches that are almost as accurate as atomic clocks. These wristwatches receive radio signals from an atomic clock. Radio signals are invisible waves that travel through space. Every day at the same time, the watches reset themselves when they receive the signals.

CRITICAL THINKING Why do scientists use atomic clocks?

Words to Know

laboratory   a place with equipment that people use to do science

microscope   an instrument used to study very small objects; it makes them appear much larger

What Is a Laboratory?

Scientists usually work in a **laboratory**, often just called a lab. A laboratory is a place with equipment that people use to do science. Much of the equipment is for doing experiments, making observations, and taking measurements. For some people, a laboratory is a small room in a hospital. It could also be a tent in the rain forest or even a submarine in the ocean.

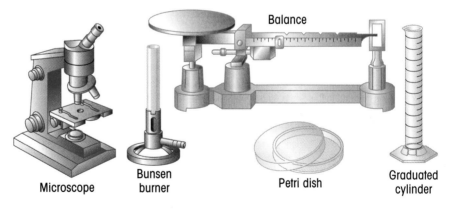

Balance

Microscope   Bunsen burner   Petri dish   Graduated cylinder

Figure 2-1 *Scientists often use this equipment in laboratories.*

Laboratory equipment includes test tubes, chemicals, and instruments, such as a **microscope.** A microscope is used to study objects that are very small. The microscope makes the objects appear much larger than they are.

✓ **How are laboratories used?**

Safety in the Laboratory

Scientists must be very careful while working in a laboratory. For example, working with fire and certain chemicals can be dangerous.

Here are ten important safety rules you should follow when working in a laboratory.

Safety Rules

1. Read all instructions carefully before beginning an experiment. Look at the list of equipment. Be sure you have everything you need.

2. Keep a very clean work area. Do not have anything out that you do not need for the experiment.

3. Always make sure your equipment is in good condition. Never use chipped glass or torn electrical cords.

4. Know how to put out fires and where to find clean, running water.

5. Never taste or touch any substance in the lab unless told to do so by your teacher or book. Do not chew gum or eat or drink anything in the lab. Keep your hands away from your face.

6. Wear eye goggles whenever you are told to do so.

7. Wear a lab apron when working with chemicals to avoid damaging your clothes.

8. Be careful when working with sharp or pointed objects, such as scissors.

9. Follow all instructions exactly.

10. If an accident occurs, tell your teacher immediately.

✓ **Why is it important to follow safety rules in a laboratory?**

Safety Alert

Before you begin work in a lab, look for possible dangers and prepare for them. Make sure there is running water and a first-aid kit nearby. Locate a fire extinguisher and fire exit. Post the phone number of a poison control center and nearby hospital.
Tell an adult what you are doing. When you are done in the lab, put away all chemicals and lab tools.

Lesson Review

1. What are some kinds of equipment you might find in a lab?

2. How can you protect yourself from fires in a lab?

3. **CRITICAL THINKING** Why is it important not to eat or taste anything while working in a lab?

Great Moments in Science

A LUCKY MISTAKE

In 1928, the British scientist Sir Alexander Fleming was studying tiny living things called *bacteria.* He grew the bacteria in small laboratory dishes. Some bacteria are harmful to people and cause disease. Fleming wanted to discover a way to fight these bacteria.

One day, Fleming made a mistake in the laboratory. He set aside a dish containing bacteria and forgot to throw it away. Some mold grew on the dish. Later, Fleming went to throw the dish away. However, something made him stop and look at the mold more closely. He noticed that no bacteria grew near the mold. The mold was killing the bacteria!

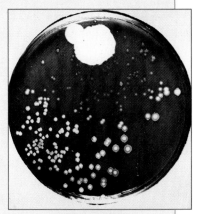

Fleming's Penicillium mold is the large white blob on top. It prevented the spots of bacteria from growing near it.

The mold that Fleming observed is called *Penicillium.* It produces a chemical that kills bacteria. The chemical is called *penicillin.* Today, people use penicillin to fight many diseases that are caused by bacteria. Fleming's mistake led to his greatest discovery. It also showed how important it is to make careful observations and to keep asking questions.

CRITICAL THINKING Why is it important to take careful notes about what happens during an experiment?

LAB ACTIVITY
Metric Measuring

BACKGROUND
Scientists often measure small amounts of things. They may need to measure lengths in millimeters. They may use milliliters for measuring small volumes of liquids.

PURPOSE
You will use a graduated cylinder and a ruler to see the importance of making accurate measurements.

MATERIALS
paper, pencil, metric ruler, book, graduated cylinder, paper cup half filled with water

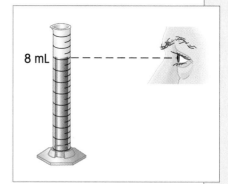

8 mL

To measure volume using a graduated cylinder, check what line the water comes to.

WHAT TO DO
1. Copy the chart to record the length of a book and the volume of water in a cylinder.
2. Work in groups of three. Take turns using the ruler to measure the length of the same side of a book in millimeters. Record your measurement. Be sure to include the units.
3. Choose one group member to pour the water from the cup into the graduated cylinder. Record the milliliter line that lines up with the bottom of the water's curve in the cylinder. (See the drawing.) Pour the water back into the cup.
4. Repeat Step 3 two more times so that each group member has a chance to measure the water's volume.

Object	Measurement
Book	
Water	

DRAW CONCLUSIONS
- Compare the measurements that your group members made. Were any of the measurements different? If so, what might have caused the measurements to be different?
- Why is it a good idea to make more than one measurement of an object?

Alice is a medical lab technician. She works in a hospital laboratory. Alice uses different kinds of lab equipment to perform tests. She uses chemicals, test tubes, microscopes, and other kinds of instruments.

Alice tests the blood and urine of patients. One of the blood tests that Alice performs is called *blood typing*. Every person has one of these types of blood: Type A, Type B, Type AB, or Type O. To find out a person's blood type, Alice mixes a drop of the person's blood with two chemicals called *anti-A serum* and *anti-B serum*. Depending on its type, the blood either clumps or does not clump with each serum. The chart below shows what happens when each type of blood is mixed with each serum.

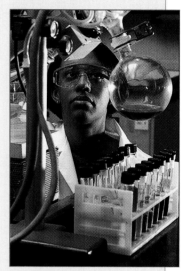

A medical lab technician performs many kinds of tests.

Look at the microscope slide below.

The slide shows two drops of a person's blood that have been mixed with anti-A serum and anti-B serum.

Anti-A	Anti-B
Clumping	No clumping

Blood Type	Anti-A Serum	Anti-B Serum
A	Clumping	No clumping
B	No clumping	Clumping
AB	Clumping	Clumping
O	No clumping	No clumping

Critical Thinking

What qualities might a person need in order to be a good medical lab technician?

1. What blood type does the person have?

2. How do you know?

Summary

Scientists use the scientific method to make new discoveries. This process includes making measurements. Scientists use equipment in labs to gather information.

Lesson 2.1

The five steps in the scientific method are: describing what the problem is, gathering information, suggesting a hypothesis, performing experiments, and drawing conclusions and reporting the results.

Lesson 2.2

Measurement is used to express the size or the amount of something. Most people in the world, and all scientists, use metric units of measurement.

Lesson 2.3

Safety in the laboratory is very important. Always read all the instructions before beginning an experiment. Follow safety rules.

Vocabulary Review

scientific method

volume

procedure

area

meter

liter

gram

microscope

Complete each sentence with a term from the list.

1. The basic metric unit of length is the _____.
2. Scientists use the five steps of the _____ to make new discoveries.
3. A _____ is equal to about one quart.
4. The _____ of an object is the number of square units needed to cover its surface.
5. A _____ is the metric unit that is used to tell how much something weighs.
6. The number of cubic units needed to fill a space is its _____.
7. The scientific method is a step-by-step _____.
8. Scientists use a _____ to look at very small objects.

Chapter Quiz

Write your answers on a separate sheet of paper.

1. What procedure do scientists use to make new discoveries?

2. What are two ways that scientists gather information?

3. Why do scientists perform experiments after suggesting an answer to a problem?

4. Why do all scientists use metric units?

5. How many times larger is a centimeter than a millimeter?

6. How many meters are in a kilometer?

7. What fraction of a gram is a milligram?

8. What equipment would you expect to find in a laboratory?

9. Before beginning an experiment, what should you do with the instructions you have been given?

10. What should you do if an accident occurs in the school laboratory?

Test Tip

Reread your answer to a question before going on to the next question. You may find a way to improve your answer.

Research Project

Research the Celsius scale. You can find information on the Internet at *http://lamar.colostate.edu/~hillger/temps.htm*. Make a chart that compares Celsius temperatures with Fahrenheit temperatures. Then use your chart to give that day's temperature in your area in degrees Celsius and Fahrenheit. Finally, find out the average temperature in the Arctic and near the equator in degrees Celsius and Fahrenheit. Include this information in your chart.

Unit 1 **Review**

Choose the letter for the correct answer to each question.

Use the diagram to answer Questions 1 to 3.

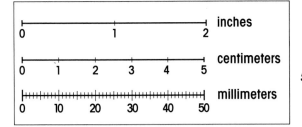

1. An inch is equal to about how many centimeters?

  A. 1

  B. 2.5

  C. 20.5

  D. 4

2. How many millimeters make up one centimeter?

  A. 2.5

  B. 10

  C. 100

  D. 1,000

3. About how many millimeters make up one inch?

  A. 25

  B. 2.5

  C. 10

  D. 1,000

4. What are the two parts of science?

  A. earth science and life science

  B. research and technology

  C. experimenting and recording results

  D. facts and the process of discovery

5. What is physical science mostly the study of

  A. plants and animals

  B. rocks and chemicals

  C. weather and climate

  D. matter and energy

6. Which of the following is not a step of the scientific method?

  A. Perform experiments.

  B. Describe the problem.

  C. Study in the lab.

  D. Suggest an answer.

7. Which of the following is an example of technology?

  A. an atom

  B. a star

  C. a television

  D. the weather

Critical Thinking

Why is it important to check all equipment before beginning an experiment?

Unit 2 ▷ Life Science: Part I

A small waterfall is a favorite place for this grizzly bear to catch fish. Scientists learn about grizzly bears and other animals mostly by observing them where they live.

Use the photo and chart to answer the following questions.

1. What things in the photo would be of most interest to a botanist?

2. What things in the photo would be of most interest to a zoologist?

3. What part of the photo might interest an ecologist the most?

Life Scientists	What They Study
Botanists	Plants
Zoologists	Animals
Ecologists	Interactions between organisms and their environment

Chapter 3 ▷ The Study of Life

This bat has a built-in radar system to hunt for insects in total darkness. What other skills do you think bats and other living things need to survive?

Learning Objectives

- Define five important fields in biology.
- Describe what an organism is.
- Explain the five main characteristics of life.
- Give examples of how an organism responds to its environment.
- Compare the life spans of different organisms.
- **LAB ACTIVITY:** Observe how behavior can be learned.
- **SCIENCE IN YOUR LIFE:** Plan a garden that will bloom from spring through fall.

Words to Know

organism	any living thing or once-living thing
biology	the study of all organisms on Earth, including plants and animals
botany	the study of plant life
zoology	the study of animal life
genetics	the study of how living things pass along certain features of themselves to their offspring
microbiology	the study of organisms too small to be seen with the eye alone
ecology	the study of interactions between organisms and their environment
characteristic	a quality or feature of a person or thing
waste	the part of food that an organism does not need after it uses the food for energy
reproduce	to make more of one's own kind of organism
environment	everything that surrounds you
life span	the amount of time an organism is likely to live

Words to Know

organism	any living thing or once-living thing
biology	the study of all organisms on Earth, including plants and animals
botany	the study of plant life
zoology	the study of animal life
genetics	the study of how living things pass along certain features of themselves to their offspring
microbiology	the study of organisms too small to be seen with the eye alone
ecology	the study of interactions between organisms and their environment

Remember
The Earth is about 93 million miles (150 million kilometers) from the sun.

The Earth is *exactly* the right distance from the sun for us and for all other life on the planet. If the Earth were just 5 percent closer to the sun, the heat would be too great. The oceans would dry up. Life could not exist. If the Earth were just 5 percent farther away from the sun, the whole planet would be completely covered with ice. Life could not exist.

Lucky for us, the Earth is well set up for life. The temperature is right. There is plenty of water. We can breathe the air.

The Variety of Living Things

The Earth is filled with life. Your schoolyard alone is home to millions of plants, animals, and other living things.

A living thing is called an **organism**. Something that once was alive is also called an organism. The study of all the organisms on Earth, including plants and animals, is called **biology**, or life science.

Differences in the sizes and shapes of organisms can be great. The blue whale is about 90 feet (27 meters) long. The adult weighs over 200,000 pounds (90,000 kilograms). This equals almost 23 elephants put together. Giant redwood trees grow to be 300 feet (90 meters) tall. Their trunks can be more than 15 feet (4.5 meters) thick. Millions of living things are so small you cannot see them.

✔ **What is the study of all the organisms on Earth?**

Dividing Up Life Science

Life science is a very big field of study. It is divided into a number of smaller fields. There are five important ones. Most life scientists choose only one of these fields to work in.

Botany is the study of plant life. **Zoology** is the study of animal life. **Genetics** is the study of how living things pass along certain features of themselves to their offspring. **Microbiology** is the study of organisms too small to be seen with the eye alone. **Ecology** is the study of interactions between organisms and their environment.

✔ **What are the five major fields of life science, or biology?**

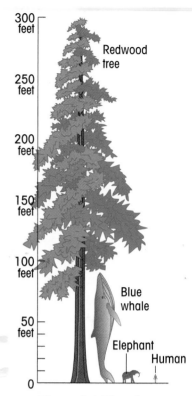

Figure 3-1 *The sizes of different organisms vary.*

Lesson Review

1. What would happen if the Earth were closer to or farther from the sun?

2. In what ways do organisms differ from one another?

3. What do people study in microbiology?

4. CRITICAL THINKING About how many times longer is a blue whale than a person? Use Figure 3-1.

On the Cutting Edge

IS THERE LIFE ON OTHER PLANETS?

SETI stands for Search for Extraterrestrial Intelligence. The SETI league is made up of scientists who believe there may be life on other planets. Presently the SETI league has two projects: Project Argus and Project Phoenix. Both projects use powerful telescopes to search the skies for radio waves.

Project Argus's telescopes search the whole sky. Project Phoenix's telescopes search only around nearby stars that are like the sun. Scientists hope that somewhere beyond the Earth, intelligent beings are sending out messages. The radio telescopes may pick up these messages.

Some scientists search for life on planets in the Andromeda galaxy. It is one of the closest galaxies to the Milky Way galaxy.

At first, most people thought SETI was a foolish idea. Today many scientists suspect that there may be life on other planets. The universe is so huge, and other planets and solar systems have been detected.

CRITICAL THINKING What might scientists think if a telescope picked up a radio signal from outer space?

What Is Life?

Words to Know

characteristic	a quality or feature of a person or thing
waste	the part of food that an organism does not need after it uses the food for energy
reproduce	to make more of one's own kind of organism
environment	everything that surrounds you
life span	the amount of time an organism is likely to live

All animals, such as this orangutan, need to eat to survive.

The Characteristics of Life

A **characteristic** is a quality or feature of a person or thing. Characteristics make one living thing different from another. A few of your characteristics include your hair color, height, shape, and personality type.

All living things share at least five important characteristics. Humans share these characteristics with blue whales, weeds, mushrooms, and every other organism on Earth. All living things have these characteristics:

1. They get and use food for energy.

2. They move.

3. They grow.

4. They reproduce.

5. They respond to their environment.

✓ **What important characteristics do all organisms share?**

Getting and Using Food

How long would you last without food and water? You might be able to live without food for a few weeks. However, you could not go without water for even four days. All living things must have food and water.

Plants make their own food. They take in water from the ground and carbon dioxide from the air. The sun's energy is used to change water and carbon dioxide into sugar. This sugar is stored in the plant as food. When the plant needs energy, it breaks down this stored food.

Some animals eat plants. Some animals eat other animals for food. Still other animals eat both plants and animals.

The food must be broken down for the organism to use it. Certain parts of the organism and chemicals that the organism produces break down the food. After using the food for energy, the animal must get rid of **waste**. Waste is the part of food that an organism does not need after it uses the food for energy.

✓ **How do plants and animals get and use food?**

Moving

Animals must be able to move. They need to find food. They must be able to move away from danger. They also need to be able to find mates. Different animals move in different ways. Some fly, others walk or run, and still others swim. Plants also move. Their movements, though, are smaller and harder to notice.

Put a green plant in a room with one window. Within a day or two, the plant's leaves will be facing the window. After several days, the whole plant will probably lean toward the window. Plants always move in the direction of sunlight. That is because plants use sunlight to make their own food.

Figure 3-2 *Plants move toward sunlight.*

✓ **Why do animals and plants move?**

Growing

All living things grow. After a certain size is reached, most organisms stop growing. People stop growing taller when they are between 15 and 20 years old. Some trees grow for hundreds of years before reaching their full height.

✓ **Which living things grow?**

Reproducing

All organisms can **reproduce** themselves. This means they are able to make more of their own kind of organism. When a cat has kittens, she has reproduced. When a human has a baby, she has reproduced.

Most animals and plants come from two parents. This is called *sexual reproduction.* Many plants, using sexual reproduction, produce seeds. These seeds fall to the Earth or are carried by wind, water, or animals to a good place to grow.

Smaller organisms often have only one parent. The organism makes a copy of itself, then divides in half. This is called *asexual reproduction.* Some plants and a few animals can also reproduce asexually. New life may grow from a bud or a part of the parent, like a cutting from a leaf or the eye from a potato.

✓ **What are the two main ways organisms reproduce?**

Science Fact

The world's largest organism may be a giant underground fungus. It was discovered in the woods on the Wisconsin-Michigan border in 1992. It covers over 37 acres, weighs over 100 tons, and is still growing.

Responding to the Environment

Everything that surrounds you makes up your **environment.** If you are in the classroom, your environment includes other students. It also includes desks and chairs, paper, a chalkboard, and the air in the room. All the things you see, hear, smell, taste, or feel around you are parts of the environment.

To respond means to react to things in the environment. If a friend grabs your arm, you will respond. You may pull away. You may turn around. You may do any number of things.

All living things respond to their environment. Zebras respond to the sight or smell of lions by running for safety. Garden plants respond to heavy watering by growing deep roots.

✓ **What does it mean to respond?**

A Closer Look

HATCHING TEMPERATURES

Newly hatched green turtles leave their nests on the beach and head for the sea. Whether they are male or female depends on how warm their nest was.

A green turtle hatchling heads for the sea.

Cooler nests (less than 82°F, or 27.7°C) produce males. Warmer nests (greater than 85°F, or 29.4°C) produce females. Nests with in-between temperatures produce both males and females.

Different beaches have different general temperatures. Some beaches produce mostly male turtles. Some produce mostly female turtles. Scientists are working on ways to protect these beaches. That way, there will always be enough green turtles of both sexes.

CRITICAL THINKING Suppose all or most of the beaches that produce female turtles are destroyed. How would this affect the number of green turtles?

How Long Do Organisms Live?

All living things die. However, different organisms have different life spans. A **life span** is the amount of time an organism is likely to live. A mayfly lives its entire adult life in one day. Most small dogs live for about 14 years. The white pine tree lives for almost 500 years. The bristlecone pine tree lives up to 5,000 years.

In the United States, the average human life span is now about 76 years. Earlier this century, the average life span was about 65 years. Progress in medical science and nutrition has helped to lengthen the human life span. Scientists hope that new discoveries will help them find a way to slow down aging. Perhaps by the year 2200, the average life span will be nearly 100 years!

✓ **How are the life spans of organisms different?**

Lesson Review

1. Name two characteristics for each of these living things:
   - tree
   - fish
   - dog
   - flower
   - cow
   - worm

2. What is included in your environment?

3. What two things have helped to lengthen the average human life span?

4. **CRITICAL THINKING** A computer is an amazing thing. Why is it not a living thing?

LAB ACTIVITY
Observing Learning

BACKGROUND

Some of the ways that you respond to your environment are learned. For example, suppose you are raking leaves on a windy day. You quickly learn that it is better to rake with the wind instead of against it. Sometimes, people and other animals learn by trial and error. That means learning by practicing and correcting mistakes.

PURPOSE

You will find out if response time can be improved with practice.

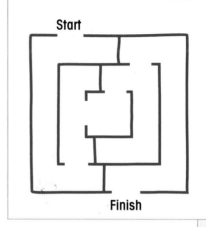

Here is a maze you can try.

MATERIALS

construction paper, pencil, marker, watch or clock with second hand

WHAT TO DO

1. Copy the chart to the right.
2. Copy the maze onto the construction paper.
3. Give your maze to a partner.
4. Time how long your partner takes to move a finger along a path from start to finish. Record the number of minutes and seconds in the chart.
5. Repeat Step 4 three more times.

Number of Tries	Amount of Time
1	
2	
3	
4	

DRAW CONCLUSIONS

- How long did your partner take to go through the maze each time?

- Did the times increase or decrease?

- What do you think caused the differences in times?

SCIENCE IN YOUR LIFE
Plan a Flower Garden

You know that plants respond to sunlight by growing and turning toward the light. The flowers of plants also respond to light.

The blooming, or flowering, of many kinds of plants depends on the lengths of days and nights. Some plants bloom only when days are shorter than the nights. These plants are called short-day plants. Short-day plants flower in spring or fall.

Long-day plants bloom when days are longer than the nights. Long-day plants flower during summer.

Some plants do not respond at all to changes in day length. They flower after several days or weeks of growing. These plants have a long flowering season.

Flower growers can control the flowering time of some plants. For example, mums are short-day plants. They usually bloom in fall, when the days are shorter than the nights. In summer, growers can cover the mums each afternoon. This makes their days shorter than their nights and causes them to bloom.

Use the table, which shows when certain flowers bloom, to answer the questions.

1. What flowers bloom in summer?

2. When do tulips and pansies bloom?

3. Make a map of a small garden. Use symbols to show the location of different flowers in your garden. Make your garden bloom from spring through fall.

Mums are normally short-day plants. They bloom in fall.

Flower	Season It Blooms
Tulip	Spring
Pansy	Spring
Poppy	Summer
Iris	Summer
Carnation	Summer
Mum	Fall
Goldenrod	Fall

Critical Thinking

Suppose a garden included tulips, pansies, and goldenrod. Would the garden have flowers from spring through fall? Explain.

Summary) | Biology, or life science, is the study of organisms.

Lesson 3.1) | Biology is broken down into five smaller fields of study. They are botany, zoology, genetics, microbiology, and ecology.

Lesson 3.2) | All organisms share five important characteristics. All organisms get and use food, move, grow, reproduce, and respond to their environments.

Vocabulary Review

Match each definition with a term from the list.

biology

genetics

microbiology

ecology

waste

reproduce

environment

life span

1. To make more of one's own kind
2. The study of how life's features are passed on to offspring
3. The number of years a type of living thing is likely to live
4. Everything that surrounds you
5. The study of all living things
6. The study of living things that you cannot see with your eye alone
7. The part of food that an organism does not need after it uses the food for energy
8. The study of interactactions between organisms and their environment

Chapter Quiz

Write your answers on a separate sheet of paper.

Test Tip
Some questions ask for a certain number of items, such as five characteristics or three reasons. Be sure to give the correct number of items in your answers.

1. Which of the following are organisms: dog, robot, dead fly, pencil? Explain how you know.

2. What would you study if you took a course in zoology?

3. What field of biology is the study of plants?

4. What five characteristics do you share with every other living thing?

5. What do plants use to make their own food?

6. What are three reasons animals must be able to move?

7. Why must plants be able to move?

8. Why are seeds important for a plant?

9. What are ten things in your environment?

10. Do all organisms have the same life spans? Give an example to explain your answer.

Research Project

Research the kinds of organisms that live in the deep ocean, especially near features called hot-water vents. Write a report on how these organisms are able to survive in such a harsh environment. Include in your report a description of the environment and drawings of the organisms.

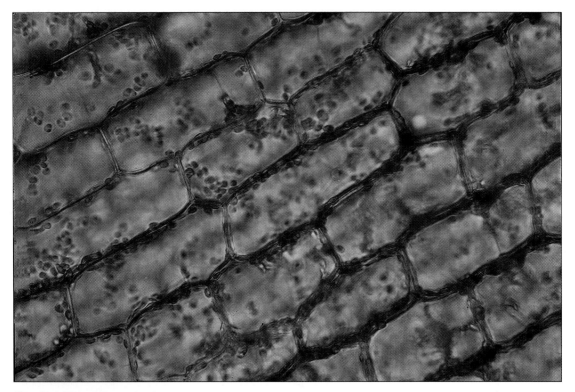

The boxlike objects in the picture might remind you of bricks in a wall. However, these objects are all alive. They make up things you see everyday. What do you think they are? Use the color as a clue.

Learning Objectives

- Explain how Robert Hooke discovered the cell.
- Compare cells, atoms, molecules, and elements.
- Describe the parts of a cell.
- Explain how cells get energy and use it.
- Compare and contrast plant cells and animal cells.
- Describe DNA and its function.
- LAB ACTIVITY: Make models of plant and animal cells.
- ON-THE-JOB SCIENCE: Compare normal cells and cancer cells.

Words to Know

cell	the smallest, most basic unit of life
element	matter that is made of only one kind of atom
chemical bond	a force that holds atoms together
molecule	two or more atoms that are joined by chemical bonds
cytoplasm	the watery substance in a cell
cell membrane	the thin covering that holds a cell together
nucleus	the part of a cell that controls all the other parts (plural, *nuclei*)
vacuole	an enclosed space in a cell that stores food molecules, water, and waste
mitochondrion	a cell part that helps the cell store and use energy (plural, *mitochondria*)
cellular respiration	the process cells use to release energy from food molecules
cell wall	the thick covering around a plant cell membrane
chloroplast	a plant cell part that stores a green material called chlorophyll
chlorophyll	the green material inside chloroplasts that absorbs sunlight so plants can make their own food
DNA	a molecule in the nuclei of cells that controls many of the characteristics of living things

Words to Know

cell	the smallest, most basic unit of life
element	matter that is made of only one kind of atom
chemical bond	a force that holds atoms together
molecule	two or more atoms that are joined by chemical bonds

The Discovery of the Cell

A microscope is a tool for viewing objects too small to be seen by the eyes alone. The first microscope was invented nearly 400 years ago. It opened up a whole new world to scientists.

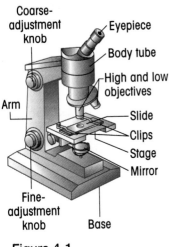

Coarse-adjustment knob — Eyepiece — Body tube — High and low objectives — Arm — Slide — Clips — Stage — Mirror — Fine-adjustment knob — Base

Figure 4-1
Compound microscope

A microscope has many parts. The *stage* is a platform where the object to be viewed is placed. The *eyepiece* is the part that you look through. It contains a *lens* that magnifies the image of the object. The *objectives* also have lenses that magnify. The *coarse-* and *fine-adjustment knobs* are used to move the stage up and down. This makes the object appear clearer.

In 1665, the English scientist Robert Hooke used a microscope to look at a piece of tree bark. Through the microscope, he saw what looked like many small boxes. Hooke thought that the boxes looked like the small rooms that monks live in. These rooms are called cells. So Hooke called the boxes that he saw in the tree bark "cells."

Robert Hooke studied many plants under the microscope. They all seemed to have cells. Hooke's discovery proved to be very important. We now know that the **cell** is the smallest, most basic unit of life.

✓ **How did Robert Hooke discover cells?**

Atoms and Elements

Cells are made of matter. Everything, living or nonliving, is matter. All matter on Earth is made of atoms.

Matter that is made of only one kind of atom is called an **element**. There are 112 different elements. Some are made only in laboratories, but most elements are found in nature. Oxygen, carbon, helium, and hydrogen are a few examples of elements. The Periodic Table of Elements in the Appendix at the end of this book lists all the elements.

Look at the pie chart. It shows the elements found in your body. The human body is 65% oxygen, 18% carbon, and 10% hydrogen. The other 7% of the human body is made of small amounts of other elements, such as nitrogen, calcium, and phosphorus.

Often, two or more atoms are joined together by chemical bonds. A **chemical bond** is a force that holds atoms together. Two or more atoms that are joined by chemical bonds form a **molecule**. A water molecule forms when two hydrogen atoms join an oxygen atom.

✔ **How many kinds of atoms are in an element?**

The Building Blocks of Life

Everything in the universe is made of atoms. But only living things have cells. Cells are the building blocks of life. Think of how bricks are put together to make a house. In this same way, cells are put together to make a living thing.

A cell is like a very tiny water balloon. It is watery inside and has a thin outer covering. All living things, including ants, flowers, and people, are made of cells.

Although you cannot see most cells without a microscope, they are much bigger than atoms and molecules. Many molecules make up a cell.

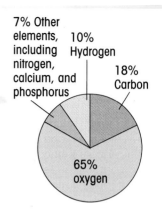

7% Other elements, including nitrogen, calcium, and phosphorus
10% Hydrogen
18% Carbon
65% oxygen

Figure 4-2 *This pie chart shows the elements in the human body.*

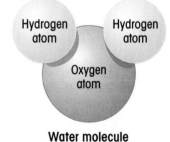

Hydrogen atom   Hydrogen atom

Oxygen atom

Water molecule

Figure 4-3 *Water molecules are made of two hydrogen atoms and one oxygen atom.*

Your own body has about 100 trillion cells. This is 20,000 times greater than the number of people in the world. However, many organisms are made of just one cell. These simple organisms can only be seen with a microscope.

✓ **What are the building blocks of life?**

Lesson Review

1. What did Robert Hooke see through his microscope?

2. What are molecules made of?

3. How many different elements are there?

4. CRITICAL THINKING Is water an element? Explain your answer.

On the Cutting Edge

CLOTH THAT CAN "BREATHE"

Water molecules are bigger than air molecules. Knowing this, Wilbert Gore and his son Bob had an idea. Why not make cloth with a weave too tight to let in water molecules but loose enough to let out air molecules? The cloth would be waterproof. It would also "breathe," meaning it would let hot air out. If you have ever worn rubber rain gear, you know what a good idea this cloth was!

It took them many years, but the Gores finally made such a cloth. They called it GORE-TEX® fabric. Today, this material is made into tents, jackets, and other things that need to be waterproof and also "breathe."

This jacket is made of a waterproof material that "breathes."

CRITICAL THINKING Why are boots that do not "breathe" less comfortable to wear?

Words to Know

cytoplasm	the watery substance in a cell
cell membrane	the thin covering that holds a cell together
nucleus	the part of a cell that controls all the other parts (plural, *nuclei*)
vacuole	an enclosed space in a cell that stores food molecules, water, and waste
mitochondrion	a cell part that helps the cell store and use energy (plural, *mitochondria*)
cellular respiration	the process cells use to release energy from food molecules
cell wall	the thick covering around a plant cell membrane
chloroplast	a plant cell part that stores a green material called chlorophyll
chlorophyll	the green material inside chloroplasts that absorbs sunlight so plants can make their own food
DNA	a molecule in the nuclei of cells that controls many of the characteristics of living things

Parts of a Cell

Most of a cell is made up of a watery, sometimes gooey, substance called **cytoplasm.** Other parts of the cell float around in the watery cytoplasm.

All cells are surrounded by a **cell membrane.** This thin covering holds a cell together. The cell membrane lets food molecules and other materials pass into the cell. It also lets wastes pass out of the cell.

Near the center of the cell is the nucleus. The **nucleus** is the cell's "command post." It controls all the other parts of the cell.

The enclosed spaces in a cell are called vacuoles. Each **vacuole** is used to store food, water molecules, and waste. A vacuole acts as a storeroom for the cell.

The cells also contain mitochondria. A **mitochondrion** is a cell part that helps the cell store and use energy. Mitochondria are the powerhouses of the cell.

✓ What are some parts of a cell?

How Cells Get Energy

Cells get their energy from food. Food molecules pass through the cell membrane into the cytoplasm. Then the molecules are broken down in the mitochondria.

Cells use oxygen to release energy from the food molecules. The oxygen gets into the cells through the cell membrane. The process cells use to release energy from food is called **cellular respiration.**

Cellular respiration also produces certain byproducts. Byproducts are products that are not needed by the cell. They are leftovers. These byproducts leave the cell through the cell membrane.

Figure 4-4
The byproducts from cellular respiration are water and carbon dioxide.

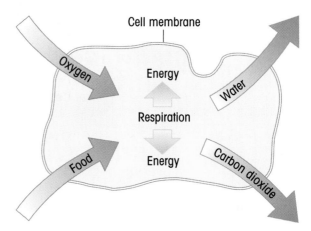

FOOD MOLECULES + OXYGEN → ENERGY + WATER + CARBON DIOXIDE

✓ How do cells get energy?

Plant Cells and Animal Cells

Plant cells are different from animal cells in a few important ways. First, a plant cell has a **cell wall**. The cell wall is the thick covering around a plant's cell membrane. It is harder and stronger than the cell membrane.

Plant cells usually have much bigger vacuoles than animal cells do. This is because plant cells must store a lot of water. Animal cells can have many small vacuoles.

Another important difference is that plant cells have chloroplasts. A **chloroplast** is a plant cell part that stores a green material called **chlorophyll**. Chlorophyll absorbs sunlight. Plants use the sunlight to make their own food.

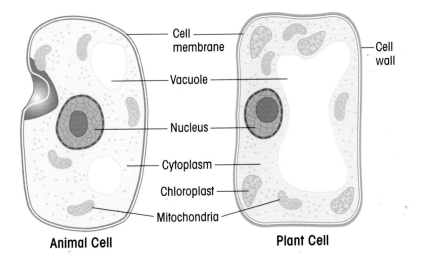

Cell membrane
Vacuole
Nucleus
Cytoplasm
Chloroplast
Mitochondria
Cell wall

Animal Cell

Plant Cell

Figure 4-5 *A plant cell has some structures that an animal cell does not.*

✔ **What are the main differences between animal cells and plant cells?**

DNA: A Code for Life

Inside the nucleus of all cells is a very important kind of molecule called **DNA.** DNA controls many of the characteristics of living things. It is one of the largest molecules found in living things. Thousands of smaller molecules join together in a certain order to make DNA. The order of the molecules makes up a kind of "life code" that controls all the activities of the cell.

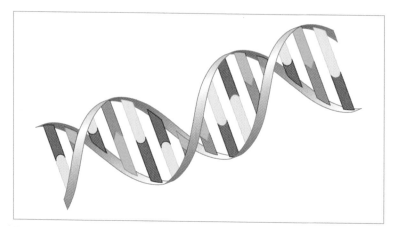

Figure 4-6 *This is a model of a DNA molecule.*

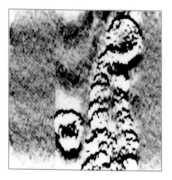

This is the first photo ever taken of DNA. See if you can find the twisted ladder.

The code in DNA controls how cells will grow and multiply. DNA controls whether an organism will grow into an anteater, a human, or any other kind of life form. DNA controls a person's eye color. It controls whether an animal will be tall or short.

In 1953, American scientists James Watson and Francis Crick formed a model of the structure of DNA. The model was shaped like a twisted ladder. The model explained how cells are able to reproduce themselves. In 1963, the two scientists received the Nobel Prize for their work. In 1989, the first photograph was taken of DNA. The photograph showed that Watson and Crick's model of DNA was correct.

Today, information about DNA is being used in criminal courts. Since every person has a different DNA code, scientists can identify people by the DNA in their cells. Sometimes, a person can be found guilty or innocent of a crime based on information about his or her DNA.

✓ How do molecules of DNA determine many of the characteristics of living things?

Lesson Review

1. What are four cell parts found in both animal cells and plant cells?

2. What are the byproducts of cellular respiration?

3. What does chlorophyll allow a plant to do?

4. CRITICAL THINKING How could police prove that a strand of hair found at the scene of a crime belongs to a suspect?

A Closer Look

DNA IN SPONGES

Sponges are animals that live on the ocean floor. They are simple animals. Yet, thanks to their DNA, sponges can do some amazing biological tricks.

If a person loses an arm or a leg, that person cannot grow a new one. A sponge can grow new parts. Its DNA has a code for growing the new parts. If part of a sponge is cut off, the cells reproduce to replace that part. In fact, if you were to cut a sponge into many pieces, each piece would grow into a complete new sponge. Now that's a pretty good trick!

Sponges can grow new body parts.

CRITICAL THINKING How does DNA help a sponge grow new parts?

South
s de   South
             Sp de

LAB ACTIVITY
Making Models of Cells

BACKGROUND

All cells have many of the same structures. However, plant cells are different from animal cells in a few important ways.

PURPOSE

You will make a model of a plant cell and an animal cell.

MATERIALS

paper, pencil, corn syrup, 2 plastic sandwich bags, 1 clear plastic cup, 2 small balls, 4 peas, 2 marbles, 1 small plastic egg, 6 peanuts in shells

WHAT TO DO

1. Use the materials to make a model of an animal cell. The first chart shows what to use for each cell part.
2. Use the rest of the materials to make a model of a plant cell. The second chart shows what to use for each cell part.
3. Describe on a separate sheet of paper how each cell part in your models is similar to the actual cell part that it represents.

Animal Cell	
For...	Use...
Cell membrane	Bag
Nucleus	1 ball
Mitochondria	3 peanuts
Vacuoles	2 marbles
Cytoplasm	Corn syrup (Fill bag.)

Plant Cell	
For...	Use...
Cell membrane	Bag
Cell wall	Cup (Put bag in cup.)
Nucleus	1 ball
Mitochondria	3 peanuts
Vacuole	Plastic egg
Chloroplasts	4 peas
Cytoplasm	Corn syrup (Fill bag.)

DRAW CONCLUSIONS

- What cell parts are found in both a plant cell and an animal cell?

- What cell parts are found in a plant cell but not in an animal cell?

- Based on the models you made, what can you say about plant cells and animal cells?

ON-THE-JOB SCIENCE
Histologic Technician

Estella is a histologic (his-tuh-LAJ-ik) technician. She works in a hospital laboratory. In the hospital, doctors who perform operations sometimes remove a sample of the patient's skin or other tissues. The cells in the tissue are then examined to see if they are healthy. The doctors send the tissue sample to Estella so that she can prepare it for an examination.

Estella checks that she has prepared her slides correctly.

Estella freezes the tissue and cuts off a very thin layer. Then she places the layer on a microscope slide. She stains the cells in the tissue with a dye. Then a doctor called a pathologist examines the cells through a microscope.

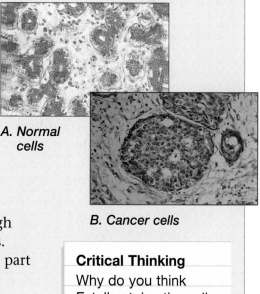

A. Normal cells

The pathologist might see cancer cells in the tissue. Cancer cells reproduce very quickly. They can crowd out and kill a person's healthy cells. Doctors treat cancer cells by removing these cells from the person's body or by destroying them with drugs or radiation.

B. Cancer cells

The photos to the right were taken through a microscope. Photo A shows normal cells. Photo B shows cancer cells from the same part of the body.

Use the photos to answer these questions.

1. How are normal cells and cancer cells alike?

2. How are the normal cells and cancer cells different?

Critical Thinking
Why do you think Estella stains the cells with a dye before a pathologist examines them under a microscope?

Summary

The cell is the basic unit of all living things. The cell has various parts that work together to keep it alive. There are many kinds of cells, including plant cells and animal cells. All cells need energy to survive.

Lesson 4.1

The invention of the microscope led to the discovery of cells. Cells are made of matter, and matter is made of atoms. Matter that is made of only one kind of atom is an element. Molecules are atoms that are joined by a chemical bond.

Lesson 4.2

The nucleus controls activities of the cell. Cells release energy from food molecules by cellular respiration. Plant cells have some parts that animal cells do not have. DNA controls many of an organism's characteristics.

Vocabulary Review

Write *true* or *false* for each sentence. If the sentence is false, replace the underlined term with another term to make the sentence true.

1. Oxygen is an <u>element</u> because it is made of only one kind of atom.

2. Food molecules pass into a cell through the <u>vacuole</u>.

3. A <u>molecule</u> covers the cell membrane in plants.

4. Cell parts that help the cell store and use energy are called <u>mitochondria</u>.

5. Plants are green because they have <u>cytoplasm</u>.

6. The <u>nucleus</u> controls all the other parts of a cell.

7. Vacuoles float in the <u>DNA</u> of a cell.

8. Chlorophyll is found in a <u>chloroplast</u>.

Chapter Quiz

Write your answers on a separate sheet of paper.

1. What did Robert Hooke discover?

2. What is the Periodic Table of Elements?

3. How are molecules formed?

4. Why is the nucleus called the cell's "command post"?

5. What three things do vacuoles store?

6. What are three reasons why cells need energy?

7. What two things must pass into a cell in order for it to get energy by cellular respiration?

8. Why are plant cells able to make their own food but animal cells are not?

9. What does the structure of a DNA molecule look like?

10. How does DNA determine a person's eye color?

Test Tip
Make flash cards of important terms to help you study for a test. Write a term on one side of the card. Write the meaning of the term on the other side.

Research Project

A cell has other parts in addition to those shown in the drawings on page 55. Use library references to find out about two other cell parts, such as ribosomes, endoplasmic reticulum, nucleolus, and lysosomes. Draw and label the cell parts and write what they do.

Chapter 5   The Kingdoms of Life

Scientists divide organisms into groups to make them easier to study. This photo shows organisms from three different groups, called kingdoms. What do you think those kingdoms are?

Learning Objectives

- Name the kingdoms of life.
- Explain the relationship between a kingdom, phylum, and species.
- Compare protists, monera, and fungi.
- Compare plants and fungi.
- Name one member of each kingdom.
- **LAB ACTIVITY:** Observe protists that live in pond water.
- **SCIENCE IN YOUR LIFE:** Identify antibacterial products in your home.

Words to Know

biologist	a scientist who studies the behavior and characteristics of living things
classification	the grouping of organisms by their type
kingdom	one of the five main groups in biological classification
phylum	the largest of the groupings of organisms below kingdom (plural, *phyla*)
species	organisms that can reproduce together and have offspring that can also reproduce
protist	a tiny one-celled organism that is neither plant nor animal but may have characteristics of both
alga	a plantlike protist (plural, *algae*)
protozoan	an animal-like protist (plural, *protozoa*)
moneran	a tiny organism that has DNA but no true nucleus (plural, *monera*)
bacterium	a tiny one-celled moneran seen only through a microscope (plural, *bacteria*)
fungus	an organism that gets its food by breaking down dead matter and absorbing useful elements from it (plural, *fungi*)

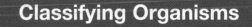

Words to Know

biologist	a scientist who studies the behavior and characteristics of living things
classification	the grouping of organisms by their type
kingdom	one of the five main groups in biological classification
phylum	the largest of the groupings of organisms below kingdom (plural, *phyla*)
species	organisms that can reproduce together and have offspring that can also reproduce

More than 1 million kinds of animals are known today. At least 324,000 kinds of plants are known. A scientist who studies the behavior and characteristics of living things is called a **biologist.** In this chapter, you will learn more about how biologists group organisms.

The Kingdoms of Life

Science Fact

Some scientists think there should be a sixth kingdom made up of some kinds of organisms now classified as bacteria.

Grouping organisms by their type is called **classification.** Biologists study many characteristics of organisms to decide how they should be grouped. In all, there are five main groups in biological classification. Each one of these is called a **kingdom.**

You already know a lot about two of the kingdoms—the Plant Kingdom and the Animal Kingdom. The biggest difference between these is the way the organisms get food. Animals must eat other organisms for food. Plants use chlorophyll and sunlight to make their own food.

The chart on the next page lists the five kingdoms. It describes some characteristics of the organisms in each kingdom. It also gives examples of organisms from each kingdom.

The Five Kingdoms of Life		
Kingdom	Description	Examples
1. Protist	Usually is one-celled Has a nucleus	Protozoa Algae
2. Moneran	One-celled Has no true nucleus	Bacteria Blue-green bacteria
3. Fungus	Single-celled and many-celled Has cell walls Has no chlorophyll	Molds Yeasts Mushrooms
4. Plant	Many-celled Has cell walls Uses sunlight and chlorophyll to make food	Seed plants Evergreens Ferns
5. Animal	Many-celled Has no chlorophyll Cannot make its own food Eats other organisms	Insects Fish Reptiles Birds Mammals

✓ **What are the main classification groups of organisms called, and how many are there?**

From Kingdoms to Species

In each of the five kingdoms, there are smaller groupings of organisms. The largest of these is called a **phylum**. The Animal Kingdom has about 20 phyla. All animals that have backbones are part of the phylum called Chordata. Within each phylum, there are many smaller groupings, including class, order, family, and genus. A **species** is all organisms that can reproduce together and have offspring that can also reproduce. Species are the smallest groupings. Humans belong to the class *Mammalia* (Mammals) and the species *Homo sapiens*.

✓ **What are the main classifications of organisms below kingdom?**

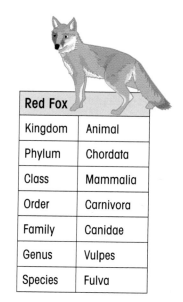

Red Fox	
Kingdom	Animal
Phylum	Chordata
Class	Mammalia
Order	Carnivora
Family	Canidae
Genus	Vulpes
Species	Fulva

Figure 5-1 *This chart shows the classification of a red fox.*

Lesson Review

1. List three features of organisms in the plant kingdom.

2. What is the smallest grouping within the biological classification system?

3. **CRITICAL THINKING** Why are turtles and butterflies two different species?

Great Moments in Science

ARISTOTLE'S CLASSIFICATION SYSTEM

Aristotle, a philosopher and scientist who lived in ancient Greece, formed one of the first classification systems. Aristotle divided living things into plants and animals. He further divided animals into three groups based on where they lived: in the air, in the water, or on land.

Aristotle (384–322 B.C.)

Aristotle's system was a good start. It was not perfect, however. For example, penguins live in the water, like fish. However, penguins have wings and feathers, not fins and scales. Today, penguins are classified as birds, even though they cannot fly.

Whales and dolphins live in the water and look like fish. Yet they breathe air, like land animals. Whales and dolphins are really mammals. They are more like humans and tigers than fish. Biologists no longer group organisms by where they live. Today's classification systems are based on characteristics such as an organism's body structure, development, and DNA.

Penguins have wings and feathers, like other birds, but they cannot fly.

CRITICAL THINKING Bats and elephants have hair. Bats and pigeons can fly. How would Aristotle have grouped these three animals? How do biologists group them today?

Words to Know

protist	a tiny one-celled organism that is neither plant nor animal but may have characteristics of both
alga	a plantlike protist (plural, *algae*)
protozoan	an animal-like protist (plural, *protozoa*)
moneran	a tiny organism that has DNA but no true nucleus (plural, *monera*)
bacterium	a tiny one-celled moneran seen only through a microscope (plural, *bacteria*)
fungus	an organism that gets its food by breaking down dead matter and absorbing useful elements from it (plural, *fungi*)

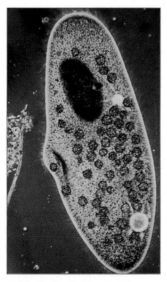

This protist is called a paramecium.

Protists

People used to believe there were only two kingdoms—plants and animals. Then the microscope was invented. It showed new kinds of organisms. Today we call these organisms protists. A **protist** is a tiny one-celled organism that is neither plant nor animal but may have characteristics of both. This is why protists were given their own kingdom. Some protists are more like plants. One plantlike protist is called an **alga.** You may have seen algae growing on lakes or floating in the sea. They are usually green, red, or brown. What you are really seeing is a giant colony of algae. A single alga is usually too small to be seen without a microscope.

One animal-like protist is a **protozoan.** Protozoa often have tiny shells. When they die, these shells pile up on the ocean floor. The chalk in your classroom is made up of these shells.

✓ **What is the main difference between algae and protozoa?**

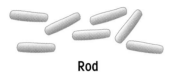

Rod

Round

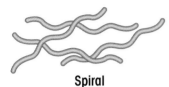

Spiral

Figure 5-2 *Bacteria shapes*

Monera

A **moneran**, like a protist, a plant, and an animal, has DNA in its cells. However, it does not have a true nucleus to hold the DNA. The DNA floats around in the cytoplasm. For this reason, scientists decided to give monera their own kingdom—the Moneran Kingdom.

The Moneran Kingdom is made up of different kinds of bacteria. A **bacterium** is a tiny one-celled organism seen only through a microscope. Like the protists, bacteria are found everywhere. They live in the ocean, the sky, and even in your skin. Many bacteria actually live inside your body.

Some bacteria are very useful. We use them to make many kinds of foods, such as cheese and yogurt. Other types of bacteria are very dangerous. They can cause sickness and even death.

Blue-green bacteria are another kind of monera. Blue-green bacteria contain chlorophyll. They are able to make their own food by photosynthesis.

✔ **How are monera different from all other organisms?**

Fungi

If you leave bread out for a long time, something soft and fuzzy might grow on it. This fuzzy substance is called *mold*. Mold is a **fungus**. A fungus is an organism that gets its food by breaking down dead matter and absorbing useful elements from it.

People used to group fungi with plants. After all, they have a lot in common with plants. They grow in one place. They do not move around looking for food, as most animals do. However, fungi are missing one important plant characteristic—chloroplasts. That means they cannot make their own food using photosynthesis. Fungi cannot be monera either, because they do have true nuclei in their cells. Finally, fungi are too big to be protists. So scientists created a kingdom just for them.

Fungi include molds, yeasts, and mushrooms. Fungi get their food from dead organisms or dead matter on an organism. For example, athlete's foot is a fungus that eats the dead skin on people's feet.

✓ How are fungi different from plants?

Lesson Review

1. Name one animal-like protist.

2. What are bacteria, and how are some of them useful?

3. How are fungi similar to plants?

4. **CRITICAL THINKING** A biologist discovers a one-celled organism without a nucleus. What kingdom must the organism belong to?

On the Cutting Edge

FIGHTING DANGEROUS PROTOZOA

Most protozoa are harmless to humans. However, some cause serious diseases. The worst of these diseases is *malaria*. More than 500 million people have malaria. Over 2.5 million people die of the disease each year. The protozoa that cause malaria are spread by mosquitoes. When a mosquito bites an infected person, the mosquito picks up the protozoa from the person's blood. It then passes the protozoa to the next person it bites.

Some mosquitoes spread malaria.

For years, scientists have tried to find a medicine to prevent malaria. Now they are studying the DNA of the malaria protozoa. Learning about the DNA may help scientists make more powerful medicines. The DNA could also be injected into a person. This may help the person's body fight off the protozoa if bitten by a mosquito.

CRITICAL THINKING Another way to fight malaria is to use poisons that kill mosquitoes. How would this help prevent malaria from spreading?

LAB ACTIVITY
Observing Protists

BACKGROUND
Have you ever looked closely at the water in a pond? It may look clear, but it is actually full of organisms. Many of the organisms in pond water are protists. Most are too small to be seen with your eyes alone. You must use a microscope to observe them.

PURPOSE
You will observe and describe some of the protists that live in pond water.

MATERIALS
paper, pencil, medicine dropper, pond water, microscope slide, coverslip, microscope

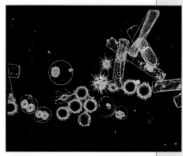

Many tiny protists can be found in a drop of pond water.

WHAT TO DO
1. Make a chart with spaces big enough for you to draw in them. Copy the column heads in the chart shown.
2. Place a drop of pond water on a microscope slide. Place the coverslip on top of the drop of water.
3. Place the slide on the microscope stage.
4. Look for protists on the slide. Use the photo on this page and on page 67 as a guide.
5. In your chart, draw each protist that you find. Also describe its color and decide whether it moves. List any other features you observe.

Drawing of Protist	Animal-like Features	Plantlike Features

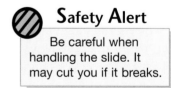

Safety Alert
Be careful when handling the slide. It may cut you if it breaks.

DRAW CONCLUSIONS
- What plantlike features did some of the protists have?
- What animal-like features did some of the protists have?
- What can you now say about protists?

SCIENCE IN YOUR LIFE
Fighting Bacteria at Home

Toshio had a serious ear infection. His doctor told him the infection was caused by bacteria. The doctor gave Toshio medicine called an antibiotic to get rid of the infection. Antibiotics are drugs that kill bacteria in your body.

You can protect yourself from harmful bacteria. Some products that you use to clean your body or your home contain chemicals called *antibacterial agents*. These chemicals help prevent infections caused by bacteria. For example, many soaps and deodorants contain antibacterial agents. Some household cleaners do, too. They fight bacteria in the kitchen and the bathroom.

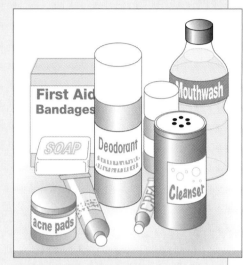

Many types of products contain antibacterial agents.

Check out the products in your home. How many contain antibacterial agents, and what do they do? Follow these steps:

1. Read the labels on all cleaning products that are kept in your kitchen or bathroom. Look for products that say they kill bacteria. Some products will have the word "antibacterial" on the label. Others may say "kills germs" or "germ fighting." All of these terms mean the same thing.
2. Divide your list into two groups:
   a. Products that kill bacteria in or on your body
   b. Products that kill bacteria on surfaces around the house

Critical Thinking

How might you find out how effective certain household products are at killing bacteria?

Summary   Scientists classify organisms to learn about them and to understand their relationships to other organisms.

Lesson 5.1   The five kingdoms are animal, plant, protist, moneran, and fungus. Each of the kingdoms is broken down into many more groups. The smallest groups of classification are called species.

Lesson 5.2   Protists can be plantlike or animal-like. Algae are plantlike protists. Protozoa are animal-like protists. Monera do not have true nuclei. Bacteria and blue-green bacteria are monera. Fungi cannot move around like animals but do not have chloroplasts. Molds, yeasts, and mushrooms are all fungi.

Vocabulary Review

fungus

alga

species

classification

biologist

protozoan

kingdom

bacterium

Complete each sentence with a term from the list.

1. The grouping of organisms by their type is called _____.

2. A _____ is a protist that cannot make its own food.

3. Bacteria belong to the Moneran _____.

4. A _____ is a scientist who studies the behavior and characteristics of living things.

5. A one-celled plantlike protist is known as an _____.

6. A _____ is a one-celled organism without a nucleus.

7. A mushroom is an example of a many-celled _____.

8. A _____ includes all organisms that can reproduce together and and have offspring that can also reproduce.

Chapter Quiz

Write your answers on a separate sheet of paper.

1. What are the names of the five kingdoms?

2. Which kingdoms contain many-celled organisms?

3. Which classification grouping includes Chordata, or all animals that have backbones?

4. What is the smallest classification grouping?

5. Which kingdom do algae belong to?

6. Which kingdom contains organisms that do not have nuclei?

7. What is the name of one kind of monera?

8. How are fungi different from plants?

9. How do fungi get food?

10. What are the names of three kinds of fungi?

Test Tip
Number all of your answers. Make sure each answer has the same number as its question.

Research Project

Simple organisms help make the following foods: bread, buttermilk, cottage cheese, miso, pickles, ricotta cheese, sauerkraut, sour cream, soy sauce, tempeh, and tofu. Research how these foods are made. Some are made with the help of bacteria, and some are made with the help of fungi. Write about one of each type. Describe how the fungi or bacteria help make the food.

The ability to move is important in the animal kingdom. These dolphins jump through the air and swim quickly through the ocean. Other animals crawl, run, or fly. How does moving around help animals to survive?

Learning Objectives

- Identify characteristics common to all animals.
- Compare animals with simpler organisms.
- Compare and contrast invertebrates with vertebrates.
- Identify groups of invertebrates.
- List characteristics of fish, amphibians, reptiles, birds, and mammals.
- LAB ACTIVITY: Identify animals by using a two-choice key.
- ON-THE-JOB SCIENCE: Relate knowledge of animal characteristics to pet store work.

Words to Know

invertebrate	an animal that does not have a backbone
parasite	an organism that lives on or in another organism, called a host, and causes harm to that organism
host	a living thing that supports a parasite
mollusk	an animal with a soft body that is not divided into segments
arthropod	an animal with an outer skeleton, jointed appendages, and a body divided into separate parts, called segments
appendage	a part that extends out from the body, such as a wing, a leg, an arm, or a claw
crustacean	an arthropod with two body segments and five pairs of legs
vertebrate	an animal with a backbone
cold-blooded	having a body temperature that changes with the environment
warm-blooded	having a body temperature that stays fairly constant
amphibian	a cold-blooded vertebrate with wet, slippery skin and two pairs of legs; able to live on both land and in water
reptile	a cold-blooded land vertebrate, usually with four legs and clawed toes
migrate	to move long distances each year to reach warm areas and better feeding grounds
mammal	a warm-blooded vertebrate that has hair on its body; the mother's body makes milk to feed its young

From Simple to Complex

You already know a lot about animals. After all, you are one. However, there are many fascinating things about animals you might not know. For example, humans have 656 muscles. That sounds like a lot, but caterpillars have about 2,000 muscles!

What Are Animals?

All protists, monera, fungi, and plants are made of cells, just as animals are. They also all share the five characteristics of life. Still, there are many differences between members of the animal kingdom and simpler organisms.

Moving
Animals can move around. Animals can fly, swim, run, or walk. Plants move their leaves and bend their stems toward sunlight. However, they cannot choose to get up and move to a different place.

Getting Food
Animals need to get food. They must find plants or other animals to eat. Plants can make their own food, using the chloroplasts in their cells.

Cell Functions
Animals have *specialized* cells. These are cells that do special jobs. Different cells carry out different functions. Plants have cells that do special jobs also. However, the cells of protists, monera, and fungi are not specialized. Each cell does the same thing.

✓ **What are the main differences between animals and other organisms?**

Remember
The five characteristics of life are getting and using food, moving, growing, reproducing, and responding to the environment.

Special Cells, Special Jobs

Most of the organisms you have read about so far are one-celled. A few organisms, like mushrooms, are made of many cells. However, the cells in a mushroom are almost all alike.

Nearly every animal cell has a nucleus, a cell membrane, mitochondria, and other cell parts. Different kinds of animal cells, though, have different shapes and sizes, depending on what jobs they do.

Remember
The nucleus is the part of a cell that controls all other parts. The membrane is the thin covering that holds a cell together. Mitochondria are cell parts that help the cell store and use energy.

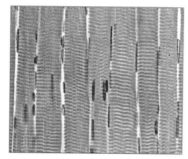

Muscle cells must be able to stretch.

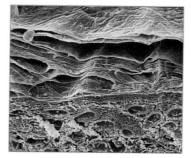

Skin cells are flat and broad. They protect the organism.

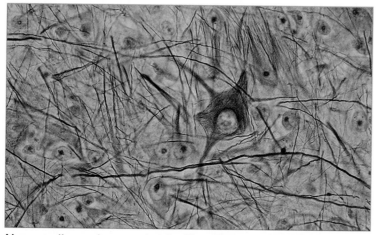

Nerve cells are long and stringlike. They carry messages around the body.

Think of a one-celled organism as a store run by only one person. That person has to do all the work. Bigger stores hire many workers. Each person has a specialized job. Some people sell, others keep track of the money, and still others are in charge of whole departments. The bigger the store is, the more specialized the jobs are. This is also true of animal cells. The more complicated the animal is, the more specialized cells it has.

✓ **How do the cells in an animal differ from the cells in a simpler organism?**

Lesson Review

1. How do animals and plants differ in how they get their food?

2. Why do animal cells have different shapes and sizes?

3. CRITICAL THINKING Why would it be hard for most animals to survive if they could not move around?

A Closer Look

SPECIALIZED CELLS IN ACTION

A heron stands still alongside a pond. Suddenly it lunges forward and plucks a fish out of the water. Lunch is served!

The heron uses its specialized cells each time it catches a fish. Cells in the bird's eyes sense the light that bounces off the fish. These cells send a message to other cells in the eyes. Nerve cells carry the message to the brain. Other nerve cells in the brain read the message: food! They send a new message to the heron's muscles: strike! The muscle cells pull against the bones in the heron's neck. That forces the heron's head into the water. The muscle cells also open the heron's jaws so it can capture the fish.

A heron fishes for its meal.

CRITICAL THINKING What would happen if a heron's cells did not do their jobs correctly?

Words to Know

invertebrate	an animal that does not have a backbone
parasite	an organism that lives on or in another organism, called a host, and causes harm to that organism
host	a living thing that supports a parasite
mollusk	an animal with a soft body that is not divided into segments
arthropod	an animal with an outer skeleton, jointed appendages, and a body divided into separate parts, called segments
appendage	a part that extends out from the body, such as a wing, a leg, an arm, or a claw
crustacean	an arthropod with two body segments and five pairs of legs

Animals come in all shapes, sizes, and colors. These features help them survive in their environments. Any body feature, process, or behavior that allows an organism to survive in its environment is called an *adaptation.* Common animal adaptations are teeth, spines, horns, poisons, odor, speed, and even the ability to stand still for a long time. Color is also important in adaptation. Many animals use color, or *camouflage,* to blend in with their environment so they can hide. Others have bright colors to attract mates.

An **invertebrate** is an animal that does not have a backbone. It is a simple creature compared to an animal with a backbone.

Science Fact

Some sponges are smaller than a penny. Others can be up to 6.6 feet (2 meters) in diameter.

Sponges

A sponge is an animal that lives in water and often grows on rocks. Sponges have existed for more than half a billion years.

Sponges have changed very little in the last half a billion years.

A sponge's body has many holes that let water pass through it. The sponge gets oxygen and food from this water. The water also carries away waste.

Most cleaning sponges found in the kitchen are synthetic, or made by people. They are not natural sponges. Perhaps you have seen a dried natural sponge. It is usually a tan color and has an uneven shape. These sponges are really the remains of once-living sponges.

Sponges are like plants in some ways. They spend most of their lives attached to one object. However, when they are young, they move around, as animals do. Also, they trap their food, as animals do.

✓ **Why are sponges called animals?**

Worms

Worms are another type of invertebrate. There are many kinds of worms. A tapeworm is a ribbonlike flatworm. Some tapeworms grow to 44 feet (13 meters) long. The tapeworm is a **parasite.** That means it lives on or in another organism and causes harm to that organism. A **host** is a living thing that supports a parasite. The tapeworm absorbs nutrients from the host's digested food.

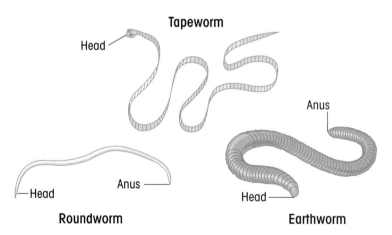

Figure 6-1 *Tapeworm, roundworm, and earthworm*

A roundworm has more parts than a tapeworm. The roundworm can digest its own food. It has a mouth and an *anus*. An anus is an opening through which waste leaves the body.

An earthworm is the kind of worm people dig up for fishing. It has even more parts than the roundworm and a segmented body. Segmented means divided into separate parts. An earthworm has a *crop* for storing food and a *gizzard* for grinding food. It also has five hearts for pumping blood throughout its body.

✓ **How is a roundworm different from a tapeworm?**

Mollusks

A **mollusk** is an animal with a soft body that is not divided into segments. The word *mollusk* means "soft-body." Snails, slugs, clams, oysters, squid, and octopuses are all mollusks. Most snails and slugs live in water. A few live on land. Many mollusks have hard shells that protect their bodies. Snails have a tonguelike structure called a *radula*, which is covered with thousands of tiny teeth. Snails that live in water use their radulas to scrape up algae.

✓ **What is the function of a mollusk's shell?**

Spiny-Skinned Invertebrates

Sand dollars and sea stars are spiny-skinned invertebrates. They belong to this group of animals that live in salt water. The name "spiny-skinned" comes from the sharp spines on their skin. The spines help to protect the animal from enemies.

Sea stars often eat oysters. A sea star uses its five strong arms to pull the oyster open. Then the sea star actually pushes its own stomach out of its mouth. It puts its stomach into the oyster shell and digests the oyster. Then it swallows its own stomach again.

✓ **Where are spiny-skinned invertebrates found?**

Sea stars use their arms to pull open the shells of clams and oysters.

Arthropods

An **arthropod** is an animal with an outer skeleton, jointed appendages, and a body divided into segments. An **appendage** is a part that extends out from beyond the body. Wings, legs, arms, and claws are appendages. Some appendages can bend. Spiders, scorpions, cockroaches, ticks, crabs, lobsters, bees, mosquitoes, ants, and grasshoppers are all arthropods.

Arthropods are divided into many groups, or classes. The number of body segments and appendages determines which class an arthropod is in. Three classes of arthropods are insects, crustaceans, and spiders.

Insects

Insects are the largest group of arthropods. Insects are by far the most common land animals. There are more than 800,000 species of insects. An insect is an arthropod with a body that is divided into three parts: *head*, *thorax*, and *abdomen*. Insects have three pairs of legs and usually two pairs of wings. They also have feelers, called *antennae*.

Many insects, such as bees and butterflies, are useful to humans. Honeybees make honey. Many bees and butterflies spread pollen. Some insects are harmful. Fleas get diseases from rats and pass them to humans. Flies and cockroaches feed on garbage and animal waste and spread harmful organisms.

Figure 6-2 *An insect has three pairs of legs. Its body is divided into three main sections.*

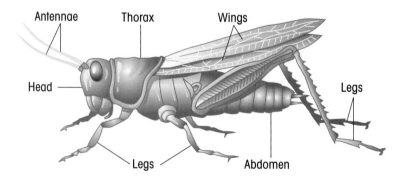

Antennae   Thorax   Wings

Head

Legs   Legs   Abdomen

Spiders

Many people think spiders are insects. However, these arthropods have only two body segments and four pairs of legs. Also, they have no antennae. Scorpions, mites, and ticks all belong to the same class as spiders.

Lyme disease is a bacterial disease humans get from the bite of a tiny tick. Most ticks pick up the bacteria from the blood of infected deer or mice. To protect yourself in yards or fields in warm weather, wear light-colored clothes, long sleeves, pants tucked into socks or boots, and insect repellent. Check for ticks daily, and remove them with tweezers only. If a rash or flu develops, see a doctor. The usual treatment is antibiotics. Other diseases transmitted to humans by ticks include Rocky Mountain spotted fever.

The female black widow spider releases a poison when she bites.

Crustaceans

The lobster is an example of a **crustacean.** Crustaceans are arthropods with two body segments and five pairs of legs. The front pair of legs are usually called claws. The other four pairs of legs are called walking legs. Crabs and crayfish are also crustaceans. Crustaceans are used by humans as food.

✓ **What are three characteristics of arthropods?**

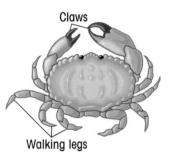

Figure 6-3 *A crab*

Lesson Review

For statements 1 to 3, decide if each one is true or false. If it is false, rewrite the statement to make it true.

1. Sponges are plants.

2. An earthworm uses its crop to protect its body.

3. Lobsters, crabs, and crayfish are all crustaceans.

4. CRITICAL THINKING Most arthropods have hard outer skeletons. However, the parts of the skeleton are connected by soft spaces. How does that help the arthropod?

Vertebrates

Words to Know

vertebrate	an animal with a backbone
cold-blooded	having a body temperature that changes with the environment
warm-blooded	having a body temperature that stays fairly constant
amphibian	a cold-blooded vertebrate with wet, slippery skin and two pairs of legs; able to live on both land and in water
reptile	a cold-blooded land vertebrate, usually with four legs and clawed toes
migrate	to move long distances each year to reach warm areas and better feeding grounds
mammal	a warm-blooded vertebrate that has hair on its body; the mother's body makes milk to feed its young

A **vertebrate** is an animal with a backbone. There are five main groups of vertebrates. Humans, snakes, zebras, birds, fish, rats, dogs, and frogs are all examples of vertebrates.

Vertebrates are more complicated organisms than invertebrates. Vertebrates have larger brains, more digestive parts, and more reproductive parts. Most vertebrates also have appendages.

Vertebrates can be **cold-blooded** or **warm-blooded**. The body temperature of cold-blooded animals changes with the environment. The body temperature of warm-blooded animals stays fairly constant. It does not change much. Fish, amphibians, and reptiles are cold-blooded. Birds and mammals are warm-blooded.

Science Fact

The whale shark is the largest cold-blooded animal in the world. It can grow to 39 feet (12 meters) long. The blue whale is the largest warm-blooded animal. It can grow to over 100 feet (30 meters) long.

Fish

The simplest vertebrates are fish. Salmon, trout, sharks, and minnows are all examples of fish. Fish are cold-blooded vertebrates with fins, scales, and gills. The fins help fish swim.

Fishes' bodies are covered with scales. Look at the picture of a scale on this page. You can see rings on it. The scales on a fish grow with the fish. Each year another ring is added to each scale. You can tell how old a fish is by counting the rings on its scales.

Fish do not have lungs to breathe air. They have gills instead. As water goes through slits in the gills, oxygen is absorbed right into the blood. The blood carries the oxygen to all parts of the fish's body.

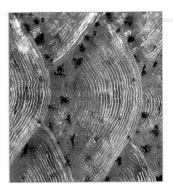

Fish scales

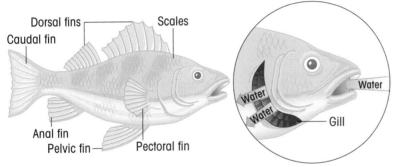

Dorsal fins Scales
Caudal fin
Anal fin
Pelvic fin Pectoral fin
Water
Water
Water
Gill

Figure 6-4 *Fish gills absorb oxygen from the water.*

✓ **What are the main characteristics of fish?**

Amphibians

Frogs, toads, and salamanders are kinds of amphibians. An **amphibian** is a cold-blooded vertebrate with wet, slippery skin and two pairs of legs. Most amphibians have sticky tongues that they use to catch insects.

The word *amphibian* means "able to live on both land and in water." Frogs, for example, spend most of their lives on land. However, they lay their eggs in water. Amphibian eggs have no shells.

Spotted salamander

Young amphibians have gills, like fish. They use their gills to get oxygen from the water. When they mature they leave the water to live on land. By then, they have developed lungs for breathing air. However, most amphibians live in wet places. They need to keep their skin wet. When a frog is completely underwater, it can absorb oxygen through its skin.

✓ **What are three kinds of amphibians?**

On the Cutting Edge

RESEARCHING FROG SLIME

Katherine Milton is a scientist from California. She learned something very important about frogs from the Mayoruna Indians of Brazil's Amazon River Basin. Milton watched the Indians collect slime from the bodies of one species of frog, called the phyllomedusa frog. The Indians dried the slime on sticks. Then they burned the skin on their arms and put the dried frog slime into their wounds.

A phyllomedusa frog

At first, the Indians got very sick and fell asleep. But when they awoke, they were able to hunt for long hours and not get tired. The Mayoruna men "take frog" at least once a month. The Mayoruna women "take frog" when they need to work long hours.

Researchers have found that frog slime is an amazing healer and pain killer. It may lead to discoveries in fighting strokes, Alzheimer's disease, and depression. Katherine Milton is not surprised. She studies the native peoples of the Amazon because she knows they have great knowledge.

CRITICAL THINKING Why do you think medical researchers should study other native peoples of the Amazon?

Reptiles

The animal known as the **reptile** is a cold-blooded land vertebrate. Most reptiles have four legs and clawed toes. Some examples of reptiles are lizards, turtles, snakes, alligators, and crocodiles. Reptiles all have lungs for breathing air. Because snakes and some lizards have no legs, they move along on their bellies. Some snakes have as many as 300 pairs of ribs.

Snakes are not slimy, as many people think. They are warm and dry. From time to time, a snake sheds the outer layer of its dry, scaly skin. Some snakes have fangs and a poison called *venom*.

Reptiles can live in very dry places. Their bodies are covered with hard scales, almost like plates. This lets a reptile bake in the hot sun for hours without drying out. The hard coating keeps in moisture.

Reptiles lay eggs. The leathery cover on an egg protects the young reptile inside. It also keeps the egg from drying out when laid on land.

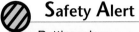

Safety Alert

Rattlesnakes, copperheads, coral snakes, and cottonmouths bite about 8,000 Americans a year. Their venom can be fatal. When hiking, do not go near any snakes. Walk slowly around them. Wear boots in tall grass and brush. Stay on hiking paths. Do not lift or climb on rocks.

Science Fact

Crocodiles swallow their food whole. A full-grown crocodile carries about 5 pounds (2 kilograms) of rocks in its stomach to grind up the food.

At 12 feet long, crocodiles are among the largest living reptiles.

✓ **Why are reptiles able to live in dry places?**

Birds

A bird is a warm-blooded vertebrate with feathers and wings for flying. Birds also have hollow bones, which make the bones lighter. Because birds are light, it is easier for them to fly. Birds also have two legs.

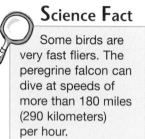

Science Fact

Some birds are very fast fliers. The peregrine falcon can dive at speeds of more than 180 miles (290 kilometers) per hour.

There are more than 8,600 different kinds of birds. Hummingbirds are the smallest. A hummingbird weighs less than 1 ounce (28 grams). Ostriches are the largest birds. An ostrich can weigh up to 300 pounds (140 kilograms). Like reptiles, birds lay eggs and make nests.

Many birds **migrate**. That means they fly long distances each year to reach warm areas and better feeding grounds. Sometimes they migrate to nest or mate. The blackpoll warbler is a bird about the size of a sparrow. It flies from Canada to New England each year. It flies during the night and rests during the day. It stays in New England for about two weeks eating insects. Then it flies to South America. This is a distance of about 2,500 miles (4,000 kilometers).

Many birds migrate long distances every year, like these snow geese.

✓ **What are three characteristics of birds?**

Mammals

A **mammal** is a warm-blooded vertebrate that has hair on its body. The mother's body makes milk to feed its young. Most mammals also give birth to live young. Most babies do not hatch from eggs. At birth, most mammals are already formed as young animals. Mammal parents take care of their young. Humans, elephants, mice, dolphins, tigers, bears, and bats are all examples of mammals.

Most mammals have big brains. They have two sets of appendages (all legs or legs and arms), and many have tails. Most mammals live on land. However, some, like whales and seals, live in water. The blue whale is the largest mammal on Earth. The shrew is the smallest mammal.

Some mammals carry a virus in their saliva that causes the disease *rabies*. Rabies is spread mostly by animal bites. Dog bites once caused most rabies in humans. Today, rabies is usually spread to humans by bats, skunks, raccoons, and foxes in the wild. Never go near unknown dogs or any wild animals. If you are bitten, go to a hospital or see a doctor right away. Rabies must be treated within 2 days of infection. It is too late once symptoms appear, about 7 to 10 days after a bite.

Some shrews weigh as little as a hummingbird.

✓ **What are three characteristics of mammals?**

Lesson Review

1. What characteristic do all vertebrates share?

2. What are the five kinds of vertebrates?

3. What two kinds of vertebrates have bodies that are covered with scales?

4. **CRITICAL THINKING** Why do you think many birds eat a lot of food before they migrate across large bodies of water?

LAB ACTIVITY
Using a Two-Choice Key

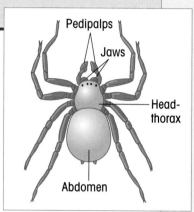

Pedipalps

Jaws

Head-thorax

Abdomen

Structure of spiders

BACKGROUND
It can be hard to identify organisms. Scientists make this task easier by using a *two-choice key*. This key is simply a list of statements about the organism. For each characteristic, there are two possible choices. Making the correct choices leads you to the name of the organism.

PURPOSE
You will identify spiders by using a two-choice key.

MATERIALS
paper, pencil

WHAT TO DO
1. Study the diagram to learn the general structure of spiders.
2. Look at spider A. Read the first two statements in the key. Decide which choice fits. Follow the direction given for that choice.
3. Continue until you come to a type of spider at the end of a choice. That will be spider A. Write the name next to the letter A on a sheet of paper.
4. Repeat Steps 3 and 4 for the other spiders.

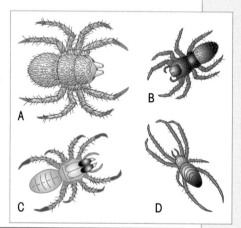

A

B

C

D

Two-Choice Key for Identifying Spiders

1. a. The entire body and all legs are covered with hairs. . . . . Go to 2
   b. Only parts of the body are covered with hairs. . . . . Go to 3
2. a. The pedipalps are curved. . . . . jumping spider
   b. The pedipalps are straight. . . . . tarantula
3. a. The jaws are large, and the head-thorax is covered by a plate. . . . . . trapdoor spider
   b. The jaws are small, and the head-thorax is not covered by a plate. . . . . argiope

---

DRAW CONCLUSIONS
• Suppose you found an animal that had antennae. Could you use this key to identify the animal? Explain.

ON-THE-JOB SCIENCE
Pet Store Worker

Rosita Hernandez works in a pet store. She helps customers find the animal they would like to have as a pet. She also helps them find the right food and supplies for that pet. She makes sure each pet is in the correct carrier when it leaves the store.

The animals that are sold in a pet store have different needs. Some must be kept in water. Others need a dry cage with a small bowl of water. Some must stay warm to survive. Others must be kept cool. Each animal eats a certain type of food. A pet store worker must understand the needs of each animal.

Rosita takes care of the animals in the pet store.

Pet store workers usually put similar kinds of animals near each other in the store. That makes it easier for customers to find what they want.

The pet store is divided into six sections: invertebrates, fish, amphibians, reptiles, birds, and mammals. The store receives the following animals:

guppies	parakeets	crayfish	hamsters
lizards	salamanders	snakes	goldfish
gerbils	turtles	frogs	canaries

Critical Thinking

How did you decide where to put the animals for Question 1 below?

Using the chart above, answer these questions.

1. Which animals would go in each section?
2. Which animals would need to be kept in water or in a wet environment?
3. Which animals could keep their body temperature constant if the temperature of their surroundings changed?

Summary — Animals are complex organisms. They are divided into two main groups: vertebrates and invertebrates. Smaller groups share characteristics such as being cold-blooded or warm-blooded.

Lesson 6.1 — Animals can move around, must get their own food, and are made of specialized cells.

Lesson 6.2 — Invertebrates do not have backbones. Sponges, mollusks, and arthropods are examples of invertebrates.

Lesson 6.3 — Vertebrates have backbones, developed brains, and digestive and reproductive parts. Fish, amphibians, reptiles, birds, and mammals are vertebrates.

Vocabulary Review

cold-blooded

reptile

arthropod

mollusk

vertebrate

parasite

migrate

appendage

Complete each sentence with a term from the list.

1. An animal with a backbone is known as a _____.

2. An insect is a type of _____.

3. Some birds _____ long distances to nest or mate.

4. The tapeworm is a _____, which means it lives on or in another living thing.

5. The body temperature of a _____ animal changes with the environment.

6. A body part that extends out from the body, such as a wing or a leg, is an _____.

7. A _____ lays eggs with a leathery cover that keeps them from drying out.

8. A _____ has a soft body that is not divided into segments.

Chapter Quiz

Write your answers on a separate sheet of paper.

1. How is an animal different from a plant?

2. How are invertebrates different from vertebrates?

3. How are parasites and hosts related?

4. What are three examples of mollusks?

5. What are the three segments of an insect's body?

6. How are spiders different from insects?

7. How are fish different from mature amphibians?

8. What are three examples of reptiles?

9. What kind of bones do birds have that make flying easier?

10. How are mammals different from other vertebrates?

Test Tip
Always try to write answers in complete sentences. This helps improve the quality of your thinking as well as that of your writing.

Research Project

You may have heard of a flock of sheep or a herd of cows. *Flock* and *herd* are the group names for these animals. Other kinds of animals have different group names. Research the group names for the following animals: geese, gorillas, fish, chicks, quail, lions, ants, and wolves. Make a chart that lists each animal and its group name.

Chapter 7

The Plant Kingdom

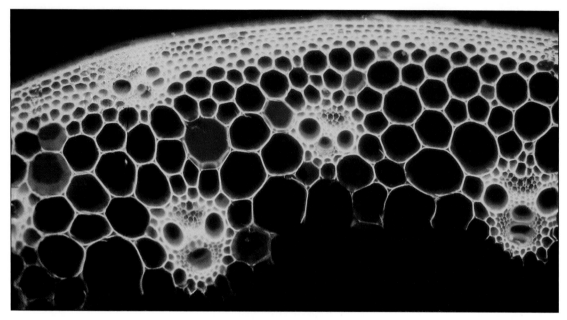

Tiny tubes inside a plant's stem carry water, minerals, and food to other parts of the plant. What other plant parts do you know about?

Learning Objectives

- Explain how plants differ from animals.
- Explain the function of seeds, roots, stems, and leaves.
- Describe photosynthesis.
- Identify the parts of a flower and their functions.
- Describe what happens during pollination.
- Describe the process of fertilization.
- Describe the process of seed germination.
- Explain the function of fruits for seed plants.
- LAB ACTIVITY: Compare how different environments affect seed germination.
- SCIENCE IN YOUR LIFE: List common items that are made from trees.

Words to Know

seed	the part of a seed plant from which a new plant can grow
root	the part of a plant below the surface of the soil; used to hold the plant in place, store extra food, and soak up water and minerals from the soil
stem	the upright part of a plant; used to carry food and water and hold a plant up so its leaves can get sunlight
leaf	the food-making part of the plant
photosynthesis	the process that plants use to make food in the form of sugar
pistil	the female part of a flower
egg cell	a female sex cell
stamen	the male part of a flower
pollen	the light, powdery dust in stamens that contains the male sex cells
sperm cell	a male sex cell
petal	one of the colorful outer parts of a flower; it attracts insects
pollination	the process of transferring pollen from the stamen of a flower to the pistil of the same or a different flower
fertilization	the process of a sperm cell and an egg cell joining
germination	the process by which a tiny new plant breaks through the hard seed coat that is protecting it
fruit	the part of a plant that holds the seeds

Plants as Food Makers

Words to Know

seed	the part of a seed plant from which a new plant can grow
root	the part of a plant below the surface of the soil; used to hold the plant in place, store extra food, and soak up water and minerals from the soil
stem	the upright part of a plant; used to carry food and water and hold a plant up so its leaves can get sunlight
leaf	the food-making part of the plant
photosynthesis	the process that plants use to make food in the form of sugar

What Are Plants?

Plants are organisms made of many specialized cells. They are different from animals in three very important ways:

Remember
A cell is the smallest, most basic unit of life. A cell wall is the thicker covering around a plant cell membrane.

1. Plants make their own food.

2. Plant cells have cell walls.

3. Plants cannot move from place to place.

There are about 265,000 kinds of plants. You can see some of them on a walk through a park. Plants you might see include trees, grasses, ferns, bushes, flowering plants such as roses and daisies, and mosses. Plants grow in most places—from the desert to the mountains. Some even grow in water.

We owe a lot to plants. Without them, humans and all other animals could not survive. We would have no food to eat and no air to breathe. In this chapter, we will see why animal life would be impossible without plants.

✓ **How are plants different from animals?**

Seed Plants

Most of the plants you see around you are *seed plants*. These are the kind you will study in this chapter. The parts of seed plants are seeds, roots, stems, and leaves.

Seeds

The **seed** is the part of a seed plant from which a new plant can grow. Some kinds of seed plants produce flowers. These plants produce seeds inside the fruit. Avocados, daisies, and plum trees are examples of flowering seed plants. Another kind of seed plant produces cones. The seeds are inside the cones. Pine trees produce cones. Seeds are important in plant reproduction.

Roots

Below the surface of the soil is the plant's **root**. Roots have several jobs. One job is to hold the plant in place. Roots also store extra food that the plant has made. However, the most important job of roots is to soak up water and minerals from the soil. Water enters a plant through its roots. From the roots, water moves to other parts of the plant. Sugar beets and carrots are examples of roots.

Stems

The **stem** is the upright part of a plant. It starts at the ground and goes up to the leaves. The stem holds a plant up so its leaves can get sunlight. It also carries water and food through long, narrow tubes that go up and down the stem. First, the roots soak up water. Then the water is carried up the stem to other parts of the plant. Some of the food that plants make is sent down the stem to the roots.

Some stems are soft and flexible, like the stem of a daisy. Other stems are hard and rigid, like the stems of trees and shrubs. These are woody stems. The wood is made of cells with thick walls. The stems of trees are called *trunks*.

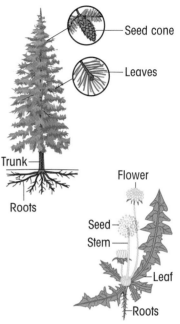

Figure 7-1 *Seed plants*

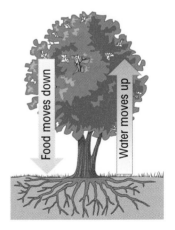

Figure 7-2 *In a tree, water moves up the trunk. Food moves down.*

You have probably eaten plant stems. Asparagus, bamboo shoots, and sugar cane are all stems. Potatoes are also stems. Many people think they are roots because they grow under the ground. However, potatoes are really just underground stem structures that store extra food.

Leaves

The **leaf** is the food-making part of a plant. Plants make their own food, using chlorophyll. Most of a plant's chlorophyll is found in its leaves.

The process that plants use to make food, in the form of sugar, is called **photosynthesis.** Four things are needed for photosynthesis: sunlight, water, chlorophyll, and carbon dioxide. Carbon dioxide is a gas in the air. It is made of carbon and oxygen molecules. Here is how photosynthesis works.

1. Water goes from the soil through the roots and stems to the leaves.

2. Carbon dioxide from the air enters small openings on the undersides of the leaves.

3. As sunlight strikes the chlorophyll in the leaves, energy is released.

4. This energy makes the carbon dioxide and water join together to make sugar and oxygen.

Remember

Chlorophyll is a green material stored inside plant structures called chloroplasts.

Science Fact

The spines of a cactus plant are really modified leaves. They protect the plant from animals that would eat it. The spines also prevent the plant from losing too much water in the hot, dry desert.

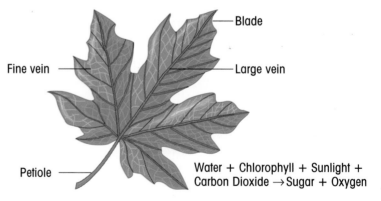

Blade

Fine vein

Large vein

Petiole

Water + Chlorophyll + Sunlight + Carbon Dioxide → Sugar + Oxygen

Figure 7-3 The leaf of the plant is where food is made. The process is shown in the formula above.

The sugar that plants make is not the kind of sugar you buy at the store. It is the basis of all food. Plants use the energy stored in sugar to carry out life processes. Animals eat the plants and get the energy stored in this sugar. People eat the animals or the plants and also get the energy. So you can see that *all* animals depend on photosynthesis for food.

Animals also get oxygen from photosynthesis. Remember that animals need oxygen to get energy from food during cellular respiration. After the plant sugar is made, there is some oxygen left over. This goes out of the plant through small openings on the underside of leaves. Without plants covering the Earth and releasing oxygen, animals could not breathe.

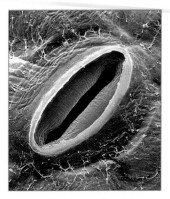

Small openings on the underside of leaves let oxygen, carbon dioxide, and water move in and out.

✓ **What are the jobs of seeds, roots, stems, and leaves on plants?**

Insect-eating Plants

There are a few plants that actually eat animals! These plants live in soil that does not have everything the plants need to grow. So the plants catch insects to get what they need.

The pitcher plant has leaf parts that are shaped like pitchers. These parts are lined with brushlike hairs. The hairs point down into the pitcher. When an insect comes along, it gets trapped in the hair and cannot get out. It slides down into the pitcher. The plant then digests the insect. The Venus' flytrap is another insect-eating plant. It catches insects on its brushlike leaves. The leaves snap closed like a trap around the insect.

Why, then, are these classified as plants rather than animals? Because they are rooted to the ground. They cannot move around at will. Also, they still make food using photosynthesis. Insects just add to their diet.

✓ **Why do some plants eat insects?**

Lesson Review

1. What four parts do all seed plants have?

2. What part of the plant makes most of its food?

3. What four things are needed for photosynthesis?

4. **CRITICAL THINKING** What job do both roots and stems do?

Modern Leaders in Science

PATRICIA SHANELY

Rain forests grow in very warm, wet places. They produce great amounts of oxygen. Also, rain forests provide food for a great many species of animals, including people.

In Brazil, people have cut down much of the thick plant growth in rain forests to create farmland. But rain forest soil is not good for growing crops. The crops use up the soil nutrients in a few years. Then people cut down more trees to make more fields.

Patricia Shanely works with the people of Brazil to help save the rain forests.

For the past ten years, Patricia Shanely has studied ways to help save the rain forests. She has worked with people who live in small villages in the rain forests of Brazil. She has taught them that selling trees to lumber companies is not the only way to earn money. Many people in the villages now gather fruits from the forest trees and sell them at markets. By saving the trees, the people will be able to hunt animals for food, use oils from the trees for medicines, and eat wild fruits. The trees also will continue to provide oxygen for all of us.

CRITICAL THINKING What are some ways you, too, can help save the rain forests?

Plant Reproduction

Words to Know

pistil	the female part of a flower
egg cell	a female sex cell
stamen	the male part of a flower
pollen	the light, powdery dust in stamens that contains the male sex cells
sperm cell	a male sex cell
petal	one of the colorful outer parts of a flower; it attracts insects
pollination	the process of transferring pollen from the stamen of a flower to the pistil of the same or a different flower
fertilization	the process of a sperm cell and an egg cell joining
germination	the process by which a tiny new plant breaks through the hard seed coat that is protecting it
fruit	the part of a plant that holds the seeds

Pollination

Seed plants reproduce using female and male plant parts found in their own flowers. The **pistil** is the female part of a flower. At the bottom of the pistil is the plant's *ovary*, where the female sex cells are stored. A female sex cell is called an **egg cell.**

The **stamen** is the male part of the flower. Flowers usually have several stamens. At the end of each stamen is a light, powdery dust called **pollen.** The pollen contains the male sex cells. A male sex cell is called a **sperm cell.**

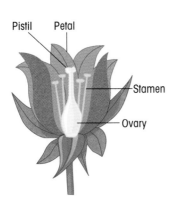

Figure 7-4 *Parts of a flower*

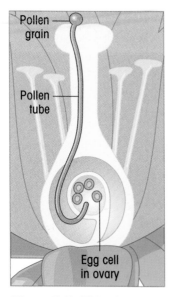

Pollen grain

Pollen tube

Egg cell in ovary

Figure 7-5 *This shows the process of plant fertilization.*

A flower **petal** is a colorful outer part of a flower. Flower petals attract insects. They also help to protect the inner parts of the flower.

For seed plants to reproduce, pollen must land on a pistil. Sometimes wind blows pollen off the stamens. That pollen may land on the pistil of the same plant or another plant. The pistil is sticky and traps the pollen. The entire process is called **pollination.** It is the transfer of pollen from the stamen of a flower to the pistil of another flower.

Bees often help with pollination. They are attracted to a flower because of its bright colors, pleasant smell, and its nectar. Nectar is a sweet liquid the plant produces. The bees use the nectar to make honey.

The bees have sticky legs. When they land on a stamen, the pollen sticks to their legs. They fly off. When they land on another flower, they leave a little pollen behind, on the pistil.

After pollination, a sperm cell travels down the pistil to the ovary of the flower. There it joins with an egg cell. Then a seed begins to grow. This process of sperm cell and egg cell joining is called **fertilization.**

✓ **What are the parts of a flower and how do they help in pollination?**

Protecting the Seed

You may have eaten sunflower seeds. These come from a sunflower. Seeds are also found in apples, squashes, and many other foods.

A seed is that part of a seed plant from which a new plant can grow. A seed includes a young new plant surrounded by a hard protective coating. Most of a seed is food for the young plant. The young plant needs a lot of food for growing. When the environment is warm and wet enough, the seed grows into a plant. This may take weeks or even years.

Wind and water can carry seeds far from the plants that made them. Sometimes animals carry seeds, too. Some kinds of seeds stick to the coats of animals. An animal may carry a seed a long way before it falls off. Some seeds never make it to a good place for growing. If a seed gets a chance, however, it will grow. The tiny new plant will break through the hard seed coat that has been protecting it. This is called **germination.**

The **fruit** of a seed plant is really a container for the seed. It may be juicy. It is the plant's ovary that has grown bigger. Inside a watermelon are a lot of black seeds. All the rest of the melon is protecting those seeds from water loss, disease, and insects.

Many of the foods we call vegetables or grains are really fruits. Anything that has seeds in it but is not a cone is a fruit. This includes tomatoes, beans, avocados, eggplants, oats, and wheat. All these fruits have seeds.

Thistle seeds

Maple seeds

Burdock seeds

Figure 7-6 *The shape of the seed helps it to travel.*

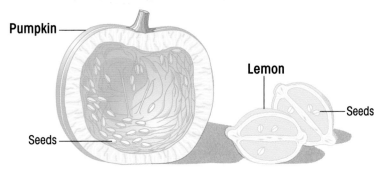

Pumpkin

Lemon

Seeds

Seeds

Figure 7-7 *Fruits protect their plants' seeds.*

✓ **How is a seed protected?**

Lesson Review

1. What happens when pollination takes place?

2. What happens when fertilization takes place?

3. CRITICAL THINKING Why do you think seeds might not germinate right away?

LAB ACTIVITY
Germinating Seeds

BACKGROUND
Seeds wait for the environment to be just right before the tiny new plant starts to grow. Then the seed breaks through the hard seed coat and germination occurs.

PURPOSE
You will see how different conditions affect how seeds germinate.

MATERIALS
paper, pencil, masking tape, 4 small plastic bowls, 4 small pieces of sponge, grass or radish seeds, water, plastic wrap, refrigerator

WHAT TO DO
1. Copy the chart to the right.
2. Write your name on four pieces of masking tape. Write "dry and warm" on one piece of tape. Write "moist and warm" on the second piece. Write "dry and cold" on the third piece, and write "moist and cold" on the fourth piece. Put one piece of tape on the outside of each bowl.

	Day 1	Day 2	Day 3	Day 4	Day 5
Dry and warm					
Moist and warm					
Dry and cold					
Moist and cold					

3. Wet two pieces of sponge. Place them in the bowls marked "moist." Put the two pieces of dry sponge in the bowls marked "dry."
4. Sprinkle half a spoonful of seeds on each piece of sponge. Cover each bowl with a piece of plastic wrap.
5. Place the bowls where your teacher tells you.
6. Check the seeds every day for 5 days. Write down what you see on each sponge every day.

DRAW CONCLUSIONS
- In which dish did the seeds begin to grow first?
- Which dish contained the most new plants?
- What can you say about which conditions are best for seed germination?

Trees produce the oxygen we need to breathe. Trees also provide humans and other animals with foods such as apples and walnuts. But people also use wood from trees. Wood from trees that have been cut down and sawed into boards is called *lumber*. Most lumber is used in building houses and in making furniture, boxes, and crates. Bits of wood can be treated with chemicals to make *wood pulp*. Wood pulp is used to make paper. In many parts of the world, people use wood as a fuel for heating and cooking.

People also use the bark of some trees. The bark of the Pacific yew tree is used to make a medicine to fight cancer. Bottle stoppers, bulletin boards, and floor materials are made from the bark of the cork oak tree.

The liquid, called *sap*, that flows in tree trunks is also used to make products. Maple syrup is made from the sap of maple trees. Turpentine, which is used in paints and varnishes, is made from the sap of pine trees.

Make a chart like the one below.

1. Look around you for products that are made from trees. List each product.

2. Tell what part of the tree it came from.

Logs are loaded onto a truck for their trip to a sawmill.

Critical Thinking

In some parts of the world, trees are being cut down for fuel faster than new trees can grow. What problems could this cause for a family in one of these areas?

Tree Product	Part of Tree

Summary

Plants make their own food and cannot move from place to place. They have specialized parts for growth and reproduction.

Lesson 7.1

The roots of a plant soak up water and minerals. They also hold the plant in place. The stem holds the plant upright. It is also a pathway for food and water. Water from the roots travels up from the stem. Food made by the leaves travels down the stem. Leaves carry out most of the plant's food-making, called photosynthesis.

Lesson 7.2

The flower of a plant is where the seed is made. Stamens, which hold pollen, are the male parts of the flower. The pistil is the female part. Pollination takes place when pollen lands on the pistil. Seeds are young plants in a protective coating. They must be in a wet, warm place to germinate. Fruits are the ovaries of plants. They protect the seeds.

Vocabulary Review

Match each definition with a term from the list.

egg cell

fruit

leaf

photosynthesis

pistil

root

stamen

stem

1. The food-making part of the plant

2. The upright part of a plant that holds the plant up and carries food and water

3. The male part of a flower

4. The part of a plant that holds the seeds

5. The process that plants use to make food in the form of sugar

6. The female part of a flower

7. The part of a plant below the surface that soaks up water and minerals

8. The female sex cell in a flower

Chapter Quiz

Write your answers on a separate sheet of paper.

1. How do plants differ from animals?

2. What four parts do all seed plants have?

3. What are three things roots do for plants?

4. What does a stem carry up a plant?

5. What does a stem carry down a plant?

6. What process in plants requires sunlight, water, chlorophyll, and carbon dioxide?

7. What happens during photosynthesis?

8. How do plants help you breathe?

9. What happens during pollination?

10. What part of a plant contains and protects the seeds?

Test Tip

Review the diagrams and the captions in the chapter before a test. Make sure you read the labels, too.

Research Project

Take a notebook and pencil to a grocery store. Create a chart of "Plant Parts We Eat." Make five headings on your paper: Stems, Leaves, Roots, Seeds, Fruits. Find as many foods as you can to list under each heading. Be sure to look at the canned and frozen foods as well as the fresh foods. Research where each of these foods is grown. Include this information in your chart. Finally, plan and write a menu for a meal that includes foods from different plant parts.

Chapter 8

Genetics:
The Code of Life

The puppies look like their mother and father. Why do you think the puppies resemble their parents?

Learning Objectives

- Explain how an organism passes on its traits.

- Compare dominant and recessive traits.

- Describe how DNA, genes, and chromosomes are related.

- Compare the number of chromosomes in body cells and sex cells.

- Explain the occurrence of mutation.

- Describe how the science of genetics is used in breeding.

- Give examples of how environment can affect an organism's traits.

- LAB ACTIVITY: Observe dominant and recessive traits.

- ON-THE-JOB SCIENCE: Relate an understanding of traits to cattle breeding.

Words to Know

trait	a characteristic that can be inherited from parents; it identifies an organism as an individual
offspring	a new organism that results from reproduction
heredity	the passing down of traits from parents to offspring
crossbreeding	the matching of parents with different traits to produce offspring with new traits
hybrid	the offspring of parents that have been crossbred
dominant	describes a trait that will show its effect no matter the effect of its partner trait
recessive	describes a trait that will be masked by a dominant partner trait
chromosome	a threadlike structure in a cell nucleus that holds thousands of bits of information about an organism's traits
gene	a bit of information in a chromosome
mutation	a change in the genetic code of an organism

The Same But Different

Words to Know

trait	a characteristic that can be inherited from parents; it identifies an organism as an individual
offspring	a new organism that results from reproduction
heredity	the passing down of traits from parents to offspring
crossbreeding	the matching of parents with different traits to produce offspring with new traits
hybrid	the offspring of parents that have been crossbred
dominant	describes a trait that will show its effect no matter the effect of its partner trait
recessive	describes a trait that will be masked by a dominant partner trait

What Is Heredity?

Have you ever wondered why you look the way you do? Do you look like some members of your family but not like others? Which of your features are like your mother's? Is your nose like hers? Which features are like your father's? Are your height and body shape like his? Do you talk or act like any of your sisters or brothers?

How are you different from the members of your family? Do you have features that none of them have?

A **trait** is a characteristic that can be inherited from parents. It identifies an organism as an individual. The way you look and act are traits. The color of your skin, hair, and eyes, and your height and shape are traits. You also have personality traits. Are you quiet or talkative? Are you careful or reckless? These are different personality traits.

Where do traits come from? All living things reproduce. This means that they produce new organisms to take their place when they die. For example, humans have babies. Plants make seeds that grow into plants. A new organism that results from reproduction is called an **offspring.** Offspring get many of their traits directly from their parents. The passing down of traits from parents to offspring is called **heredity.**

Genetics is the scientific study of heredity. The science of genetics is very new compared to other sciences. The study of genes began about 135 years ago. Yet, today, genetics is one of the fastest growing sciences.

✓ **How do people get many of their traits?**

The Beginning of Genetics

Some basic laws of genetics were first discovered in the mid-1800s. An Austrian monk named Gregor Johann Mendel grew 22 different kinds of pea plants in his garden. He bred these plants to study how their traits were passed from parents to offspring. *Breeding* means producing offspring, especially with the idea of getting new or better kinds.

Some of Mendel's pea plants were short and bushy. Others were tall and climbing. Some plants had white flowers. Others had purple flowers. Some produced round seeds. Others produced wrinkled seeds.

Mendel used the pollen from a tall plant to pollinate a short plant. This is called **crossbreeding.** Crossbreeding is the matching of parents with different traits to produce offspring with new traits.

Mendel also crossbred white-flowered plants with purple-flowered plants. Then he crossbred plants that had round seeds with plants that had wrinkled seeds. When parents with different traits are crossbred, the offspring is called a **hybrid.**

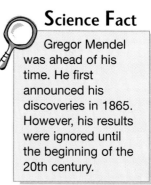

Science Fact

Gregor Mendel was ahead of his time. He first announced his discoveries in 1865. However, his results were ignored until the beginning of the 20th century.

Gregor Mendel (1822–1884)

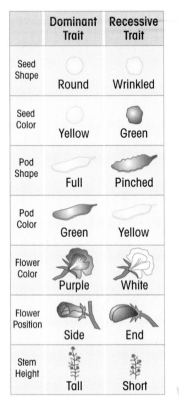

	Dominant Trait	Recessive Trait
Seed Shape	Round	Wrinkled
Seed Color	Yellow	Green
Pod Shape	Full	Pinched
Pod Color	Green	Yellow
Flower Color	Purple	White
Flower Position	Side	End
Stem Height	Tall	Short

Figure 8-1 *This table shows the seven characteristics that Mendel studied in pea plants.*

Mendel's results may surprise you. When he crossed tall plants with short plants, he always got tall plants. When he crossed purple-flowered plants with white-flowered plants, he always got purple-flowered plants. When he crossed round seeds with wrinkled seeds, he always got round seeds.

Mendel had discovered that there are two kinds of traits. One kind may cover or hide the other kind. In pea plants, being tall is a trait that can hide the trait of shortness. The color purple can hide the color white. Roundness can hide wrinkling in seeds.

In an organism, a **dominant** trait is one that will show its effect no matter the effect of its partner trait. A **recessive** trait is one that will be masked by a dominant partner trait. Recessive traits are not lost. They may show up in later generations. This explains how two brown-eyed parents can have a blue-eyed child. Both parents carry a recessive trait for blue eyes. They both pass on that trait to the child.

✓ **What two kinds of traits did Gregor Mendel discover?**

Lesson Review

1. What are four traits that you inherited from your parents?

2. What are three traits that Mendel studied in pea plants?

3. How is a hybrid created?

4. **CRITICAL THINKING** If you crossed a short pea plant with another short pea plant, what kind of offspring would be produced?

The Building Blocks of Heredity

Words to Know

chromosome	a threadlike structure in a cell nucleus that holds thousands of bits of information about an organism's traits
gene	a bit of information in a chromosome
mutation	a change in the genetic code of an organism

Chromosomes and Genes

A **chromosome** is a threadlike structure in a cell nucleus. It is made up of DNA. Scientists now know that traits are controlled by DNA. Each chromosome holds thousands of bits of information about an organism's traits. Each of these bits of information is called a **gene.** A gene consists of a DNA code that controls a trait. Genes are the basic building blocks of heredity. They form the *genetic code* of life.

Remember
DNA is a special kind of molecule found in the nuclei of cells. It controls many of the characteristics of living things.

Chromosomes come in pairs. Half an organism's chromosomes are from the father. Half are from the mother. Genes come in pairs, too. Most inherited traits are controlled by at least one pair of genes. These genes will be either dominant or recessive, like the traits they control. However, traits are often controlled by more than one pair of genes.

Science Fact

Scientists often use fruit flies to study genetics. That is because fruit flies have hundreds of offspring at a time, and they reproduce every ten days. Scientists can easily and quickly observe the passing of traits over many generations.

Each species has a certain number of chromosomes. Humans have 23 pairs. This means that every nucleus in every human body cell has 46 chromosomes. Fruit flies have only 4 pairs. Every body cell in a fruit fly has 8 chromosomes in its nucleus.

✓ What is the relationship between a chromosome and a gene?

On the Cutting Edge

A POWERFUL WEAPON AGAINST DIABETES

Scientists have found the gene in human cells that controls the making of a hormone called insulin. Insulin is made by the pancreas, an organ in the digestive system. A serious disease called diabetes keeps the body from making insulin or using it properly.

When you eat carbohydrates, your body breaks them down into a simple sugar called glucose. The body uses glucose for energy. In 1922, researchers found that glucose was controlled by insulin.

This lab uses bacteria to produce insulin.

Insulin can be injected into the body to control diabetes. Insulin used to be very expensive and hard to get. Today, however, insulin can be made in the laboratory. The gene from human DNA is removed and attached to the DNA of bacteria. This causes the bacteria to make insulin. Bacteria reproduce very quickly. Today, bacteria "factories" make insulin quickly and at little cost.

CRITICAL THINKING How does the making of insulin-producing bacteria help people who have diabetes?

Fertilization

Remember
All living things are made of cells. The male sex cells are called sperm cells, and the female sex cells are called egg cells.

Most cells reproduce by dividing in half. One cell divides into two cells. However, before the cell divides, it copies its chromosomes exactly. This way, both of the new cells are complete and are exactly the same.

Many organisms, including humans, begin with two special kinds of cells called sex cells. Like body cells, the sex cells reproduce by dividing. However, sex cells divide twice. The second time, they do not make copies of the chromosomes. As a result, each new sex cell gets only half the number of chromosomes found in body cells.

When organisms reproduce, a sperm cell and an egg cell join. This is fertilization. The two cells become one cell with a full set of chromosomes. The offspring that results has genes from both the sperm cell and the egg cell.

✓ **What happens to the chromosomes of the parents during fertilization?**

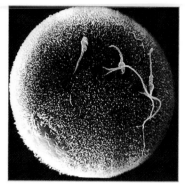

Fertilization

Where Do New Traits Come From?

New traits may suddenly appear in organisms. For example, a purple-flowered plant may have a single red flower. Then some of its offspring may have only red flowers. The new trait may be the result of a change in the organism's DNA. This change in the genetic code of an organism is called a **mutation.**

Most mutations are harmful and can cause an organism's early death. These mutations are not usually passed on to offspring. For example, a bird born with a soft beak would not be able to crack nuts or dig for worms. It would die young.

Sometimes, a helpful mutation occurs. Imagine a mutation that causes a giraffe to have a longer neck. The giraffe could reach more leaves on a tree than other giraffes could. The giraffe would pass along this mutation to its offspring.

✓ **What can cause a new trait to appear in an organism?**

Lesson Review

1. On what structures are genes located?

2. How are sex cells different from body cells?

3. CRITICAL THINKING What might cause a frog to be born with only one leg?

Plant and Animal Breeding

Long before scientists knew anything about DNA, people used genetics. For example, farmers have used genetics to control the traits of the offspring of their plant crops and animals. Even in ancient times, farmers bred the best fruit trees to get better fruit. They bred the best milk cows to get better milk.

Today, scientists, farmers, and gardeners carefully choose plants and animals for breeding. This is called *selective breeding*.

✓ **What is selective breeding?**

The Environment and Traits

Your genes do not control everything about you. Your environment also plays a big part in forming your traits. Your environment includes the air you breathe, the food you eat, the education you get, and other things in your surroundings.

Suppose, for example, that a woman has the genes to be a very fast runner. Yet, she has a poor diet and never exercises. These environmental influences would probably keep the woman from running very fast.

A tomato plant may be the offspring of parents that produced big, juicy tomatoes. The young plant has very good genes for producing delicious fruit. Yet, suppose the plant is rooted in poor soil and does not get enough water. Despite its good genes, the tomato plant may not produce any fruit at all because of its environment.

✓ **Besides genes, what else can affect the traits of an organism?**

Transferring Genes

Today, scientists can produce new traits in organisms by removing a gene from the DNA of one organism and transferring it to the DNA of another organism. As a result, the organism that receives the gene has the trait that is controlled by that gene. You read on page 114 that scientists transferred a human insulin gene into bacteria. With this gene, the bacteria produce human insulin. The process of transferring a gene from one organism to another is called *genetic engineering*.

✓ **How does genetic engineering produce new traits?**

Lesson Review

1. How do farmers use genetics to produce better plants?

2. What is the result of genetic engineering?

3. **CRITICAL THINKING** How might a person's environment affect his or her height?

A Closer Look

CLONING ANIMALS

An animal has a combination of traits from its mother and its father. But scientists have found a way of producing an animal that gets all its traits from one parent. The animal, which is identical to the parent, is called a clone.

Scientists make a clone by removing the nucleus from an animal's egg cell. Then they remove the nucleus from a body cell of an animal of the same species. This nucleus is inserted into the egg cell. The egg cell now has a full set of chromosomes. Scientists place the egg cell into an adult female, where it grows. The offspring is identical to the animal from which it got its chromosomes.

This sheep, called Dolly, is a clone.

CRITICAL THINKING How can cloning be helpful to farmers?

LAB ACTIVITY
Observing Dominant and Recessive Traits

BACKGROUND

All organisms have traits. Your eye color, skin color, and height are a few human traits. Some traits are dominant. Others are recessive. A dominant trait will show its effect no matter the effect of its partner trait.

PURPOSE

You will observe some dominant and recessive human traits.

MATERIALS

mirror

WHAT TO DO

1. Copy the chart.
2. Look at the three human traits shown in the drawing. Note whether each trait is dominant or recessive.
3. Find out which of the traits you have. Use a mirror to observe your features.
4. In the chart, record your traits. Then write whether each trait is dominant or recessive.
5. Count up and record the number of students in your class who have the dominant trait for each feature. Then count up and record the number of students who have the recessive trait for each feature.

Pointed hairline
Dominant

Smooth hairline
Recessive

Hanging earlobe
Dominant

Attached earlobe
Recessive

Long eyelashes
Dominant

Short eyelashes
Recessive

Human traits

Feature	Trait	Dominant or Recessive?
Hairline		
Earlobe		
Eyelashes		

DRAW CONCLUSIONS

- Which dominant traits do you have?
- Which recessive traits do you have?
- Do more students in your class have dominant traits or recessive traits for each feature? Why do you think this is so?

ON-THE-JOB SCIENCE
Cattle Breeder

Jacob is a cattle breeder. He selects cattle for their traits. For example, the cattle may be selected for producing high-quality meat or large amounts of milk. When the selected cattle produce offspring, Jacob chooses the offspring that show the best traits. Then these offspring reproduce. Jacob continues to select the best offspring for several generations. Eventually, a new breed of cattle with the best traits is produced. The chart below describes some traits of four breeds of dairy cattle.

Cattle breeders select cattle for certain traits.

Name of Dairy-Cattle Breed	Size	Average Amount of Milk Produced Each Year	Average Percent of Milk That Is Butterfat
Holstein-Friesian	Largest	14,700 lb	3.5%
Brown Swiss		12,800 lb	4.0 %
Guernsey		10,300 lb	4.8 %
Jersey	Smallest	9,400 lb	5.2 %

Suppose you wanted to produce a new breed of dairy cattle with improved traits. Think about the following questions: *Do you want the new breed to be large or small? Do you want the breed to produce large amounts of milk? Should the milk have a lot of butterfat?*

On a separate sheet of paper, describe the new cattle breed that you would like to produce.

Tell which of the breeds in the chart you would allow to reproduce to create the new breed. Explain why you selected those breeds.

Critical Thinking
Some cattle produce good-tasting meat *and* a lot of milk. How do you think breeders produced these cattle?

| Summary | Genetics is the study of heredity. Heredity, along with other things, determines who and what you are. |

| Lesson 8.1 | Many traits are passed from parents to offspring. This is heredity. Gregor Mendel used pea plants to study genetics. He discovered that some traits can be dominant or recessive. |

| Lesson 8.2 | Genes are parts of chromosomes. A gene contains DNA, which controls traits in an organism. Offspring get half their chromosomes from each parent. A change in the genetic code is called a mutation. |

| Lesson 8.3 | Selective breeding can produce plants and animals with better traits. The environment also affects the traits of organisms. Genetic engineering also can produce new traits. |

Vocabulary Review

Write *true* or *false* for each sentence. If the sentence is false, replace the underlined term to make the sentence true.

1. In pea plants, white flower color is a <u>dominant</u> trait because it is masked by purple flower color.

2. A <u>mutation</u> may result in a new trait in an organism.

3. <u>Crossbreeding</u> matches parents with different traits.

4. <u>A trait</u> is a new organism that results from reproduction.

5. <u>Heredity</u> is the passing of traits from parents to offspring.

6. A <u>clone</u> results from crossbreeding.

7. A <u>gene</u> contains a DNA code.

8. <u>A chromosome</u> is found in the nucleus of a cell.

Chapter Quiz

Write your answers on a separate sheet of paper.

Test Tip
Before you begin a test, look it over. Try to decide how much time you will need for each question. Set aside enough time for more difficult questions.

1. What does an organism pass along to its offspring?

2. Does a recessive trait disappear forever? If not, when may it reappear?

3. Mendel produced pea plants that were hybrid for seed shape. Why did the hybrid plants have round seeds instead of wrinkled seeds?

4. Where are the genes in your cells located?

5. How many chromosomes are in human sex cells? How many chromosomes are in human body cells?

6. What does a cell make copies of before it divides?

7. Why are harmful mutations usually not passed on to offspring?

8. How do farmers use genetics to produce better livestock?

9. How can the environment affect an organism's traits? Give two examples.

10. How did scientists produce bacteria that make human insulin?

Research Project

Choose any plant or animal to research. The organism might be at home or near your school. On a separate sheet of paper, name as many of the organism's traits as you can. Be sure to include its size, shape, and color. Describe how the organism acts. Name three traits that are caused by the organism's genes. Name a trait that is caused by the organism's environment.

This is a skeleton of a saber-toothed tiger that lived millions of years ago. There are no saber-toothed tigers on Earth today. How was this animal like the tigers of today? How was it different?

Learning Objectives

- List the ways scientists learn about theories of evolution.
- Describe Lamarck's theory of evolution.
- Identify the four main parts of Darwin's theory of evolution.
- Compare and contrast natural selection and mutation.
- Explain the role of mutations in the theory of evolution.
- LAB ACTIVITY: Explore how natural selection works.
- SCIENCE IN YOUR LIFE: Relate use of pesticides to natural selection of pests.

Words to Know

evolution	the process of change in a species over time, usually over thousands or millions of years
extinct	no longer existing on Earth
fossil	the remains of an organism that lived long ago
paleontology	the scientific study of fossils
theory	an explanation about something that is supported by data
naturalist	a scientist who studies living things in nature
natural selection	the way organisms that are best suited to their environment survive and pass on their helpful traits to offspring

Words to Know

evolution	the process of change in a species over time, usually over thousands or millions of years
extinct	no longer existing on Earth
fossil	the remains of an organism that lived long ago
paleontology	the scientific study of fossils

What Is Evolution?

Remember
Protists are tiny one-celled creatures.

Most scientists believe that life first appeared on Earth about 3 billion years ago. The organisms were a lot like protists that live in the ocean today.

It is possible that all the plants and animals alive today came from those first creatures. The evidence suggests that humanlike creatures have only been around for about 5 million years. That is really not very long. Remember that the Earth has existed for about 4.6 *billion* years.

The woolly mammoth evolved into the elephant.

Species change over time. For example, the woolly mammoth no longer exists. Yet that species slowly changed into what we know today as the elephant. Dinosaurs do not exist anymore, either. However, some scientists think that the ancestors of today's birds were dinosaurs. This process of change in a species over time, usually over thousands or millions of years, is called **evolution**. To evolve is to change with time. From those first one-celled creatures, evolution may have formed all the organisms alive today.

✓ **What happens to species over time?**

Putting Together the Puzzle of the Past

Scientists have put together a picture of evolution from many clues. For example, woolly mammoths have been **extinct** for a long time. Something that is extinct is no longer existing on Earth. The species has died out and is gone forever. However, the bones and teeth of dinosaurs and other extinct animals have been found. Scientists have found woolly mammoths in Siberia. Ice had preserved them for 25,000 years. Extinct insects have also been found trapped in hardened tree sap.

This fossil is the impression of a plant that lived long ago.

The remains of an organism that lived long ago is called a **fossil.** Bones and teeth are fossils. Footprints preserved in rock are also fossils. Fossils show how organisms from the past are different from organisms on Earth today. They also show that today's organisms evolved from these older species.

Early horse   Modern horse

Figure 9-1 *Early horses were the size of large modern dogs.*

The scientific study of fossils is called **paleontology.** By studying fossils, paleontologists learned that early horses were about the size of large modern dogs. These horses had four toes on each front foot and three toes on each back foot. Modern horses have only one toe per foot.

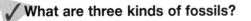 **What are three kinds of fossils?**

DNA and Other Clues to Evolution

In addition to fossils, scientists also look at other clues. They study an organism's DNA to learn about evolution.

Remember
DNA holds the genetic code of an organism.

For example, scientists have found that the DNA in humans is 98 percent the same as the DNA in chimpanzees. This means that our genetic codes are very much alike. Scientists believe that it also means that humans and chimpanzees could have evolved from the same ancestor.

Scientists also compare the bones of different living animals for clues about evolution. For example, the bones in a lion's foreleg, a bat's wing, and a dolphin's flipper are very similar. Scientists say this is because these animals have a common ancestor.

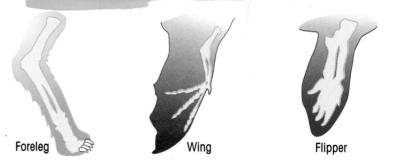

Foreleg   Wing   Flipper

Figure 9-2 *The lion's foreleg, bat's wing, and dolphin's flipper all have similar bone structures.*

✓ **Why do scientists study an organism's DNA?**

Lesson Review

1. What process may have formed all the organisms alive today?

2. Why do scientists search for fossils?

3. **CRITICAL THINKING** Scientists have found DNA in the fossils of some extinct organisms. What can they learn by comparing this DNA to the DNA of living organisms?

Theories of Evolution

Words to Know

theory	an explanation about something that is supported by data
naturalist	a scientist who studies living things in nature
natural selection	the way organisms that are best suited to their environment survive and pass on their helpful traits to offspring

An Early Theory

In 1809, the French biologist Jean Baptiste Lamarck came up with a **theory** of evolution. A theory is an explanation about something that is supported by data. Lamarck suggested that organisms develop traits by using or not using parts of the body. If a part of the body is used a lot, it becomes larger and stronger. If it is not used, it becomes smaller and weaker. Lamarck also believed that the traits an organism developed during its lifetime could be passed on from parents to offspring. A species evolves by inheriting traits such as these.

Lamarck used the giraffe as a model for his theory. He assumed that early giraffes had short necks and ate grass. Then the environment changed, and the grass died. The giraffes began to eat leaves on trees instead. They stretched their necks to reach the leaves on high branches. This made their necks grow longer. The new trait was passed on.

Figure 9-3 *Lamarck mistakenly believed that giraffes grew longer necks by stretching to reach leaves.*

Lamarck did not have much evidence to support his theory. Eventually it was proven wrong. Although his explanation for evolution was wrong, Lamarck was the first person to propose that new species evolved from older species.

✓ **What was Lamarck's theory of evolution?**

Darwin and Natural Selection

*Charles Darwin
(1809–1882)*

Charles Darwin was an English scientist who played an important role in developing the modern theory of evolution.

In 1831, when Darwin was only 22 years old, he sailed around the world. Darwin was the ship's **naturalist.** A naturalist is a scientist who studies living things in nature.

Darwin's job was to list and describe all the plants and animals he saw on the trip. His observations led him to his theory of evolution.

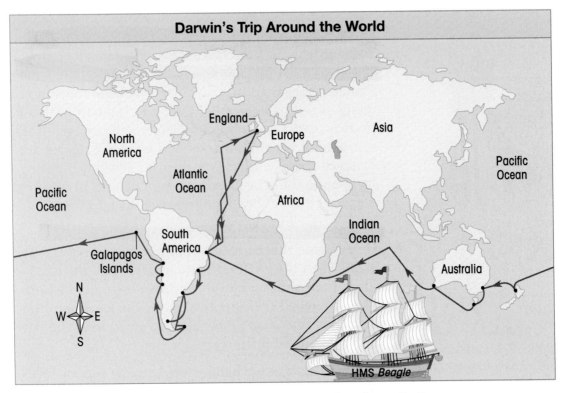

Figure 9-4 *Darwin worked as a naturalist aboard the* Beagle *on its five-year voyage.*

When Darwin returned to England, he studied his notes. He also studied all the existing theories on the origins of different animals, including humans. Then, in 1858, he wrote a book on his theories. His ideas became the basis of the modern study of evolution.

An important part of Darwin's theory of evolution was **natural selection.** Natural selection is the way organisms that are best suited to their environment survive and pass on their helpful traits to offspring.

Remember that when organisms reproduce by sexual reproduction, the offspring get half of their genes from each parent. Each parent's genes control thousands of traits. So, each offspring has a new combination of genes.

Over time, some gene combinations increase the ability of an organism to survive and reproduce. Other combinations lead to an early death of the organism. Since these individuals die before they can reproduce, their gene combinations are lost.

There are four main ideas that make up Darwin's theory of natural selection.

1. **Most organisms have more offspring than can survive.** For example, an insect lays many, many eggs in its lifetime. Only a few of these eggs will survive to become full-grown insects. Dandelions release thousands of seeds. Only a few of these seeds will be carried by the wind or animals and land somewhere good for growing into plants.

2. **Offspring must compete for food and space.** Many of an organism's offspring do not survive and reproduce. That is because there is not enough food and living space for all of them. Only those young organisms that can get food and living space will survive. A seed that lands in a dry, dark place will not grow into a plant. A kitten born in a field where there are five full-grown cats may not catch enough mice to eat and survive. There is too much competition.

3. **Organisms that survive have traits that are best suited to their environment.** Remember that there is not enough food and space for all organisms. To survive, an organism must be able to get food and protect itself from enemies. The strong, fast cats will probably get the mice before the slow, weak ones. Brown rabbits living in the forest are better camouflaged from enemies than white rabbits.

4. **Natural selection passes along helpful traits to offspring.** Strong, fast cats will live longer than weak, slow ones. So the strong, fast cats are more likely to have offspring. They will pass on their genes to their kittens.

✓ **Why are helpful traits more likely to be passed on to offspring?**

Mutations and Evolution

Scientists today know a lot more about evolution than Darwin did. By studying DNA, they have learned some of the ways that changes in species come about.

Mutations, for example, can cause a species to change. Change due to a mutation is different from change due to natural selection. Change by natural selection occurs through new combinations of existing genes. Mutation occurs when a whole new gene is formed. A mutation is a kind of genetic mistake. Many mutations are harmful. Sometimes, however, a mutation introduces a helpful trait to a species.

Remember that the early horses had several toes. This made them slow runners. Perhaps a mutation caused a horse to be born with fewer toes. This horse, and its offspring, could run faster from enemies. These offspring survived better than those with several toes. Over time, the horses with several toes died out.

✓ **How can mutations change the course of evolution?**

Lesson Review

1. What kind of traits did Lamarck believe are passed from parents to offspring?

2. Which offspring of an organism are most likely to survive and reproduce?

3. CRITICAL THINKING Suppose a brown rabbit has a mutation that makes its fur white. Would that mutation be helpful or harmful in a snowy environment? Explain why.

Great Moments in Science

JUMPING GENES

Barbara McClintock was a biologist. She spent her life studying corn in order to learn more about genes. In the 1940s, McClintock discovered that genes were not found in only one place. They moved around on chromosomes.

McClintock gave talks and wrote reports about her "jumping genes." No one paid any attention. Forty years later, other scientists finally caught up with her ideas. They, too, found that genes jump on chromosomes. This discovery helped explain how many new combinations of genes are formed. It helped scientists understand how organisms evolve. At the age of 81, McClintock won the Nobel Prize.

McClintock showed that the colors of corn kernels could change when certain genes moved on the chromosomes.

CRITICAL THINKING McClintock repeated her experiments many times. How did that make it easier for other scientists to finally accept her idea?

LAB ACTIVITY
Studying Natural Selection

BACKGROUND

Organisms pass their helpful traits to their offspring. One helpful trait for many animals is having a color that blends into their environment.

PURPOSE

You will see how a helpful trait can be passed on due to natural selection.

MATERIALS

brown and white dots, white cloth, stopwatch

WHAT TO DO

1. Copy the chart to the right.
2. Get 40 brown dots and 40 white dots from your teacher. Each dot represents an animal in the first generation.
3. Spread the cloth on the floor. The cloth represents the environment. Scatter all the dots on the cloth.
4. Pick up as many dots as you can, one at a time, as your partner times you for 30 seconds.
5. Count the number of brown dots and white dots that are left on the cloth. They represent brown animals and white animals that have survived and can now reproduce. Double the number of each color by scattering more dots on the cloth. For example, if there are 10 brown dots and 30 white dots left, add 10 more brown dots and 30 more white dots.
6. Count the number of brown dots and white dots that are now on the cloth. These dots represent animals in the second generation. Enter the numbers in your chart.
7. Repeat steps 4 to 6 to get the third generation.

Generation	Brown Dots	White Dots
1	40	40
2		
3		

DRAW CONCLUSIONS

• How many "animals" of each color were in each generation?

• How does this activity show that natural selection helps pass along certain traits?

SCIENCE IN YOUR LIFE
Changing the Course of Natural Selection

Rey is having a birthday party at his home. It is summer, and the weather is sunny and warm. His guests will play volleyball and eat in the back yard.

However, there are many mosquitoes outside. Rey is worried that the mosquitoes will bite his guests and ruin the party. He decides to spray the yard with a *pesticide*, a poison that kills insects. The pesticide gets rid of most of the mosquitoes. The party is saved.

Chemical poisons can cause the natural selection of pests that are resistant.

Rey did not know that by using the pesticide, he could be helping future generations of mosquitoes. Most mosquitoes are killed by the pesticide, but some survive. One of the survivors might have a mutation that makes it *resistant to*, or unharmed by, the pesticide. When it reproduces, its offspring may be resistant, too. If the pesticide is used often, most of the mosquitoes may be resistant after many generations. The same thing can happen with other kinds of pests, such as bacteria and weeds. This is the process of natural selection.

To see how pests can become resistant to pesticides, answer these questions.

1. Suppose there are 1,000 normal mosquitoes and one resistant mosquito in a field. What fraction of the mosquitoes are resistant?

2. The field is sprayed with a pesticide. The resistant mosquito survives, and so do one out of every hundred of the normal mosquitoes. How many normal mosquitoes survive?

3. Each of the survivors produces 100 offspring. How many resistant offspring are there? How many normal offspring are there?

4. As a group, have the mosquitoes become more resistant, less resistant, or stayed about the same?

Critical Thinking

What would happen to the resistant mosquitoes if a new pesticide was used?

Summary

The theory of evolution explains how species change over time. The current theory of evolution, including the theory of natural selection, was developed by Charles Darwin.

Lesson 9.1

Scientists study fossils for answers about evolution. Scientists also study the DNA and bone structure of living organisms.

Lesson 9.2

Charles Darwin developed his theory of evolution in the mid-1800s. His theory of natural selection explains how helpful traits are passed on to new generations. Mutations help explain how new traits can appear. A helpful mutation will be passed on to offspring.

Vocabulary Review

extinct
evolution
fossil
naturalist
natural selection
paleontology
theory

Match each definition with a term from the list.

1. An explanation about something that is supported by data

2. The way organisms that are best suited to their environment survive and pass on their helpful traits to their offspring

3. No longer existing on Earth

4. The process of change in a species over time, usually over thousands or millions of years

5. The remains of an organism that lived long ago

6. A scientist who studies living things in nature

7. The scientific study of fossils

Chapter Quiz

Write your answers on a separate sheet of paper.

1. What does a species do when it evolves?

2. What can scientists learn by studying fossils?

3. How do scientists use DNA to find out about evolution?

4. How do the limbs of lions, bats, and dolphins show that these animals came from the same ancestor?

5. What did Lamarck believe happens to the traits that an organism develops during its lifetime?

6. What are the four main ideas in Darwin's theory of natural selection?

7. What idea of natural selection is shown by a kitten catching a mouse?

8. What idea of natural selection is shown by a white rabbit in the snow?

9. How is change by natural selection different from change due to a mutation?

10. What kinds of mutations are most likely to cause a species to change?

Test Tip
If you cannot think of an answer, try to remember a picture of something related to that topic. It may help you recall the answer.

Research Project

Use the Internet or the library to find out about an extinct organism such as the dodo bird, passenger pigeon, or dinosaur. Look for a picture of the organism. Study the picture. Then write a paragraph that describes the organism. What did it look like? When did it live? Where did it live? How was it different from organisms of today?

Unit 2 Review

Choose the letter for the correct answer to each question.

Use the diagram to answer Questions 1 to 3.

1. Which characteristic do the organisms above *not* share?

    A. growing

    B. reproducing

    C. living without water

    D. responding to the environment

2. The tree can make its own food because each leaf cell has which of the following?

    A. cytoplasm

    B. a cell membrane

    C. a nucleus

    D. chloroplasts

3. To which kingdom does the mushroom belong?

    A. Moneran

    B. Fungus

    C. Protist

    D. Animal

4. All animals have which of the following?

    A. specialized cells

    B. jointed appendages

    C. lungs

    D. a backbone

5. What is the male part of a flower called?

    A. pistil

    B. stamen

    C. stem

    D. petal

6. What is the threadlike structure in a nucleus that holds thousands of bits of information called?

    A. gene

    B. trait

    C. hybrid

    D. chromosome

7. Which of the following is an example of a fossil?

    A. DNA

    B. a mutation

    C. a footprint in rock

    D. a living tree

Critical Thinking

Many biologists think that plants evolved from algae and that animals evolved from protozoa. Why might biologists think that?

Unit 3 ▶ Life Science: Part II

Humans have complex body systems and large brains. These help them to survive in many different environments, even underwater.

Use the chart below to answer the questions.

1. Which body system allows the diver to breathe in oxygen from the air tank?

2. Which body system helps the diver move through the water?

3. A wetsuit protects the diver from the environment. What organ is like the wetsuit?

Some Human Body Systems		
System	**Main Function**	**Organ in the System**
Immune	Protects from the environment	Skin
Muscular	Allows movement	Biceps (arm)
Nervous	Receives and sends messages	Brain
Respiratory	Takes in oxygen from air	Lungs

Chapter **10** The Human Body

Humans have thumbs to grasp things and large brains to figure things out. This man is repairing a communications tower. What special human abilities is he using?

Learning Objectives

- Define body tissue and organ.
- Compare two body systems.
- Identify the control center of the human body.
- Name the five sense organs.
- Compare the uses of bones and muscles.
- Describe the reproductive system and puberty.
- **LAB ACTIVITY:** Explore how taste and smell work together.
- **ON-THE-JOB SCIENCE:** Relate checking heart rates to fitness instruction.

Words to Know

tissue	a group of similar cells that work together to do a job
organ	a body part made up of one or more kinds of tissue
system	a group of organs working together to do a job
hormone	a substance made by organs called glands
skeleton	the bones that support, allow movement, and protect the organs of an animal with a backbone
calcium	a mineral found in teeth and bone
joint	a place where two bones meet
tendon	a tough band of tissue that attaches muscle to bone
puberty	the time in life when the reproductive organs develop
testes	the male organs where sperm cells are made
ovaries	the female organs where egg cells are stored
uterus	the female organ in which a fetus develops
fetus	an unborn baby that develops in a woman's uterus
menstruation	the monthly flow of blood from the uterus of a woman who is not having a baby

Words to Know

tissue	a group of similar cells that work together to do a job
organ	a body part made up of one or more kinds of tissue
system	a group of organs working together to do a job
hormone	a substance made by organs called glands

The Basic Plan

Remember
Cells are the smallest units of living matter. All animals have specialized cells that do different jobs.

The human body is made up of many kinds of **tissue**. A tissue is a group of similar cells that work together to do a job. Blood tissue is made up of blood cells.

An **organ** is a body part made up of one or more kinds of tissue. The heart is an example of an organ. It is a pump made mostly of muscle tissue. A **system** is a group of organs working together to do a job. The heart is part of the circulatory system. The circulatory system sends blood around the body.

Vein from body to heart

Artery from heart to body

— Fat

Muscle —

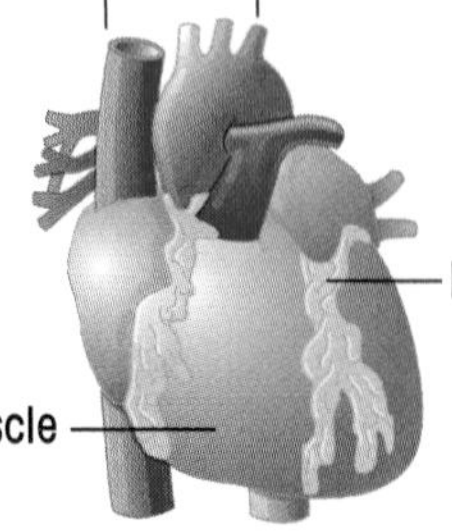

Figure 10-1
The human heart

Human Body Systems		
System	**Main Function**	**Organ in the System**
Circulatory	Sends blood around the body	Heart
Digestive	Breaks down food into usable parts	Stomach
Immune	Protects from the environment	Skin
Muscular	Allows movement	Biceps (arm)
Nervous	Receives and sends messages	Brain
Reproductive	Makes offspring	Ovaries/Testes
Respiratory	Takes in oxygen from air	Lungs
Skeletal	Supports body and protects organs	Backbone

✓ **How are tissues, organs, and systems related?**

The Body's Control Center

The brain is the control center of the human body. It is made up of billions of nerve cells, or *neurons*. The brain sends messages around the body. It also receives messages. The brain controls many of the body's functions. It also stores information.

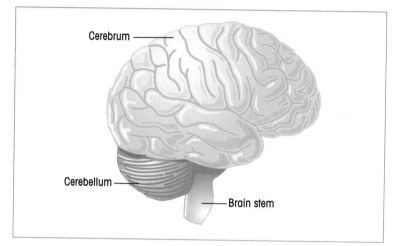

Cerebrum

Cerebellum

Brain stem

Figure 10-2 *The human brain*

Messages go from your brain down to your *spinal cord*. The spinal cord is like a big rope of neurons. It runs along the inside of your backbone.

The spinal cord connects to neurons all over your body. Messages travel from one neuron to the next until they reach their destinations. The brain, spinal cord, sense organs, and neurons are all parts of the nervous system.

Another way body functions are controlled is by hormones. A **hormone** is a substance made by organs called *glands*. Some glands make hormones that circulate in the blood and cause changes in the body.

✔ **Why is the brain said to be the control center of the human body?**

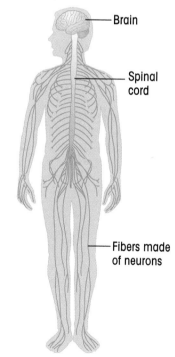

Brain

Spinal cord

Fibers made of neurons

Figure 10-3
The nervous system

The Five Senses

Humans have five senses: sight, hearing, taste, smell, and touch. Each of these senses has an organ. These sense organs are also part of the nervous system.

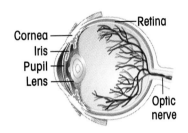

Figure 10-4
The human eye

Sight

Eyes are the organs of sight. Light bounces off objects and enters your eyes. This light triggers nerves in the back of the eyes. These nerves send messages to your brain, and you see an object.

Most people depend more on their sight than on their other senses. However, blind people learn to depend on their hearing and touch. These other senses become much sharper when the sense of sight is taken away.

Hearing

Ears are the organs of hearing. All sounds are made by vibrations. Vibrations are quick back and forth movements of air. Think of a violin. When you pluck a string, you make it vibrate. The vibrations travel long distances in waves. The sound waves enter the ears. Tiny bones inside the ears are moved by the vibrations. Nerves pick up the movement and send a signal to the brain. You hear this as sound. People sometimes cup their hands behind their ears to hear better. This directs the sound to the inner ear.

Safety Alert

Listening to very loud noises can damage parts of the ear, especially cells that line the inner ear. This can lead to hearing loss.

Taste

The tongue is the organ of taste. People can taste only four types of flavors: sour, sweet, salty, and bitter. Different areas of the tongue taste different flavors. The tip tastes sweet and salty things. The sides taste sour things. The back tastes bitter things. Not all animals have the same sense of taste. Cats do not taste sweet things.

Smell

The nose is the organ of smell. Think of smelling an onion. Tiny molecules from the onion drift up to your nose. There, the molecules from the onion trigger nerve cells that send a message to your brain.

Touch

Skin is the organ of touch. Some areas of skin, such as the fingertips, are very sensitive to heat, cold, touch, and pain. These areas have more nerve cells than other areas. The sense of touch protects the body from harm. It works like an alarm system. If something sharp or hot touches your body, you know to move away.

Skin is the human body's largest organ. It serves many functions besides passing sensory messages to the brain. For example, it keeps the body from drying out. As part of the immune system, it also keeps out some harmful bacteria.

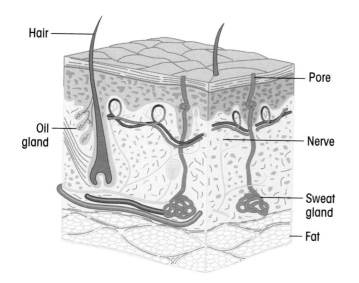

Figure 10-5 *Cross section of human skin*

Skin has sweat glands in it. Sweat glands make sweat. Sweat is made mostly of water and salt. The water in sweat cools the body when a person gets overheated. So skin also helps the human body stay at the right temperature.

✓ **What are the five sense organs and what do they do?**

How Are Humans Unique?

The human body is a lot like the bodies of other animals. The human brain, though, is larger and more complex. This is what makes humans special, or unique. Scientists say the human brain may be one of the most complex things in the universe.

Humans cannot run as fast as cheetahs. We cannot smell as well as dogs. We cannot fly like birds. Many animals have more muscle power than we do.

However, we make up for much of this with our large brains. We use our brains to design cars and airplanes that move fast. We make telescopes and microscopes to see things that other animals cannot see.

We build machines to do some of our muscle work for us. We send rockets into space. We can write stories and beautiful music and paint wonderful pictures. The human animal is indeed unique.

✓ **What organ is it that most sets us apart from other animals?**

Lesson Review

1. What is the control center of the human body?

2. Name the four types of flavors humans can taste.

3. What is the most important difference between humans and other animals?

4. CRITICAL THINKING Nails cover the skin on the ends of fingers and toes. What do you think the nails are for?

Your Body at Work

Words to Know

skeleton	the bones that support, allow movement, and protect the organs of an animal with a backbone
calcium	a mineral found in teeth and bone
joint	a place where two bones meet
tendon	a tough band of tissue that attaches muscle to bone

Getting Some Support

The human body has 206 bones in it. These bones all connect together. They are called your **skeleton.** The skeleton gives your body support and allows you to move. You would not be able to sit, walk, or stand without a skeleton.

The skeleton also protects many of your most important organs. The narrow bones, called *ribs*, form a cage around your heart and lungs. Another part of your skeleton forms a hard shell, called a *skull*, that protects your brain.

Bones are made of living cells and also the mineral called **calcium.** Calcium is found in teeth, too. You get calcium from the foods you eat. Foods rich in calcium are milk, yogurt, and cheese.

The place where two bones meet is called a **joint.** You have joints at the wrists, the knees, and on your fingers. The elbows, hips, and shoulders also contain joints.

The largest bone in the human body is the thigh bone. The smallest, called the *stirrup*, is in the ear. A child has more bones than an adult. As the child grows, some of the bones join together.

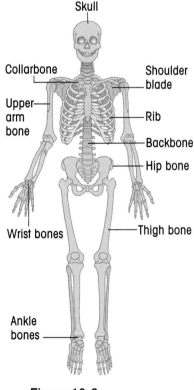

Skull

Collarbone

Upper arm bone

Shoulder blade

Rib

Backbone

Hip bone

Wrist bones

Thigh bone

Ankle bones

Figure 10-6
The human skeleton

✓ **What are bones are used for?**

Muscles on the Move

You can tighten, or flex, many of your muscles. Try flexing your arm muscle. The arm muscle is attached to your arm bone by tendons. A **tendon** is a tough band of tissue that attaches muscle to bone. Muscles that help you move parts of your skeleton are called *voluntary muscles*.

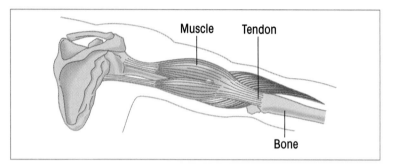

Muscle   Tendon

Bone

Figure 10-7 *Arm muscles are attached to bones by tendons. As the muscle tightens, the tendon pulls the bone into a new position.*

Some muscles work without bones. When you swallow food, certain muscles push the food down into your stomach. Other muscles cause blood to move throughout your body. These muscles are not attached to bones. They are called *involuntary muscles*.

✓ **What do tendons do?**

Lesson Review

1. How many bones are in the human body? What two purposes do they serve?

2. What are the two kinds of muscles?

3. **CRITICAL THINKING** The heart automatically pumps blood around the body. Other involuntary muscles control the blinking of your eyes, breathing, and the digesting of food. Why do you think involuntary muscles control those actions?

Words to Know

puberty	the time in life when the reproductive organs develop
testes	the male organs where sperm cells are made
ovaries	the female organs where egg cells are stored
uterus	the female organ in which a fetus develops
fetus	an unborn baby that develops in a woman's uterus
menstruation	the monthly flow of blood from the uterus of a woman who is not having a baby

Puberty

The human reproductive system does not fully develop until **puberty.** Puberty is the time in life when the male and female reproductive organs develop. During puberty, certain glands begin producing hormones. These chemicals cause physical changes in the body.

For instance, during puberty girls develop breasts and broader hips. Boys develop broader shoulders and more muscles. Both boys and girls grow hair under their arms and around their reproductive organs. Boys' voices get lower. Puberty for girls usually begins between the ages of 10 and 13. It usually begins for boys between the ages of 13 and 16.

During the time of puberty, males begin producing the sex cells known as sperm cells. The male organs that make sperm cells are called the **testes.** An adult male makes millions of sperm cells a day. Certain hormones that affect sexual development are also produced in the testes.

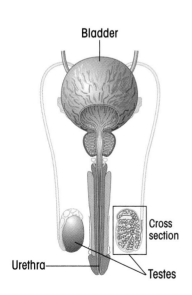

Bladder

Cross section

Urethra

Testes

Figure 10-8
The male reproductive system

✓ **What happens at puberty?**

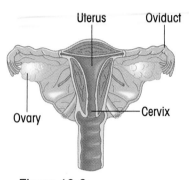

Figure 10-9
The female reproductive system

The Female Cycle

Females are born with all the egg cells they will ever have. The egg cells along with certain hormones are stored in the female organs called the **ovaries.** Each month, starting at puberty, an egg cell is released from one of the ovaries. When this happens, the walls of the **uterus** become thick with blood. The uterus is the organ in which a **fetus** develops. A fetus is an unborn baby.

If no baby is created, the extra blood that lines the uterus leaves the body. This monthly flow is called **menstruation.** When a woman grows older, menstruation stops. This usually happens around the age of 50.

✓ **What are the female reproductive organs?**

The Developing Baby

If the egg cell is fertilized by the sperm cell, a fetus will begin to grow in the uterus. The extra blood will not be lost. It will remain to feed the fetus. Because the uterus is made of mostly muscle tissue, it can stretch. This gives room for the developing baby.

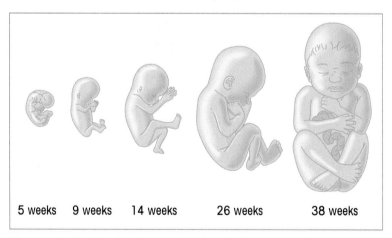

5 weeks   9 weeks   14 weeks   26 weeks   38 weeks

Figure 10-10 *Most fetuses develop in the uterus for nine months before emerging as babies.*

For the first two months, the fetus, called an *embryo*, does not look human. By four months, the fetus has developed many human features. By seven months, most of its organs are developed and working.

✓ **What happens when an egg cell is fertilized?**

Lesson Review

1. What is puberty? When does it usually happen?

2. What happens during menstruation?

3. CRITICAL THINKING Look carefully at the pictures of the fetus on page 148. Describe the changes you see taking place from week to week.

A Closer Look

PREMATURE BABIES

Babies born before about nine months in the mother's uterus are called premature babies. Babies born between the eighth and ninth month are usually developed enough to survive. They do well if they get proper care. Babies born before this are at great risk. Many die. Those that survive often have lifelong health problems. They can have brain damage. They may have trouble breathing, walking, or talking.

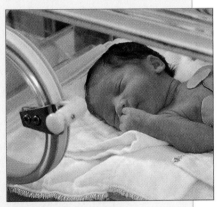

A premature baby must often live in a germ-free, warm environment.

About 250,000 premature babies are born each year in the United States. Nearly 75,000 of these are born in the seventh month or earlier. Premature births cost families and society millions of dollars each year.

CRITICAL THINKING How could seeing a doctor help a woman who is expecting a baby?

LAB ACTIVITY
Tasting What You Smell

BACKGROUND
The tongue is the organ for taste. But your tongue can only sense four basic flavors: sweet, salty, sour, and bitter. Your sense of smell is much stronger than your sense of taste. Often, when you think you are tasting something, you are really smelling it.

Safety Alert
If you are allergic to these foods, do not taste them.

PURPOSE
You will see how taste and smell work together to help you recognize and enjoy foods.

MATERIALS
blindfold, onion, potato, apple, mint leaf, paper plates, plastic spoons, paper towels, water, plastic cups

WHAT TO DO
1. Copy the chart to the right.
2. Work with a blindfolded partner. Put a tiny piece of each food on the plate. Have your partner hold his or her nose closed. Using the spoon, give your partner the food to taste but not swallow.
3. Ask your partner to describe the taste and name the food. Write this down in the chart. Have your partner remove the food, put it into the paper towel, and rinse his or her mouth with water. Repeat Steps 2 and 3 with each food sample.
4. Now have your partner leave his or her nose open. Repeat the activity. Again, write down the guesses.
5. Now you be the taster. Repeat Steps 1 to 4.

Food	Nose Closed	Nose Open
Onion		
Potato		
Apple		
Leaf		

DRAW CONCLUSIONS
- Which foods did you recognize with your nose closed?
- Which foods did you recognize with your nose open?
- What can you say about how taste and smell work together?

ON-THE-JOB SCIENCE
Fitness Instructor

Jennifer is a fitness instructor. She knows that heart rate is one measure of how healthy people are. Regular exercise strengthens the heart. A stronger heart pumps more blood throughout the body with each beat. This lets the heart beat more slowly, or less often.

Regular exercise strengthens the heart.

Jennifer's students check their heart rate three times during a workout. They check it when they are "warming up," or slowly building up their pace. They check it when they are working hard, or going at a strong, steady pace. They check it a third time when they slow down their pace. During this cooldown, the heart rate slowly returns to normal.

Some fitness machines exercise both your arms and legs at once. Here is one exercise plan you might use in a gym that has those machines.

Time (in minutes)	Activity	Heart Rate (beats per minute)
5	Warm-up	125
15	Steady pace	145
5	Cooldown	125

An exercise bicycle must be ridden longer because you are not using your arms.

Create a good exercise plan for a bicycle. Write the time and heart rate for each activity.

1. Warm-up

2. Steady pace

3. Cooldown

Critical Thinking
What body systems do you think are most affected by exercise? How are they helped by doing the exercise?

Chapter

10 ▶ Review

Summary   The human body has complex body systems and a large brain. These systems control all the body's activities.

Lesson 10.1   Cells form tissues and organs. Organs form into complex systems. The nervous system's main organ is the brain, which receives and sends messages. Hormones also control some body functions and growth. The sense organs are the eyes, ears, nose, tongue, and skin.

Lesson 10.2   Bones give the body support. Muscles allow movement.

Lesson 10.3   At puberty boys and girls develop sexually. This means they can reproduce, using the organs of the reproductive system.

Vocabulary Review

Complete each sentence with a term from the list.

tissue

hormone

system

fetus

organ

skeleton

joint

puberty

1. The heart is an example of an _____ in the body.

2. A _____ is a group of cells that all do the same job.

3. Organs working together form a body _____.

4. Another name for an unborn baby is _____.

5. After a _____ is produced by a gland in the body, it may be circulated in the blood.

6. The time of life that boys and girls develop sexually is called _____.

7. There are 206 bones in the _____ of an adult.

8. A _____ is where two bones meet.

Chapter Quiz

Write your answers on a separate sheet of paper.

1. What are two kinds of body tissues?

2. What are two organs? What do they do?

3. What are two body systems? What do they do?

4. What are the five senses and the organs that go with each sense?

5. Which body organ helps keep you at a steady temperature? How does it do this?

6. Where are billions of your nerve cells found?

7. What are important uses of your bones?

8. What is one kind of voluntary muscle? What is one kind of involuntary muscle?

9. What chemicals cause changes in the body at puberty?

10. What are male and female sex cells called? Where are they made?

Test Tip

Always reread the questions and your answers at the end of a test if you finish early. Many times you know the right answer, but rushing may cause you to make a mistake.

Research Project

Bones continue to grow throughout the teens. To keep them strong and healthy, you need to take in enough calcium in the food you eat. Research how much calcium is needed by an adult man, a 13-year-old boy or girl, and a woman over 50. Write up a daily menu for each person that includes food containing enough calcium.

Everything you do during the day requires energy. The more active you are, the more energy your body needs. Which people in the picture are using the most energy? Which are using the least energy?

Learning Objectives

- Describe the digestive system and what it does.
- Describe the respiratory system and what it does.
- Describe the circulatory system and what it does.
- Explain how blood pressure and heart disease are linked.
- LAB ACTIVITY: Measure the air in your lungs.
- SCIENCE IN YOUR LIFE: Show how different forms of physical activity affect the health of the heart and other muscles.

Words to Know

digestion	the process of breaking down food into molecules the cells can absorb
enzyme	a body chemical; in digestion, it helps break down food
esophagus	a long tube leading from the throat to the stomach
respiration	the process that gets oxygen to the body's cells and removes waste gases
larynx	a box-shaped structure below the throat
trachea	a long tube leading from the larynx to smaller branching tubes that go to the lungs; also called the windpipe
bronchi	two small tubes that branch off from the trachea and enter the lungs
circulation	the process of moving blood around the body
blood vessel	a tube that carries blood around the body
artery	a blood vessel that carries blood away from the heart
vein	a blood vessel that returns blood to the heart
capillary	a tiny blood vessel that connects an artery to a vein
plasma	the liquid part of blood
red blood cell	a blood cell that carries oxygen and carbon dioxide throughout the circulatory system
white blood cell	a blood cell that fights off bacteria and sickness in the body
platelet	a part of the blood that helps stop injuries from bleeding

Digestion

Words to Know

digestion	the process of breaking down food into molecules the cells can absorb
enzyme	a body chemical; in digestion, it helps break down food
esophagus	a long tube leading from the throat to the stomach

Eating for Life

Your body depends on the food you eat. It changes the food into energy that you need to carry out your daily activities. These activities include walking, talking, breathing, thinking, and sleeping. The process of breaking down food into molecules the cells can absorb is called **digestion.**

Suppose you ate cereal for breakfast this morning. By the afternoon, that cereal has probably been broken down into molecules. Those molecules would already be in your blood, traveling to your cells to be turned into energy.

✓ **What do you get from the food you eat?**

The Digestive System

The first step in the process of digestion is taking a bite of food and then chewing it. This helps break the food down into smaller pieces. Enzymes in your mouth help break down these pieces further. An **enzyme** is a body chemical.

After you chew the food, you swallow it. It goes down your **esophagus.** This is a long tube leading from your throat to your stomach. Involuntary muscles along the esophagus help to push the food down.

Remember
Involuntary muscles are muscles that are not attached to bone.

Your stomach contains involuntary muscles and enzymes, too. These muscles move in a wavelike motion. This breaks down the food even more.

From the stomach, food moves into your small intestine. By now, the food has become just a lot of molecules ready to enter your cells. These molecules pass through the walls of your small intestine and into the blood.

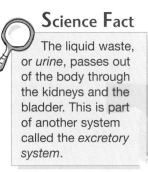

Remember
A molecule is a group of two or more atoms that are joined by chemical bonds.

However, not all the food you eat reaches your blood. Parts of it cannot be used. These parts are waste. The solid waste, called *feces*, passes from the small intestine to the large intestine. The feces pass out of the body through an opening below the large intestine called the *anus*.

Science Fact

The liquid waste, or *urine*, passes out of the body through the kidneys and the bladder. This is part of another system called the *excretory system*.

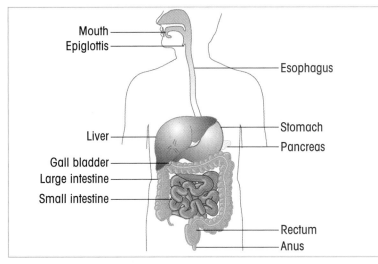

Mouth
Epiglottis
Esophagus
Liver
Stomach
Pancreas
Gall bladder
Large intestine
Small intestine
Rectum
Anus

Figure 11-1 *The digestive system breaks down food.*

✓ **What does your digestive system do?**

Lesson Review

1. What gives your body the energy it needs?

2. What are three ways that food is broken down?

3. **CRITICAL THINKING** If your body stopped making enzymes, how would that affect you?

Words to Know

respiration	the process that gets oxygen to the body's cells and removes waste gases
larynx	a box-shaped structure below the throat
trachea	a long tube leading from the larynx to smaller branching tubes that go to the lungs; also called the windpipe
bronchi	two small tubes that branch off from the trachea and enter the lungs

Breathing for Life

Remember
All cells, including plant cells, use oxygen to release energy from food. This process is called cellular respiration.

You learned that digestion gets food molecules to all your cells. However, your cells need oxygen, too. **Respiration** is the process that gets oxygen to the cells and removes waste gases. This oxygen, you recall, was produced by plants. Both animals and plants use oxygen in the air to carry out respiration.

 How does respiration help animals?

The Respiratory System

Science Fact
Plants need carbon dioxide for photosynthesis. Humans breathe out carbon dioxide with every breath.

When you take a breath, you bring air into your body. You breathe in through your nose or your mouth. From there, the air goes down your throat past the **larynx**. This box-shaped structure below the throat is also called the voice box because it contains organs known as vocal cords. Vocal cords produce the sounds for speech. The air then goes down a long tube called the **trachea**. The trachea is also called the windpipe. From the trachea, the air enters two small tubes called **bronchi**, which enter the lungs.

Your lungs are like sponges. They have many small pockets called *air sacs* in them. When you breathe in, the sacs fill with air. The oxygen in the air passes from the air sacs into your blood.

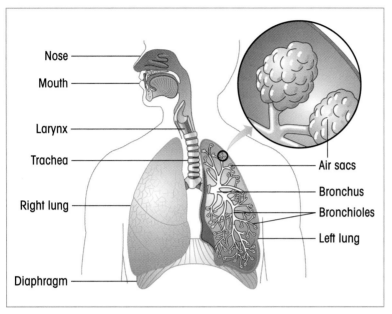

Figure 11-2 *The respiratory system gets oxygen to your cells.*

Your blood carries the oxygen to all of your cells. The oxygen combines with the food molecules in the cells. Energy is released. Carbon dioxide and water vapor are produced as byproducts. The blood carries these byproducts to the lungs. When you breathe out, you release these byproducts into the air.

✓ **What does the respiratory system do?**

Lesson Review

1. What path does air take after entering the body?

2. How does oxygen pass from your lungs into your blood?

3. CRITICAL THINKING How are we dependent on plants?

Words to Know

circulation	the process of moving blood around the body
blood vessel	a tube that carries blood around the body
artery	a blood vessel that carries blood away from the heart
vein	a blood vessel that returns blood to the heart
capillary	a tiny blood vessel that connects an artery to a vein
plasma	the liquid part of blood
red blood cell	a blood cell that carries oxygen and carbon dioxide throughout the circulatory system
white blood cell	a blood cell that fights off bacteria and sickness in the body
platelet	a part of the blood that helps stop injuries from bleeding

Pumping for Life

Circulation is the process of moving blood around the body. The blood brings food and oxygen to all the body's cells. It also carries wastes away from the cells. The most important organ of the circulatory system is the heart. It is a muscle about the size of your fist.

The heart is made up of four sections called *chambers*. The upper chambers are called the *atria*. The lower chambers are called the *ventricles*. Each chamber acts as a pump, squeezing together to push blood to every part of the body. Valves between the atria and the ventricles open and close to control the flow of blood. Tubes connected to the heart take blood to or away from the heart.

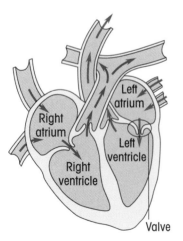

Figure 11-3 *The heart*

✔ **What is the purpose of the circulatory system?**

The Circulatory System

The circulatory system has many blood vessels. A **blood vessel** is a tube that carries blood around the body. There are three kinds of blood vessels.

- An **artery** is a blood vessel that carries blood *away* from the heart. The blood goes to all the body's cells.

- A **vein** is a blood vessel that *returns* blood to the heart.

- A **capillary** is a tiny blood vessel that connects an artery to a vein. Capillaries are the smallest blood vessels in the circulatory system. In some, only one blood cell can pass through at a time.

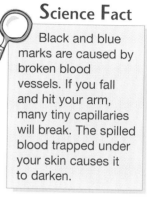

Science Fact

Black and blue marks are caused by broken blood vessels. If you fall and hit your arm, many tiny capillaries will break. The spilled blood trapped under your skin causes it to darken.

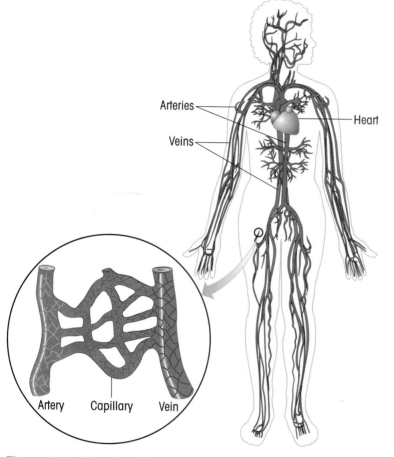

Figure 11-4 *The circulatory system moves blood around the body.*

Blood is made up of a liquid part and three solid parts. **Plasma** is the liquid part of blood. Plasma is made up mostly of water. It carries the food molecules, wastes, and other materials around the body.

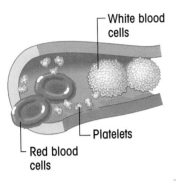

White blood cells

Platelets

Red blood cells

Figure 11-5 *Blood has three solid parts.*

The three types of solids in the blood are red blood cells, white blood cells, and platelets. A **red blood cell** carries oxygen and carbon dioxide throughout the circulatory system. A **white blood cell** fights off bacteria and sickness in your body. When people get sick, the body produces a lot of white blood cells. A **platelet** is a part of the blood that helps stop injuries from bleeding. Platelets group together to close off a cut.

✓ **What is blood made up of?**

Heart Disease

Blood pressure is a measure of how hard it is for blood to get through blood vessels. The narrower the blood vessels, the higher the pressure is. High blood pressure can damage the heart and lead to heart disease. Heart disease kills hundreds of thousands of Americans each year.

A heart attack happens when blood vessels to the heart muscle become clogged. The heart cannot get the oxygen it needs to continue pumping. Without the heart pumping, the rest of the body suffers. It cannot get the oxygen it needs to stay alive.

Scientists are learning how to prevent heart disease. Here are some ways to keep your heart healthy:

- Do not smoke.
- Eat fewer fatty foods. They can cause blood vessels to become clogged.
- Get plenty of exercise. Exercise makes your heart pump more blood through the circulatory system. This makes your circulatory system stronger.

Remember
The respiratory system and the circulatory system work together to bring oxygen to all the body cells.

Lesson Review

1. What is the purpose of the circulatory system?

2. What is the difference between an artery and a vein?

3. **CRITICAL THINKING** Why is it important to keep blood vessels to the heart muscle open?

Modern Leaders in Science

ANTONIA COELLO NOVELLO

Antonia Coello Novello was the first woman and the first Hispanic to serve as Surgeon General of the United States. She served from 1990 to 1993.

Research had shown that more than 3,000 teenagers become regular smokers each day. This concerned Dr. Novello greatly. In the United States, about 390,000 people die every year from heart and lung diseases caused by smoking. Cigarette smoke damages the lungs and prevents the body from getting the oxygen it needs. Dr. Novello fought to have more educational programs on the dangers of smoking.

Antonia Coello Novello was the first female Surgeon General of the United States.

CRITICAL THINKING How did Dr. Novello help people?

LAB ACTIVITY
How Much Air Is There?

BACKGROUND
When you breathe in, air sacs in your lungs fill with air. This is how oxygen enters your body. Your lungs must be able to hold a lot of oxygen.

PURPOSE
You will see how much air people's lungs hold.

MATERIALS
clear plastic bottle with a cap, small tub of water, a flexible drinking straw per student, marking pen or masking tape, ruler

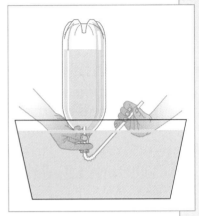

WHAT TO DO
1. Form small groups.
2. Copy the chart to the right. Add as many rows as there are people in your group.
3. Fill the bottle completely with water. Screw the cap onto the bottle. Turn the bottle upside down and place it in the tub of water. Carefully unscrew the cap underwater.
3. Place one end of the straw into the bottle. Bend the straw so that the other end is above the water.
4. Have one member of the group take a deep breath and then breathe out through the straw into the bottle. Mark the level of the water on the bottle at the end of the breath.
5. Use the ruler to measure the distance from the bottom of the bottle to the mark. Write the distance on the chart.
6. Repeat Steps 1 to 5 until each member in the group has recorded a breath measurement.

Name	Deep Breath Out
	____ inches
	____ inches
	____ inches

DRAW CONCLUSIONS
- What happened to the water level when you breathed into the straw? Why did this happen?
- Whose lungs in your group hold the largest amount of air?

Keeping the heart and other muscles of your body healthy is a lifelong responsibility. There are different types of physical activity. Each one has different health benefits.

Carmen works hard to keep her body in good physical shape. She uses the Physical Activity Pyramid to plan her weekly fitness routine. She knows that activities from the bottom three sections of the pyramid are especially good for the circulatory system.

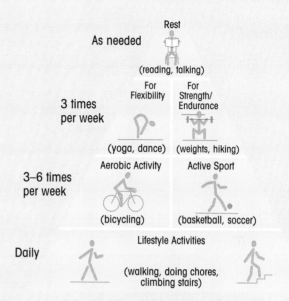

Physical Activity Pyramid

Make a chart like the one below.

Use the pyramid to plan a weekly routine. Then fill in the chart with the names of activities to do each day. An activity should be continued for at least 15 minutes to be recorded.

Day	Lifestyle	Aerobic	Active Sport	Flexibility	Strength/ Endurance	Rest
Su						
M						
T						
W						
Th						
F						
S						

Critical Thinking

How is the Physical Activity Pyramid useful for someone who is not very active?

Chapter

11 ▷ Review

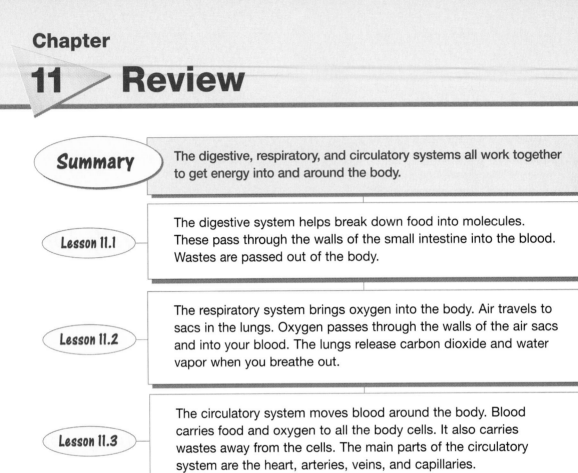

Summary

The digestive, respiratory, and circulatory systems all work together to get energy into and around the body.

Lesson 11.1

The digestive system helps break down food into molecules. These pass through the walls of the small intestine into the blood. Wastes are passed out of the body.

Lesson 11.2

The respiratory system brings oxygen into the body. Air travels to sacs in the lungs. Oxygen passes through the walls of the air sacs and into your blood. The lungs release carbon dioxide and water vapor when you breathe out.

Lesson 11.3

The circulatory system moves blood around the body. Blood carries food and oxygen to all the body cells. It also carries wastes away from the cells. The main parts of the circulatory system are the heart, arteries, veins, and capillaries.

Vocabulary Review

Write *true* or *false* for each sentence. If the sentence is false, replace the underlined term to make the sentence true.

1. An <u>enzyme</u> is a substance that breaks down food.

2. The <u>bronchi</u> are the tubes that enter the lungs.

3. Air travels down the larynx to the <u>esophagus</u>.

4. A <u>capillary</u> connects an artery to a vein.

5. The liquid part of the blood is called <u>urine</u>.

6. A <u>red blood cell</u> helps stop injuries from bleeding.

7. A <u>white blood cell</u> fights off bacteria and sickness.

8. An <u>artery</u> returns blood to the heart.

Chapter Quiz

Write your answers on a separate sheet of paper.

1. Where does food go after you have chewed it?

2. Where does food go that is not digested?

3. What systems get oxygen to the cells?

4. Where do the bronchi lead?

5. What two byproducts do you breathe out into the air?

6. What do the valves of the heart do?

7. What are the three different kinds of blood vessels?

8. What are three solids found in blood? Describe their jobs.

9. Is high blood pressure good for a person or bad? Explain your answer.

10. What can you do to keep your heart healthy?

Test Tip
Reread your answers to all the questions. Be sure that you have answered both parts of any two-part question.

Research Project

CPR stands for cardiopulmonary resuscitation. It is a procedure used to save lives. It is a way to restart a person's heart and breathing. A person who has stopped breathing is not taking in oxygen. Do some research on CPR. Find out when it is used, the basics of the procedure, and how you can learn CPR in your community. Write a report on what you find out.

Chapter 12 > Staying Healthy

The foods we eat can help our bodies grow strong. These people are eating many different kinds of foods. Why is it important to eat a variety of foods?

Learning Objectives

- Explain the causes of disease.
- Describe how the immune system fights disease.
- Identify the nutrients needed for a healthy diet.
- Describe the Food Guide Pyramid.
- Explain how to guard your health.
- LAB ACTIVITY: Compare the nutrients in different foods.
- ON-THE-JOB SCIENCE: Apply using the Food Guide Pyramid to serving healthy foods.

Words to Know

disease	a kind of illness or sickness, often caused by tiny organisms such as bacteria
defense	a way your body fights off harmful organisms
virus	a very small disease-causing particle
nutrition	the study of food and eating right to stay healthy
nutrient	a substance usually found in food that body cells need to stay healthy and grow
carbohydrate	a sugary or starchy food that gives people energy
fat	a nutrient in foods that supplies the body with energy
cholesterol	a substance found in some fats and also in the body, which is needed in small amounts
protein	a nutrient in foods that builds and repairs body tissues
vitamin	a nutrient found in tiny amounts in many plant and animal foods; it is needed by the body to stay healthy
mineral	an inorganic substance found in water and some foods; tiny amounts of some minerals are needed by the body to stay healthy

Words to Know

disease	a kind of illness or sickness, often caused by tiny organisms such as bacteria
defense	a way your body fights off harmful organisms
virus	a very small disease-causing particle

What Is Disease?

A **disease** is a kind of illness or sickness. Many diseases are caused by tiny organisms, such as bacteria. Some diseases, like the common cold, are not usually serious. Other diseases are very serious.

In the 1300s, a terrible disease swept through Europe. Almost a quarter of the population died of it in only 20 years. The disease was called the Plague, or the Black Death. No one knew how it started or how it was passed along. Today we know that bacteria caused the Plague.

Since the 1300s, scientists have learned a lot about what makes people sick. They have also learned a lot about how to prevent disease. They know that people can catch diseases from other animals. For example, mosquitoes, fleas, and pigs can carry disease.

Humans also pass diseases to one another. This is why it is important to cover your mouth when you cough or sneeze. It is also why you should wash your hands often.

✓ **How do people usually catch diseases?**

Science Fact

The bacteria that started the Plague of the 1300s infected rats. Fleas bit the rats. The fleas then spread the bacteria to humans. The Plague still exists. However, there are now medicines to treat it.

The Immune System

The human body has many ways to fight disease.
These are your defenses. A **defense** is a way your body
fights off harmful organisms. Your immune system
defends you from harmful organisms.

Skin and Hair

The skin is an important defense. It keeps harmful
microscopic organisms from reaching most of your
organs. The hairs in your nose also keep harmful
organisms out of your body. These hairs filter the
air you breathe.

White Blood Cells

Some bacteria still find their way into the body.
The white blood cells then go to work to destroy the
invaders. Suppose that bacteria enter your body. White
blood cells in the blood will surround the bacteria and
try to break them down. The bacteria may reproduce
faster than the white blood cells can handle, though.
In that case, your body will begin to produce more
white blood cells. Until there are enough to fight off
the invader, you might feel very sick.

Your immune system works best when you are already
healthy. If you eat right and get enough exercise and
rest, there is less chance of your getting sick.

Remember
White blood cells are found
in the circulatory system
along with red blood cells
and platelets.

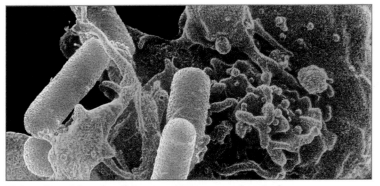

*This white blood cell is attacking some bacteria,
shown here in blue.*

✓ **What does the immune system do for the human body?**

Viruses

A **virus** is a very small disease-causing particle that is often mostly DNA. It is smaller than a bacterium. Viruses cause many diseases, such as AIDS, influenza (the flu), colds, polio, chicken pox, measles, and mumps.

Scientists still do not fully understand viruses. In fact, they are not even sure whether viruses should be considered living or nonliving particles.

Viruses do not appear to be alive. They do not carry out normal cell functions. Viruses invade living cells. Once in a cell, the virus uses parts of the cell to make more viruses. The cell itself is eventually destroyed.

Many diseases caused by viruses can now be prevented. Some, though, are still deadly.

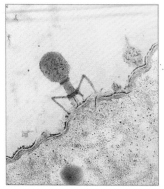

Close-up of a virus

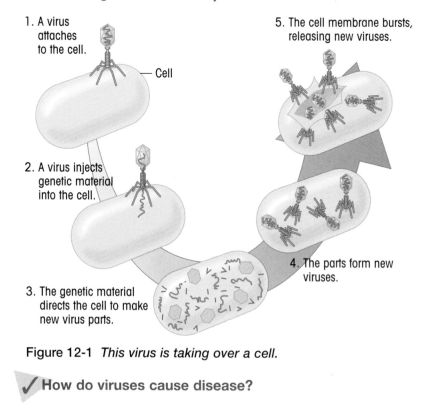

1. A virus attaches to the cell.

Cell

2. A virus injects genetic material into the cell.

3. The genetic material directs the cell to make new virus parts.

4. The parts form new viruses.

5. The cell membrane bursts, releasing new viruses.

Figure 12-1 *This virus is taking over a cell.*

✓ **How do viruses cause disease?**

Lesson Review

1. What are some differences between bacteria and viruses?

[handwritten: V-smaller? living or non living, invade cells]

2. What are some diseases caused by viruses?

[handwritten: Aids, flu, colds, polio, chicken]

3. CRITICAL THINKING What happens if bacteria find their way into your body?

A Closer Look

THE FIGHT AGAINST AIDS

AIDS stands for *acquired immune deficiency syndrome*. It is a disease caused by a virus. This virus is called *human immunodeficiency virus,* or HIV. AIDS harms the body's ability to fight other diseases. Since the disease was first recognized in 1981, over 30 million people have been infected with HIV. Over 10 million people have died from AIDS. There is still no known cure.

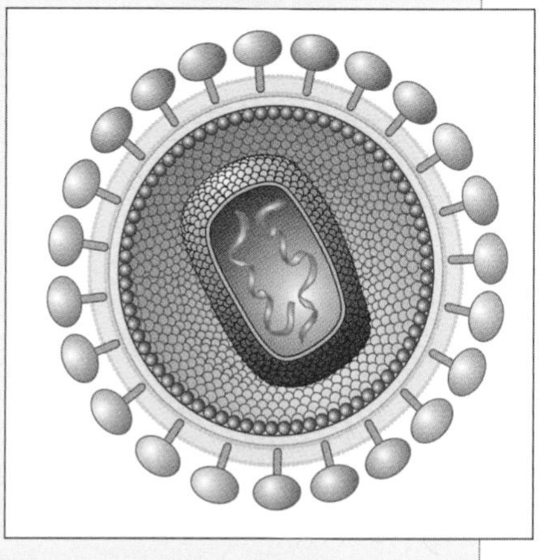

This is the AIDS virus, called HIV.

However, there are ways to protect yourself from getting AIDS. HIV is passed through bodily fluids. It is passed along in four main ways: 1) through sexual contact; 2) by sharing needles used for drugs; 3) through a transfusion of blood from a person who was infected; 4) from a pregnant woman who has AIDS or HIV and passes it to her unborn child. You *cannot* get HIV from mosquitoes, shaking hands, or being near or touching someone with AIDS or HIV.

Some medicines exist to help control HIV. In some cases, medicines have kept people who have HIV from getting AIDS. Scientists are working hard to develop medicines that will stop the spread of HIV.

CRITICAL THINKING How can you avoid getting AIDS?

Words to Know

nutrition	the study of food and eating right to stay healthy
nutrient	a substance usually found in food that body cells need to stay healthy and grow
carbohydrate	a sugary or starchy food that gives people energy
fat	a nutrient in foods that supplies the body with energy
cholesterol	a substance found in some fats and also in the body, which is needed in small amounts
protein	a nutrient in foods that builds and repairs body tissues
vitamin	a nutrient found in tiny amounts in many plant and animal foods; it is needed by the body to stay healthy
mineral	an inorganic substance found in water and some foods; tiny amounts of some minerals are needed by the body to stay healthy

You Are What You Eat

Science Fact

Rickets is a painful disease that weakens bones. It is caused by a lack of Vitamin D. You can get Vitamin D by eating tuna, salmon, or eggs, or drinking milk that has Vitamin D added to it.

Have you ever heard the expression, "You are what you eat"? There is certainly some truth to that. If you eat well, you are more likely to feel well and avoid disease. The study of food and eating right to stay healthy is called **nutrition.**

Good nutrition requires eating the right combination and amounts of nutrients. A **nutrient** is a substance usually found in food that body cells need to stay healthy and grow. There are six main kinds of nutrients: carbohydrates, fats, proteins, vitamins, minerals, and water. If any of these nutrients is missing from your diet, your health may be in danger.

 **What is good nutrition?**

The Nutrients

Carbohydrates

A **carbohydrate** is a sugary or starchy food. Carbohydrates give you energy. Fruits, vegetables, grains, potatoes, and pasta are all sources of carbohydrates.

Another kind of carbohydrate is fiber. Humans cannot digest fiber, but it helps move food and wastes through the digestive system. Fiber is found in whole grains and the skins of fruits and vegetables.

Fats

A **fat** is a nutrient in food that also supplies the body with energy. However, your body does not break down fats as quickly as it does carbohydrates. Most people eat more fat than they should. Fat can build up on blood vessel walls and lead to heart disease. Butter, ice cream, and red meat are all sources of unhealthy fat.

Cholesterol is a substance found in some fats and also in the human body. You need small amounts of it to digest food and produce certain substances in the body.

However, too much cholesterol can be unhealthy. Cholesterol causes fat to build up in the arteries and block the flow of blood.

It is a good idea for people to limit the amount of cholesterol from animal fats in their diet. Eating less red meat and fewer eggs and foods containing butter, cheese, or cream helps. Also, adults should have their cholesterol levels checked by a doctor once a year.

Remember
There are three ways to help prevent heart disease.
1. Do not smoke.
2. Cut back on fatty foods.
3. Get plenty of exercise.

Proteins

Foods containing the nutrient **protein** build and repair body tissue. Almost every part of your body is made of protein. This includes your hair, fingernails, blood, muscles, and organs. Meat, fish, nuts, beans, and dairy products are all sources of protein.

Some Vitamins Used by the Body	
Vitamin	**Used by Body For**
A	Normal sight; healthy skin; defending against infection
B	Nerve and heart functions
C	Bone tissue and growth; healing wounds
D	Bone growth and repair

Some Minerals Used by the Body	
Mineral	**Used by Body For**
Potassium	Nerve and muscle functions
Calcium	Boot and tooth growth
Iron	Forming red blood cells and muscle cells

Vitamins and Minerals

To stay healthy, people need vitamins in their diet. A **vitamin** is a nutrient found in tiny amounts in many plant and animal foods. A **mineral** is an inorganic substance found in water and some foods. The body needs tiny amounts of some minerals to stay healthy. Potassium, calcium, and iron are examples of minerals the body needs.

Many people take vitamin and mineral pills. Some scientists believe that taking a few of these nutrients in large amounts can prevent disease. Others say that a well-balanced diet with a variety of foods gives you all the vitamins and minerals you need.

Water

Water is also an important nutrient. All body cells contain water. To stay healthy, it is important to drink 8 glasses of water a day.

✓ **What are the six kinds of nutrients?**

The Food Guide Pyramid

Eating the right amount of nutrients takes practice. Your meals throughout the day should contain a balance of nutrients.

Scientists have created a tool to help you choose foods for a healthy diet. That tool is called the Food Guide Pyramid.

The Food Guide Pyramid groups foods according to the number of servings you should eat daily. The foods you should eat most often are at the bottom of the pyramid. For a healthy diet, start with plenty of bread, cereal, rice, pasta, fruits, and vegetables. Then add foods from the milk group and the meat group. Keep in mind that the meat group not only includes meat, fish, and poultry but also eggs, dry beans, and nuts.

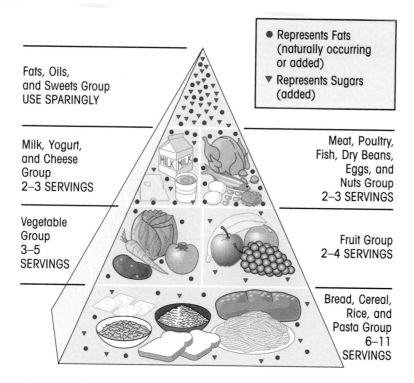

Fats, Oils,
and Sweets Group
USE SPARINGLY

Milk, Yogurt,
and Cheese
Group
2–3 SERVINGS

Vegetable
Group
3–5
SERVINGS

- Represents Fats
  (naturally occurring
  or added)
▼ Represents Sugars
  (added)

Meat, Poultry,
Fish, Dry Beans,
Eggs, and
Nuts Group
2–3 SERVINGS

Fruit Group
2–4 SERVINGS

Bread, Cereal,
Rice, and
Pasta Group
6–11
SERVINGS

Figure 12-2 *The Food Guide Pyramid shows what you should eat every day.*

Notice that fats, oils, and sweets are at the top of the pyramid. They take up the least amount of space. That means you should eat them the least of all foods.

✓ **What three food groups should most of your foods come from, according to the Food Guide Pyramid?**

Lesson Review

1. What nutrients do you need to stay healthy?

2. Why should people be concerned about cholesterol?

3. What is the purpose of the Food Guide Pyramid?

4. CRITICAL THINKING Using the Food Guide Pyramid, how would you change a diet that was too high in fat?

Only you can guard your health. In Chapter 11, you learned about heart disease. Heart disease is the number one cause of death in the United States. Good nutrition is one way you can protect yourself against heart disease. Not smoking and getting exercise will also help protect you from heart disease.

Nicotine is a substance in cigarettes that can make you sick. It causes blood vessels to become narrow. Narrow blood vessels make it difficult for blood to flow freely through your body. Over time, this can lead to heart disease. Smoking also causes many respiratory diseases such as lung cancer and emphysema. Cancer is the second most deadly disease in the United States.

Safety Alert

People can get addicted to substances, such as nicotine, caffeine, alcohol, certain medicines, and illegal drugs. *Addicted* means "having a habit that cannot be broken easily." People addicted to a substance can have serious health problems and should get help.

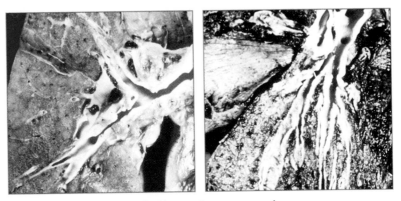

This photo compares the lung of a non-smoker with the lung of a smoker.

Exercise keeps your muscles in good working order. Your heart is a big muscle. It needs exercise just as other muscles in your body do. By exercising, you keep your heart strong. Exercise also keeps your blood vessels open wide. This helps prevent heart disease.

✓ **What are three ways to guard your health?**

Lesson Review

1. How does nicotine affect the body?

2. What are the benefits of exercise?

3. **CRITICAL THINKING** How can you best protect yourself from heart disease?

On the Cutting Edge

USING ELECTRICITY TO KILL BACTERIA

Every year, millions of people become sick by eating foods that contain harmful bacteria. Scientists have tried to develop ways to stop the bacteria from growing in the foods we buy. One process that many companies use to kill bacteria in food is called *gamma irradiation*. However, some groups are concerned about the safety of this process, which exposes the food to harmful rays.

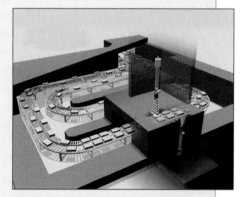

This is a model of an electronic pasteurization factory.

Now there is a new process that kills 99.9 percent of the bacteria found in food and may be safer than gamma irradiation. The new process is called *electronic pasteurization*. It uses electricity to stop bacteria from reproducing. It does not change the taste or quality of the food.

The U.S. government has approved the new process. Electronically pasteurized foods should appear in markets soon.

CRITICAL THINKING Why is it important to kill bacteria in the food we buy?

LAB ACTIVITY
Making a Healthy Meal

BACKGROUND

Healthy meals provide a variety of nutrients in the right amounts. So, to plan healthy meals, you need to know what nutrients the foods contain.

PURPOSE

You will use the number of grams of protein, carbohydrate, and fat in different foods to make a healthy meal.

MATERIALS

paper, pencil

WHAT TO DO

1. Look at the list of foods to the right.
2. Choose foods from the list to make a healthy lunch. Write your choices in a notebook. Try to make a lunch that has about 20 grams of fat, 20 grams of protein, and 90 grams of carbohydrates. You can be a few grams over or under for each nutrient.
3. You can choose more than one serving of a food, but try to use a variety of foods.

Food	Serving Size	Protein (grams)	Carbohydrate (grams)	Fat (grams)
Banana	1		30	
Apple	1		15	
Pork chop	1 oz	7		5
Chicken (white)	1 oz	7		1
Rice	1/3 cup	3	15	
Biscuit	1	3	15	5
American cheese	1 slice	7		8
Skim milk	8 oz	8	12	1
Whole milk	8 oz	8	12	5
Broccoli (cooked)	1/2 cup	2	5	
Beans	1/3 cup	3	15	1
Pasta	1/2 cup	3	15	1
Bread	1 slice	3	15	1
Spaghetti sauce	1/2 cup	3	15	5
Tuna	1 oz	7		1
Juice (grape or cranberry)	1/3 cup		15	

DRAW CONCLUSIONS

- What can you say about the variety of foods you chose?

- Raul and Katrina make meals that each include 20 grams of fat, 20 grams of protein, and 90 grams of carbohydrates. Raul's meal includes two kinds of foods. Katrina's meal includes six kinds of foods. Which meal is probably healthier? Explain why.

ON-THE-JOB SCIENCE
Cafeteria Attendant

Shawn is a cafeteria attendant. He works half-days at an elementary school. He helps serve breakfast and lunch to the students.

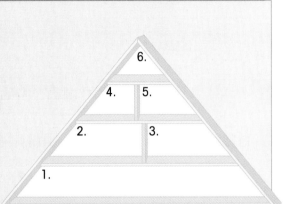

Shawn built a wooden Food Guide Pyramid with shelves in the shape of a triangle. Each day, he displays the breakfast and lunch foods in the pyramid. This helps the students learn more about nutrition and shows that they are getting healthy meals.

Help Shawn display the foods for today's lunch.

A. Cabbage   B. Pasta   C. Tomatoes   D. Milk

E. Bread   F. Chicken   G. Cookies   H. Apple

Draw an outline of the pyramid on a sheet of paper. Number the sections 1 to 6. Then write the letter of each food shown above in the correct section of the Food Guide Pyramid. Use the pyramid on page 177 to help you.

Critical Thinking
A student asked Shawn if he could have another serving of cookies instead of the apple. What should Shawn say about the nutrition of this meal?

Summary

Many diseases are caused by bacteria and viruses. Your immune system helps you avoid disease. You can also help protect yourself from getting sick by following good health habits.

Lesson 12.1

Skin, hair, and white blood cells form your body's defenses against disease. Viruses invade living cells and use parts of the invaded cell to make more viruses.

Lesson 12.2

You need the right balance of nutrients in your diet to stay healthy. The six nutrients are: carbohydrates, fats, proteins, vitamins, minerals, and water.

Lesson 12.3

Having good nutrition, getting exercise, and not smoking are ways you can help protect yourself from disease.

Vocabulary Review

virus
vitamin
disease
protein
carbohydrate
defense
nutrition
cholesterol

Complete each sentence with a term from the list.

1. A _____ is a kind of illness or sickness.

2. A way your body fights off harmful organisms is called a _____.

3. A _____ invades living cells.

4. The science of food and eating right is called _____.

5. A sugary or starchy food is a _____.

6. People often take a _____ pill to get more of this nutrient, which is found mostly in fruits and vegetables.

7. You should limit the amount of _____ in your diet.

8. A nutrient that builds and repairs body tissue is called a _____.

Chapter Quiz

Write your answers on a separate sheet of paper.

1. What are three animals that carry diseases?

2. How do hairs in your nose help your body fight diseases?

3. How do white blood cells destroy bacteria?

4. What are three diseases caused by viruses?

5. What are the six kinds of nutrients you need for a healthy diet?

6. What do carbohydrates do for your body?

7. If you needed more protein in your diet, what foods would you need to eat?

8. What kinds of foods should you eat the least of? Why?

9. What are two diseases caused by smoking cigarettes?

10. How does exercise help you to stay healthy?

Test Tip

When you are asked questions that begin with *How* or *Why,* answer in complete sentences. Read your answers to make sure they are sentences and that they answer the question.

Research Project

Make a poster of a food pyramid based on the Food Guide Pyramid on page 177. Look through newspapers and magazines for pictures of foods. Choose one food from each food group to research. Find out how many grams of protein, carbohydrates, and fat are in one serving of each. Also look for amounts of cholesterol. Put all of this information on the poster.

Chapter 13

Depending on Each Other

Zebras live in Africa on grasslands called savannas. What living things do zebras need to live and grow? What nonliving things do zebras need?

Learning Objectives

- Identify resources that are recycled in nature.
- Compare populations and communities.
- Describe how organisms interact with nonliving things in an ecosystem.
- Give an example of a food chain and a food web.
- Identify energy sources from the past.
- Explain the water and air cycles.
- Identify reasons for conserving natural resources.
- LAB ACTIVITY: Make models of food chains.
- SCIENCE IN YOUR LIFE: Relate recycling of garbage to preserving natural resources.

Words to Know

recycling	reusing a substance over and over again
habitat	the place where an organism lives
population	all the members of a species living in the same place
community	a group of different populations living in the same place and interacting with each other
ecosystem	a community and all the nonliving things that the community interacts with
food chain	the path of food through a community
producer	an organism that makes its own food
consumer	an organism that eats other organisms
food web	a group of food chains that are linked to each other
decomposer	an organism that breaks down and absorbs nutrients from dead matter
fossil fuel	a fuel made of organisms that died millions of years ago
solar energy	energy from the sun
evaporation	the process by which a liquid changes to a gas
condensation	the process by which a gas changes to a liquid
natural resource	a substance found in nature that is useful to humans
conservation	the wise and careful use of natural resources

Words to Know

recycling	reusing a substance over and over again
habitat	the place where an organism lives
population	all the members of a species living in the same place
community	a group of different populations living in the same place and interacting with each other
ecosystem	a community and all the nonliving things that the community interacts with

Recycling Resources

Take a breath of air. That same air might have been breathed by Christopher Columbus in 1492 or even Cleopatra in ancient Egypt. The air that our bodies use has been around for millions of years. We breathe it again and again. In fact, all the air, water, and food our bodies take in has been used before. Reusing a substance over and over is called **recycling**.

Nature recycles its resources. A resource is anything that an organism can use to live. All organisms share resources on Earth. Also, many organisms depend on each other to meet basic needs, such as eating food.

✓ **What happens to nature's resources on Earth?**

Habitats

A **habitat** is the place where an organism lives. A habitat can be a small place or a big place. For example, a bird's habitat is the tree in which it builds its nest. However, the entire forest where the bird lives can also be called its habitat.

All the members of a species living in the same place make up a **population**. For example, all the bullfrogs in a pond are a population. All the pine trees in a forest are a population. All the people in a city are a population.

One place can be the home of many populations. A group of different populations living in the same place and interacting with each other is called a **community**. All the plants and animals living in a desert make up the desert community. All the organisms living in a mud puddle make up the mud puddle community.

Organisms in a community interact with each other. Animals eat plants and other animals. Plants make oxygen for animals. Dead organisms provide bacteria with food.

✓ **How are habitats, populations, and communities related to each other?**

Ecosystems

An **ecosystem** is a community and all the nonliving things that the community interacts with. For example, animals breathe in oxygen from the air. Plants take in water from the soil through their roots. All living things depend on each other and on nonliving things.

Remember
The study of how living things depend on each other is called ecology.

Figure 13-1 *A desert community includes all the organisms that live there.*

Ecosystems are made up of many parts working together, just like the systems in the human body. An ecosystem that works smoothly is said to be in balance. A balanced ecosystem helps the organisms in it to survive.

✓ **What happens in a balanced ecosystem?**

Changing Communities

Over time, communities can change. For example, over many years, leaves and branches fall into a pond. Soil washes into the pond, too. As it fills up, the pond becomes shallower. The fish in the pond die and sink to the bottom. Nutrients from the dead fish make the soil on the pond floor rich. More and more plants grow in that soil. Slowly, the pond fills in. The pond becomes a meadow. Mice and rabbits move onto the meadow. Grass grows. Then bigger bushes grow. Finally, trees take root. The pond has become a forest.

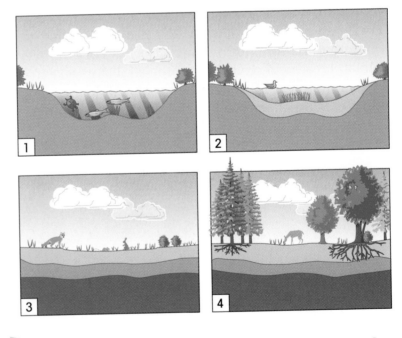

Figure 13-2
Over hundreds or even thousands of years, a pond may change into a forest.

✓ **What may happen to a community over the years?**

Lesson Review

1. What are three resources that nature recycles? *AIR, H2o, food*

2. What makes up a community? *diff pop. living + interacting together.*

3. List two nonliving things that organisms interact with in an ecosystem. *H2o + O*

4. CRITICAL THINKING As a pond changes into a forest, what happens to the types of organisms that make up the community?

A Closer Look

CHANGING COMMUNITIES

On May 18, 1980, the volcano Mount St. Helens in Washington blew its top. Rocks, ash, and hot gases swept across the forest nearby. Trees burned down or snapped in half. A thick layer of rock and ash settled over the land. Many plants, animals, and other organisms were killed. The forest community was destroyed.

Life is returning to Mount St. Helens.

With time, plants and animals moved into the area. Winds blew seeds and insects onto the land. The insects ate the seeds. Deer mice arrived. They ate the seeds and the insects. Some of the seeds grew into small plants. The soil became richer as the organisms died and decayed. Larger plants can now grow in the richer soil. They will provide food and shelter for other animals. Eventually, a forest will cover the area once again.

CRITICAL THINKING Why didn't the deer mice move into the area before the seeds and insects?

Words to Know

food chain	the path of food through a community
producer	an organism that makes its own food
consumer	an organism that eats other organisms
food web	a group of food chains that are linked to each other
decomposer	an organism that breaks down and absorbs nutrients from dead matter
fossil fuel	a fuel made of organisms that died millions of years ago
solar energy	energy from the sun
evaporation	the process by which a liquid changes to a gas
condensation	the process by which a gas changes to a liquid
natural resource	a substance found in nature that is useful to humans
conservation	the wise and careful use of natural resources

Food Chains and Webs

All the organisms in a community need food. The plants make their own food. Some of the animals eat the plants. Other animals eat the animals that feed on the plants. The path of food through a community is called a **food chain.** A community may have many food chains.

Remember
Green plants make food from chlorophyll, sunlight, water, and carbon dioxide.

Every food chain begins with a **producer.** A producer is an organism that makes its own food. Green plants and other organisms that have chlorophyll in their cells are producers. Many producers are eaten by consumers. A **consumer** is an organism that eats other organisms. Animals, fungi, most bacteria, and some protists are consumers.

Most consumers eat several kinds of food. They are part of more than one food chain. So the different food chains in a community are usually linked to each other. Together, the linked food chains make up a **food web.**

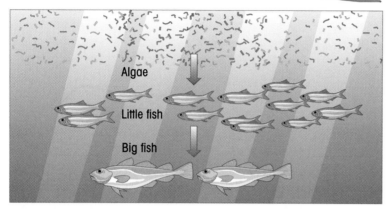

Figure 13-3 *In the ocean, algae are at the beginning of the food chain.*

Some consumers, such as certain bacteria and fungi, are also decomposers. A **decomposer** is an organism that breaks down and absorbs nutrients from dead matter. Decomposers break down the large molecules in dead organisms into smaller molecules. Some of these molecules are absorbed as food for the decomposer. Others become part of the soil. Plants use the molecules to live and grow. The continuous movement of food through a community forms a *food cycle.*

✓ **What is the difference between a producer and a consumer?**

Energy from the Past

When you drive a car, you are using dead plants and animals. That is because gasoline is a **fossil fuel.** A fossil fuel is made of organisms that died millions of years ago. Deep in the Earth, heat and pressure slowly changed the remains of dead organisms into coal, oil, and natural gas. People discovered that they could burn these materials for energy.

Remember
Fossils are the remains of organisms that lived long ago.

The Earth has only limited amounts of fossil fuels. Other sources of energy are needed. Scientists are working on ways to trap the sun's energy. Energy from the sun is called **solar energy**. Solar energy is often used today to heat homes.

✓ **What kind of energy that comes from the past do we use today?**

The Water Cycle

There is only a certain amount of water on Earth. People and other organisms use that water again and again. The water continuously moves to different parts of the Earth. Rainwater falls to the ground. Water in the ground runs into streams. Streams run into rivers. Rivers run into lakes and oceans.

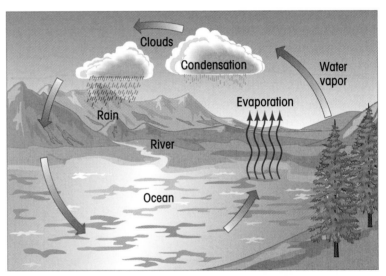

Figure 13-4 *Water is recycled in the water cycle.*

When water heats up, it changes into a gas called water vapor. This process is called **evaporation**. The sun's energy causes water to evaporate from the land and bodies of water. Plants and other organisms release water vapor into the air.

When water vapor cools, it changes to a liquid. This process is called **condensation**. As water vapor rises into the sky, it condenses and forms clouds. Later, the water falls to Earth again as rain or snow. The continuous movement of water on Earth is called the *water cycle*.

✓ **What are two processes in the water cycle?**

The Oxygen and Carbon Dioxide Cycle

The recycling of air involves two processes that you already know about—photosynthesis and respiration. When green plants carry out photosynthesis, they give off oxygen as a byproduct. People and other organisms use this oxygen for respiration.

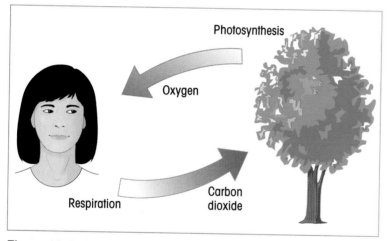

Figure 13-5 *Plants and animals constantly recycle oxygen and carbon dioxide.*

Remember that carbon dioxide is a waste product of respiration. Carbon dioxide is a gas that plants need for photosynthesis. As you can see, oxygen and carbon dioxide constantly cycle between plants and animals. Organisms need each other.

✓ **What two gases are recycled by organisms?**

Natural Resources and Conservation

Water, air, soil, minerals, forests, wildlife, and fossil fuels are substances found in nature that are useful to humans. Each is a **natural resource.** For example, people use fossil fuels to produce energy. Air and water are needed for our health. Some things in nature, such as mountains and waterfalls, are called natural resources simply because they are pleasing to our senses.

Resource	How People Use It
Water	For living and growing, cooking, washing, producing electricity, manufacturing, transportation
Air	For breathing, inflating tires and other objects, manufacturing
Soil	For growing plants
Minerals	For getting nutrients, fertilizing, manufacturing
Forests	For making furniture, paper, fuel, recreation
Wildlife	For food, medicine, recreation
Fossil fuels	For fuel for vehicles, factories, and electric power plants

There are more people on Earth today than ever before. We are using up many of our natural resources. Very old forests have been chopped down. Many plant and animal species have been killed off. The loss of any type of organism can harm other populations in that organism's habitat. For example, an organism could be a food source for other organisms. Its loss can destroy the balance of a whole ecosystem.

Conservation is the wise and careful use of natural resources. More and more people are realizing how delicate the Earth's ecosystems are. These people argue that we must save the Earth's natural resources for the future. They say we must keep the air and water clean.

We must stop the extinction of species. This will help preserve our planet's ecosystems.

✓ **List three examples of natural resources.**

Lesson Review

1. Draw and label a food chain that includes big fish, algae, and little fish.

2. How does water move in the water cycle?

3. How do the processes of photosynthesis and respiration help recycle the air?

4. **CRITICAL THINKING** Why is it important to use fossil fuels wisely?

On the Cutting Edge

LESS GASOLINE FOR CARS OF THE FUTURE

In 1974, the average car used 1 gallon (about 4 liters) of gasoline for every 14 miles (about 23 kilometers) it traveled. Today, many cars can travel twice as far on 1 gallon of gasoline. Even so, researchers are working on designing cars that use even less gasoline. One way to make cars go farther on less fuel is to make them lighter in weight. The lighter the car, the less gasoline it uses. Researchers are now designing and testing cars made of materials, such as aluminum and plastic, that are lighter than steel. Researchers hope that within the next few years, cars will be up to 40 percent lighter and be able to travel 100 miles (160 kilometers) per gallon.

Lightweight cars, such as this car made of aluminum, use less gasoline.

CRITICAL THINKING What other qualities should lightweight materials that are used for cars have?

LAB ACTIVITY
Making Models of Food Chains

BACKGROUND
The plants in a community make their own food. The animals eat the plants or other organisms. The path of food through a community is called a food chain.

Desert Organisms	Foods They Eat
Plants	Make their own food
Lizards	Grasshoppers
Rats	Plants, Grasshoppers
Hawks	Snakes, Rats
Grasshoppers	Plants
Snakes	Rats

PURPOSE
You will make models of two different food chains to see how organisms depend on each other.

MATERIALS
pencil, 6 hole-punched index cards, pieces of yarn, paper

WHAT TO DO
1. Write the name of each organism from the chart above on a separate index card.
2. The chart lists some foods that the organisms eat. Use the information in the chart to make a model food chain. Include at least three of the organisms. Remember that a food chain begins with a producer. Make the model food chain by using the yarn to connect the correct index cards.
3. Draw and label the model you made on a separate sheet of paper.
4. Now make a second food chain, following Steps 1 to 3. You may need to take apart your first model.

DRAW CONCLUSIONS
- What can you now say about the organisms in a community?

- What would you have if you arranged several different food chains so that the organisms were connected?

SCIENCE IN YOUR LIFE
Recycling Garbage

People in the United States produce hundreds of millions of tons of garbage every year. These wastes must be thrown out, or disposed of, properly to avoid health problems.

Most of the solid wastes that we produce are buried in large pits called *landfills*. Some wastes are burned. But there are problems with these methods of waste disposal. Many of the landfills are filling up quickly. Burning wastes pollutes the air.

Recycling garbage can help solve the problem of waste disposal. When people recycle garbage, they reuse the wastes instead of disposing of them. The pie graph on this page compares the amounts of different kinds of wastes that people produce. Notice that about 38% of the wastes are paper. Paper, glass, metal, plastics, and yard wastes can all be recycled. That is more than 70% of all the wastes we produce.

Many communities collect garbage and take it to a processing center. The garbage is sorted and then melted, shredded, or crushed. The new material is used to make products such as newspapers and aluminum cans.

Find out how much recyclable garbage you and your family produce.

1. Copy the chart. Collect the different types of garbage listed in the chart for one week.

2. Record the number of items you collected of each type of garbage.

If possible, take everything you have collected to a recycling center.

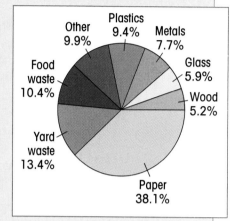

Different types of wastes are produced by people.
Source: Environmental Protection Agency

Type of Recyclable Garbage	Number of Items Collected
Paper	
Plastic	
Glass	
Metal	

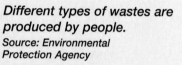

Critical Thinking
What can you do to produce less garbage?

Summary

Organisms depend on each other for food. They also depend on nonliving things, such as air, water, soil, and sunlight. Many of our natural resources are recycled so they can be shared.

Lesson 13.1

A community is a group of different populations living in the same place. A community and the nonliving things it interacts with make up an ecosystem. Most communities change over time.

Lesson 13.2

All organisms are part of food chains and food webs. Water, oxygen, and carbon dioxide constantly cycle between organisms and different parts of the Earth. Water, air, soil, forests, wildlife, minerals, and fossil fuels are all natural resources that must be used wisely.

natural resource

conservation

habitat

condensation

recycling

solar energy

ecosystem

food web

Vocabulary Review

Match each definition with a term from the list.

1. A community and all the nonliving things with which the community interacts

2. Reusing a substance over and over again

3. The place where an organism lives

4. A substance found in nature that is useful to humans

5. Energy from the sun

6. The process by which a gas changes to a liquid

7. A group of food chains that are linked to each other

8. The careful use of natural resources

Chapter Quiz

Write your answers on a separate sheet of paper.

1. What is the difference between a population and a community?

2. How do plants get water in an ecosystem?

3. What happens to many communities over long periods of time?

4. Rabbits eat plants. Foxes eat rabbits. Do rabbits, foxes, and plants form a food chain? If yes, draw a diagram of the chain.

5. Are you a producer or a consumer? Explain your answer.

6. How do decomposers help plants?

7. What are three fossil fuels?

8. What process causes water to leave the ocean and enter the air?

9. What two processes are involved in the recycling of air?

10. Why should people conserve natural resources?

Test Tip

Answer the questions you are sure of first. Then go back and answer those you need to think more about. Be sure that the number of each answer matches the number of its question.

Research Project

Research one food chain for each of five different ecosystems. For example, you could find food chains for a desert community, an ocean community, a rain forest community, a woodlands community, and an Arctic community. Draw and label the food chain. Label the producers, the consumers, and the decomposers.

Unit 3 Review

Choose the letter for the correct answer to each question.

Use the diagram below to answer Questions 1 and 2.

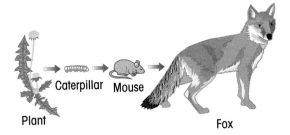

Plant   Caterpillar   Mouse   Fox

1. Which organisms in the food chain diagram above are consumers?

   A. fox, mouse, and caterpillar

   B. fox and mouse

   C. mouse and caterpillar

   D. plant and caterpillar

2. Which is the producer?

   A. fox

   B. mouse

   C. plant

   D. caterpillar

3. What is a group of food chains that are linked to each other called?

   A. a food cycle

   B. a food web

   C. photosynthesis

   D. an ecosystem

4. What carries messages between your brain and other parts of your body?

   A. glands

   B. brain stem

   C. tendons

   D. neurons

5. What are the main organs of the respiratory system called?

   A. lungs

   B. feet

   C. ears

   D. kidneys

6. Which cells help the body fight disease?

   A. red blood cells

   B. bacteria

   C. white blood cells

   D. viruses

7. Which nutrients should make up the smallest part of your diet?

   A. carbohydrates

   B. fats

   C. proteins

   D. water

Critical Thinking

The organs and systems of the human body all work together to help a person survive. How is this like an ecological community?

A pitcher throws a baseball very fast. He wants it to cross home plate before the batter can hit it.

When a pitcher throws a baseball, energy is passed from the pitcher to the ball. The speed of the ball depends partly on how much energy is passed along. The table shows the speed of pitches and the time it takes for each one to get to home plate. Use the table to help you answer the questions.

Speed and Time for a Ball to Get to Home Plate	
Speed	**Time**
88 feet per second	0.7 second
65 feet per second	1.0 second
50 feet per second	1.3 seconds

1. How fast is a ball moving if it takes 1.0 second to travel from the pitcher to home plate?

2. How soon will a ball reach home plate if it is traveling at 50 feet per second?

The large stone in this necklace is called the Hope diamond. It has been valued and admired for hundreds of years. How is the Hope diamond different from the diamonds that surround it?

Learning Objectives

- Compare chemistry and physics, the two branches of physical science.
- Identify elements.
- Describe an atom and identify its parts.
- Use properties to identify matter and its three states.
- Explain how density affects mass.
- Compare and contrast compounds, mixtures, and solutions.
- LAB ACTIVITY: Explore how some substances will form solutions and some will not.
- ON-THE-JOB SCIENCE: Relate working with mixtures to making concrete.

Words to Know

property	a way to describe matter, such as color, shape, odor, and hardness
chemistry	the scientific study of what matter is made of and how it reacts when it comes into contact with other matter
physics	the scientific study of what energy is and how it interacts with matter
electron	a part of an atom that has a negative electrical charge and is found outside the atom's nucleus
neutron	a part of an atom that has no electrical charge and is found inside the atom's nucleus
proton	a part of an atom that has a positive electrical charge and is found inside the atom's nucleus
density	the measure of how much mass something has for its size
solid	matter that has a definite shape and volume
liquid	matter that has a definite volume but no definite shape
gas	matter that has no definite shape or volume
compound	a substance that is formed when the atoms of two or more elements join together chemically
mixture	a substance made of two or more elements or compounds that are mixed together but not chemically joined
solution	a kind of mixture in which one substance dissolves, or seems to disappear, into another substance

Words to Know

property	a way to describe matter, such as color, shape, odor, and hardness
chemistry	the scientific study of what matter is made of and how it reacts when it comes into contact with other matter
physics	the scientific study of what energy is and how it interacts with matter
electron	a part of an atom that has a negative electrical charge and is found outside the atom's nucleus
neutron	a part of an atom that has no electrical charge and is found inside the atom's nucleus
proton	a part of an atom that has a positive electrical charge and is found inside the atom's nucleus

What Is Physical Science?

What do you have in common with a sandwich? How about sand, a race car, a tree, a pig, or the air you breathe? Not much, you might say. Well, you have one important thing in common with all these things. You are made of matter, along with everything on Earth that takes up space.

Remember
Matter is made up of tiny units called atoms. Atoms join to make molecules.

Matter has properties. A **property** is a way to describe matter. Some properties of matter are color, shape, odor, and hardness. The scientific study of the properties of matter is *physical science*.

✓ **What is the study of the properties of matter called?**

Physics and Chemistry

There are two branches of physical science. Some physical scientists study what matter is made of and how it reacts when it comes into contact with other matter. This field of study is called **chemistry.** Other scientists focus on energy. They try to understand what energy is and how it interacts with matter. This field of study is called **physics.**

Chemists must understand a lot about physics, however. Physicists must also understand a lot about chemistry. As you read on, you will see that the study of matter and energy go together.

✓ **How are chemistry and physics related?**

The Elements

All matter is made up of elements. There are at least 112 known elements. Eighty-eight of these elements are found in nature. The rest of the elements have been made in laboratories. Gold, silver, helium, oxygen, and nitrogen are examples of elements found in nature.

Elements are substances that cannot be broken down into simpler substances. Chemists use symbols to write about elements. A symbol is a shorthand way of writing a name. The chart on this page lists some of the elements and their symbols. For example, the symbol for the element hydrogen is H. The symbol for oxygen is O. See the Periodic Table of Elements in Appendix B for the symbols for all the elements.

There are two main groups of elements, *metals* and *nonmetals*. Gold and silver are metals. Helium, oxygen, and nitrogen are nonmetals.

Within the two main groups of elements are smaller groups called *families*. Families of elements share certain characteristics. In the Periodic Table of Elements, different colors show the different families.

Element	Symbol
Aluminum	Al
Arsenic	As
Calcium	Ca
Carbon	C
Chlorine	Cl
Chromium	Cr
Cobalt	Co
Copper	Cu
Fluorine	F
Gold	Au
Helium	He
Hydrogen	H
Iron	Fe
Lead	Pb
Mercury	Hg
Oxygen	O
Platinum	Pt
Silver	Ag
Sulfur	S
Tin	Sn
Zinc	Zn

Figure 14-1
Common elements and symbols

Not all substances that are made of the same element have the same properties. A diamond is one form of the element carbon. A diamond is the hardest natural substance known. Diamonds are used to make cutting tools and, of course, jewelry. Graphite is another form of the element carbon. It is black, soft, and slippery. It is used in the moving parts of machines to help them work more smoothly. It is also what is used in pencils.

✓ **Why are elements considered the simplest substances on Earth?**

The Structure of an Atom

Elements are made up of atoms. Atoms have four main parts: a nucleus, electrons, neutrons, and protons. This is true for all elements except hydrogen, which has no neutrons.

The Nucleus
One part of an atom is its central core. This core is called a *nucleus*. A cell has a nucleus, too. However, this nucleus is different from the nucleus of an atom.

Electrons
An atom has one or more electrons. An **electron** is a part of an atom that has a negative electrical charge. Electrons are found outside the atom's nucleus. Clouds of electrons actually circle around the nucleus. Different elements have different numbers of electrons. A hydrogen atom has only one electron. A uranium atom has 92 electrons. Electrons travel at very high speeds.

Neutrons and Protons
An atom has neutrons and protons. A **neutron** is a part of an atom that has no electrical charge. Neutrons are found inside the atom's nucleus. A **proton** is also found inside the nucleus. However, protons have a positive electrical charge.

Every atom has the same number of protons as it has electrons. The number of neutrons varies.

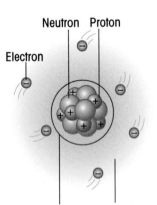

Neutron Proton

Electron

Nucleus Electron cloud

Figure 14-2 *An atom of carbon has six electrons.*

Electrons and protons have opposite electrical charges. They attract each other. This attraction is what holds electrons close to the nucleus of the atom.

✓ **What are the four main parts of an atom?**

Lesson Review

1. What are some properties of matter?

2. What are the two branches of physical science?

3. What are the two main groups of elements? Into what smaller groups are they broken down?

4. CRITICAL THINKING An atom has 12 protons. How many electrons does the atom have?

On the Cutting Edge

LOOKING AT ATOMS

Everything around you is made up of atoms. However, to see atoms themselves, you need a computer and special microscopes. One such microscope is called the scanning tunneling microscope, or STM.

An STM uses beams of electrons instead of beams of light. The electron beams move over, or scan, a surface. Signals are sent from the microscope to a computer. Then the computer shows an image of the atoms on the surface. The atoms appear as bumps on the surface. Scientists have used STMs to view metals, human tissue, and the twisted-ladder shape of a DNA molecule.

Individual atoms appear as bumps or peaks in this computer image from an STM.

CRITICAL THINKING How would it be helpful to see images of atoms?

Words to Know

density	the measure of how much mass something has for its size
solid	matter that has a definite shape and volume
liquid	matter that has a definite volume but no definite shape
gas	matter that has no definite shape or volume
compound	a substance that is formed when the atoms of two or more elements join together chemically
mixture	a substance made of two or more elements or compounds that are mixed together but not chemically joined
solution	a kind of mixture in which one substance dissolves, or seems to disappear, into another substance

Telling Things Apart

The properties of a substance make it possible to tell it apart from another substance. A few properties of matter are color, shape, odor, and hardness. You could describe an element such as mercury as silver-colored and a liquid. It also does not have a strong smell.

Another property of a substance is its mass. Mass is the amount of matter in something. For example, a volleyball is about the same size as a bowling ball. However, there is much more matter in a bowling ball than in a volleyball. It has a greater mass.

Another property of matter is **density.** Density is the measure of how much mass something has for its size. Scientists define density as the *measure of mass per unit volume.* The meaning of *per unit volume* is "for any given space." So, density is the amount of mass in a given space.

Science Fact

Iron pyrite is often called "fool's gold." It has many of the same properties as gold. However, a few drops of acid will dissolve iron pyrite and give off a bad smell. Real gold will not change under "the acid test."

Think of a loaf of bread. Imagine balling it up and squeezing it together as tightly as possible. The balled-up bread would take up less space than the original loaf. It would have a smaller volume than it did before you balled it up. The amount of bread would be the same. The mass per volume, or density, however, would be greater.

Now think of a cork in water. The cork is less dense than water. This causes the cork to float. Lead, however, is denser than water. It sinks to the bottom.

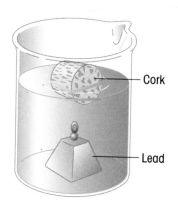

Figure 14-3
Cork floats in water while lead sinks.

✓ **How are mass and density related?**

The Three States of Matter

Matter has three different states, or ways of existing. These states are solid, liquid, and gas. A **solid** is matter that has a definite shape and volume. A **liquid** is matter that has a definite volume but no definite shape. A **gas** is matter that has no definite shape or volume.

Matter can change between the different states. For example, water is usually in liquid form. If you freeze water, it becomes a solid, as ice. When a solid melts, it turns back into a liquid. When you heat water, it turns to a colorless gas called water vapor and then disappears. This is called *evaporation*. A gas changes back to liquid during *condensation*. When a cold window fogs up, the fog is water vapor that has turned back into a liquid.

Like solids, liquids have a definite volume. However, they do not have a definite shape. Think of a glass of water. If you poured that water into a bowl, the volume of water would still be the same. It would take up the same amount of space. The shape of the water would change, though. It would take on the shape of the bowl. Now think about moving a solid, such as a peach, from a glass to a bowl. The peach would not change shape or volume.

Gas is also matter. That is, it takes up space. However, it does not have a definite shape or a definite volume. A gas will spread out over a container of any size or any shape.

Think of a small bathroom after a hot shower. The water vapor fills the whole bathroom. Suppose you took a shower in a much bigger bathroom. The same amount of water vapor would spread out in the bigger room. Air, hydrogen, helium, oxygen, and carbon dioxide are all gases.

The molecules in all substances are constantly moving. However, the molecules in solids are packed very tightly together. They move very little. The molecules in liquids have more room. They move around more freely. The molecules in gases have even more room to move.

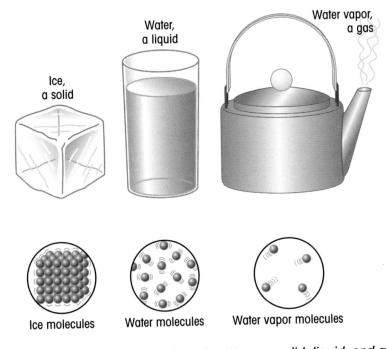

Water vapor, a gas

Water, a liquid

Ice, a solid

Ice molecules   Water molecules   Water vapor molecules

Figure 14-4 *The three states of matter are solid, liquid, and gas.*

✔ **What are the three states of matter?**

Compounds, Mixtures, and Solutions

A substance that is formed when the atoms of two or more elements join together chemically is called a **compound.** The elements in a compound have a chemical connection, or *bond.* In most chemical bonds, atoms share electrons. Water is a compound made of oxygen and hydrogen. The oxygen and hydrogen atoms share electrons. Rust is a compound made by a chemical bond of iron and oxygen. Sugar, salt, and soap are also compounds.

A **mixture** is different from a compound. A mixture is a substance made of two or more elements or compounds that are mixed together but not chemically joined. For example, if you mix soil and water, they are still separate. You can pour the mixture through a filter. The soil will stay on the filter, and water will come out the other end.

A **solution** is a special kind of mixture. In a solution, one substance *dissolves,* or seems to disappear, when it is put into another. However, it is not gone. It has only spread out evenly throughout the other substance.

Salt water is a solution. If you put a small amount of salt in water, the salt will dissolve. However, if you let the salt water stand in a sunny place for several days, the water will evaporate. You will be left with the salt.

✓ **How can different elements join together?**

Lesson Review

1. Which of the three states of matter have a definite volume?

2. How is a mixture different from a compound?

3. CRITICAL THINKING Which has greater density, a jar filled with air or a jar filled with water? Explain your answer.

LAB ACTIVITY
Part of the Solution

BACKGROUND

A mixture can be separated by a filter. A solution cannot.
You must use evaporation to separate a solution.

PURPOSE

You will add solids to water. Then you will test to see
if you have a mixture or solution.

MATERIALS

paper, pencil, 4 plastic cups, water,
teaspoons, salt, chalk dust, 2 coffee filter
papers, 2 saucers

Solid	Does It Dissolve in Water?	Contents of Filter Paper	Contents of Saucer
Salt			
Chalk			

WHAT TO DO

1. Copy the chart to the right.
2. Fill two of the plastic cups halfway with water.
3. Add a teaspoon of salt to one cup and stir. Then add a teaspoon of chalk dust to the other cup and stir. Record your observations in the second column of the chart.
4. Place one coffee filter paper in the top of another cup. Pour the water-salt mixture into the filter paper.
5. Save the filter paper with any contents in it. Label it. Pour some of the filtered liquid from the cup into a saucer. Let it sit overnight or until the water evaporates.
6. Repeat Steps 4 and 5 on the water-chalk mixture.
7. The next day, compare the contents of the two filter papers and the two saucers. Complete the chart.

DRAW CONCLUSIONS

- Which solid dissolved in water and which did not?
- Which solid formed a mixture with the water?
- Which formed a solution with the water?

ON-THE-JOB SCIENCE
Concrete Worker

Al Hernandez is a concrete worker. He mixes cement, sand, gravel, and water to make a thick, wet mixture of concrete. He then pours the concrete into a mold. The cement in the concrete causes the mixture to harden.

Concrete must contain the correct type and amount of each ingredient. If the wrong type of cement is used, the concrete might not harden correctly. If the concrete contains too much water, sand, or gravel, it might not be strong enough.

Look at the drawings. Note the differences among concrete Mixtures A, B, and C. Concrete will be stronger if the sand and gravel mixture is very dense.

Concrete must have the right mix of ingredients to be strong.

  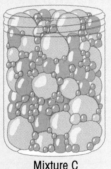

Mixture A   Mixture B   Mixture C

Answer these questions, using the drawings.

1. Which mixture has the most amount of space between particles?

2. Which mixture is most tightly packed? Why?

3. Which mixture above would make the strongest concrete? Why?

Critical Thinking

When too much water is added to concrete, small holes form in the concrete as it dries. What do you think these holes will do to the concrete?

Chapter

14 ⟩ Review

Summary

Properties are used to identify matter. Properties of matter include mass, density, and state.

Lesson 14.1

Chemistry and physics are two branches of physical science. Elements are made up of atoms. Atoms contain a nucleus, electrons, neutrons, and protons.

Lesson 14.2

The state of matter can be solid, liquid, or gas. When the atoms of elements bond, they form a compound. When they mix but do not bond, they form a mixture. A solution is one kind of mixture.

Vocabulary Review

Write *true* or *false* for each sentence. If the sentence is false, replace the underlined term to make the sentence true.

1. The scientific study of matter is called <u>chemistry</u>.

2. The state of matter that has no definite shape or volume is a <u>liquid</u>.

3. When atoms of two elements bond, a <u>mixture</u> is formed.

4. The particle that has no electrical charge and is found in the nucleus of the atom is an <u>electron</u>.

5. A <u>property</u> can be used to identify matter.

6. The scientific study of energy is called <u>physics</u>.

7. Matter with a definite volume and shape is a <u>liquid</u>.

8. The positively charged particle in an atom is a <u>proton</u>.

Chapter Quiz

Write your answers on a separate sheet of paper.

1. You are studying the properties of an apple. Are you studying chemistry, or are you studying physics? Explain.

2. What are three properties of a pumpkin?

3. What are the four main parts of an atom? Where are they located?

4. What keeps electrons close to the nucleus?

5. What is density a measure of?

6. What happens to a gas when it is moved from a small container into a big container?

7. Are the molecules farther apart in water, steam, or ice? Explain.

8. Iron and oxygen atoms bond to form rust. Is rust a compound or a mixture? Explain.

9. Why is muddy water a mixture and not a compound?

10. What happens to salt when it dissolves in water?

Research Project

The breakfast you ate this morning, the clothes you wear, and the book in front of you are all made of compounds. These compounds are made up of elements. Choose an element listed in the Periodic Table of Elements found in Appendix B. Find out all you can about the element's properties. For example, find out its boiling point, melting point, density, and any other properties. The Internet and reference books are good sources of information.

Chapter 15 — Energy and Matter

Yesterday, these trees were green and growing. Today, leaves and branches are being changed by fire. How are these changes in the trees different from just chopping the trees down?

Learning Objectives

- Identify energy and matter.
- Explain the difference between potential energy and kinetic energy.
- Identify the different forms of energy.
- Describe how heat energy changes matter.
- Compare and contrast physical and chemical changes.
- LAB ACTIVITY: Explore how energy can be transformed from one form to another.
- SCIENCE IN YOUR LIFE: Relate cooking to the ways that energy changes substances.

Words to Know

potential energy	energy that is stored in matter
kinetic energy	energy that comes from movement
light energy	energy in the form of moving waves of light
heat energy	energy in the form of moving molecules
electrical energy	energy in the form of electrons moving through a substance
chemical energy	energy stored in molecules
mechanical energy	energy in the form of parts moving in a machine
nuclear energy	energy stored in the nucleus of an atom
nuclear fission	the breakup of the nucleus of an atom
nuclear fusion	the joining together of two or more atomic nuclei

Words to Know

potential energy	energy that is stored in matter
kinetic energy	energy that comes from movement

What Is Energy?

The whole world is made up of matter. It takes energy to power all that matter. Energy is the ability to do work or produce heat. In science, to do work means to make something move. Energy makes things move. Without energy, rivers would not flow. The Earth would not go around the sun. You would not move a muscle. Nothing would move at all.

Energy has no mass. Yet it is as real as matter. There is energy in all things, whether they are moving or they are standing still.

The universe has all the energy it will ever have. Energy cannot be created or destroyed. However, it can change form.

✓ **What does it mean to do work?**

Potential and Kinetic Energy

There are two main kinds of energy. One kind can be stored in matter. This is called **potential energy**. Energy can also be released from matter, which sometimes sets matter in motion. The kind of energy that comes from such movement is called **kinetic energy.**

A stick of wood stores energy. When the wood burns, it releases energy. The energy it releases is in the form of heat and light.

Figure 15-1 *The rocks on the ledge have potential energy.*

Figure 15-2 *The falling rocks have kinetic energy.*

Water held back by a dam has potential energy. A running river has kinetic energy. A rock perched on the edge of a cliff has potential energy. If the rock begins to fall, the potential energy changes into kinetic energy. During the change from one kind of energy to another, some of the energy is given off as heat.

Where do you get your energy? The energy your body needs comes from the food you eat. It is stored in your cells. As you move around, walk to school, think about a math problem, or play sports, digested food provides you with power in the form of kinetic energy.

✓ **When does an object have kinetic energy?**

Lesson Review

1. What is needed to make something move?

2. What are the two main kinds of energy?

3. Where does the human body get the energy it needs to function?

4. **CRITICAL THINKING** You stop your bicycle at the top of a hill. What change in energy happened?

Words to Know

light energy	energy in the form of moving waves of light
heat energy	energy in the form of moving molecules
electrical energy	energy in the form of electrons moving through a substance
chemical energy	energy stored in molecules
mechanical energy	energy in the form of parts moving in a machine
nuclear energy	energy stored in the nucleus of an atom
nuclear fission	the breakup of the nucleus of an atom
nuclear fusion	the joining together of two or more atomic nuclei

Light Energy

Potential and kinetic energy can exist in many different forms. Energy in the form of moving waves of light is called **light energy.** The main source of light energy on Earth is the sun. This is also what we know as solar energy. Many people use solar energy to heat their homes.

✓ **What is the main source of light energy on Earth?**

Heat Energy

Energy in the form of moving molecules is called **heat energy.** Hot objects contain more heat energy than cold objects. The molecules in a hot object move faster. By rubbing your hands together, you can increase the amount of heat energy in your palms. Notice how they become warmer.

✓ **Which object has more heat energy, a hot cup or a cold cup? Why?**

Electrical Energy

Energy in the form of electrons moving through a substance is called **electrical energy.** Remember that electrons have a negative electrical charge. The electrical energy is carried along by a flow of electrons. Lightning is a form of electrical energy.

✓ **What part of the atom produces electrical energy?**

Chemical Energy

Energy stored in molecules is called **chemical energy.** When molecules react with each other, the energy stored in them may be released. Cars use chemical energy stored in gasoline. Humans use chemical energy stored in food.

✓ **What form of energy is stored in food?**

Mechanical Energy

The energy in the form of parts moving in a machine is called **mechanical energy.** A windmill changes the mechanical energy of the spinning blades into electrical energy. A power plant turns the mechanical energy of a spinning turbine into the electrical energy that you use every day.

✓ **What form of energy do the moving parts of a machine have?**

Nuclear Energy

The energy stored in the nucleus of an atom is called **nuclear energy.** This energy is released when the nucleus is broken apart. The breakup of the nucleus is called **nuclear fission.** Nuclear fission of a large number of atoms results in a huge release of energy. Nuclear power plants use nuclear fission to make electricity.

Lightning is a form of electrical energy.

Bicycles also use mechanical energy.

Nuclear power plants produce electricity from nuclear fission.

Huge amounts of energy are also released when two or more nuclei join together, or fuse. This process is called **nuclear fusion.**

✓ **What is it called when a nucleus breaks up and releases energy?**

Energy in Different Forms

You have learned that energy can neither be created nor destroyed. However, it can change form. Solar panels on a house can change light energy into heat energy. The chemical energy in a battery can get turned into electrical energy. A water wheel can turn the kinetic energy of a river into mechanical energy. This ability of energy to change forms is a property of energy.

✓ **What is a special property of energy?**

Lesson Review

1. What are the names of six different forms of energy?

2. What type of energy does chemical energy become when you turn on a battery-operated radio?

3. CRITICAL THINKING Which form of energy is most important to your life? Explain your answer.

Matter and Heat Energy

All changes in matter need some kind of energy. Heat energy can change matter. It causes the molecules in a substance to move faster and farther apart. When enough heat is added, many solids will change to liquids. This is the process of melting. Ice is the solid form of water. When you add enough heat to ice, it melts.

When you add more heat to a liquid, the molecules move even faster. They also move farther apart. With enough heat, molecules will begin to break away from the substance. The substance then changes into a gas. This is the process of evaporation.

Remember
The process of a liquid changing to a gas is called evaporation. Condensation is the process of a gas changing to a liquid.

Heat energy can be taken away from matter. When enough heat is taken away from a gas, the gas turns into a liquid. This is the process of condensation. If you take enough heat away from a liquid, it becomes a solid. This is the process of freezing.

You have probably noticed a light mist of water on the grass in the morning. This is called *dew*. Dew is caused by condensation. At night, the air cools. This cooling causes water vapor in the air to change into liquid water. As the sun warms the ground, the dew will evaporate.

✓ **What causes matter to change its state?**

Two Ways to Change Matter

Physical Change
A physical change affects only the state, shape, or volume of matter. If you drop a plate and break it, for example, the shape has changed. However, it is still a plate. No chemical change has occurred.

Crushing, tearing, and grinding are all examples of physical changes. Freezing, melting, boiling, and condensation are also physical changes. Ice has the same chemical makeup as water. It just has less heat energy in it.

Chemical Change

In a chemical change, a substance that has new properties is produced. Compounds are always the result of a chemical change. For example, a kind of acid is formed when milk sours. A change in odor tells you a chemical change has taken place.

Another example of a chemical change is burning wood. The wood and oxygen from the air combine to turn the wood into ashes. Several new gases are also released into the air.

Sometimes you know that a chemical change has taken place by the way something looks. When iron rusts, you can tell a new substance has formed by looking at it. But not all chemical changes are easily seen.

One sign that a chemical change has happened is that energy is released, as when a match burns. Or energy might be absorbed, as when a cake bakes. Another sign is the release of a gas, such as the exhaust fumes from a car.

✓ **What are the two main kinds of changes matter can undergo?**

Figure 15-3 *Chopping vegetables causes a physical change.*

Figure 15-4 *Cooking vegetables causes a chemical change.*

Lesson Review

1. What happens to a liquid if you take away enough heat energy?

2. An apple rots. What two things show you that a chemical change happened?

3. Is frying an egg a physical change or a chemical change? Explain your answer.

4. **CRITICAL THINKING** If you place a blown-up balloon in the freezer and take it out in a few minutes, you will see drops of water inside the balloon. How did the drops of water get inside the balloon?

Modern Leaders in Science

ROY PLUNKETT

In 1938, the Du Pont company asked Roy Plunkett to make a new *refrigerant*. A refrigerant is a gas used to cool the air in refrigerators and air conditioners. So Plunkett mixed up a bottle of gas chemicals that he thought might work. Then he put the bottle aside.

Roy Plunkett

When Plunkett returned to the bottle, he found something very strange. Instead of a gas, the bottle contained a very slippery, white powder.

Plunkett did not know it right away, but he had created one of the first plastics. Today we know this plastic as Teflon. It is used as a nonstick coating on pans and cooking utensils.

CRITICAL THINKING What type of change does Plunkett's discovery show?

LAB ACTIVITY
Changing Forms of Energy

BACKGROUND
When you turn on a hair dryer, electrical energy changes to mechanical and heat energy. When you eat an apple, chemical energy changes to heat energy in your body. You know that energy is neither created nor destroyed. It just changes its form.

PURPOSE
You will observe how energy changes from one form to another.

MATERIALS
paper, pencil, safety goggles, sand, plastic container with lid, alcohol thermometer, timer

WHAT TO DO
1. Copy the chart to the right.
2. Put on your safety goggles. Do not take them off until everyone is done with the activity.
3. Place sand in a plastic container until it is about half full.
4. Place the end of the thermometer in the middle of the sand. Leave the thermometer in the sand for about two minutes. Remove the thermometer. Record the temperature of the sand in the "Before" part of the table.
5. Place the lid firmly on the container. Shake the container rapidly for three minutes.
6. Remove the lid. Right away, take the temperature of the sand. Record this reading in the "After" part of the table.

Measure the temperature of the sand.

Temperature of Sand	
Before	After

DRAW CONCLUSIONS
- What happened to the temperature of the sand when it was shaken?
- What can you say about the energy change that took place?

SCIENCE IN YOUR LIFE
Cooking and Energy

Energy and foods are related to each other in several ways. One way involves the changes that occur in foods when they are cooked. You have probably eaten cooked eggs. However, you have probably never eaten raw eggs. Cooking greatly improves the taste of eggs.

Cooking involves adding energy to food. Chemical changes occur in food when energy is added. Cooking changes the taste, appearance, and texture of the food. It might also kill bacteria that are in the raw food.

The food itself contains energy. Your body changes the chemical energy in food into energy that can be used for all body functions.

The amount of chemical energy in food is measured in units called *calories*. If you look at a food label, it will tell you how many calories are in a certain amount of the food.

Adding energy to food causes chemical changes to occur.

Use the calorie chart to write a healthy meal plan that contains 500 to 600 calories.

Calories in One Serving of Certain Foods			
Food	**Calories**	**Food**	**Calories**
Apple	80	Grapes	40
Bagel	200	Ground beef	245
Banana	105	Kiwi fruit	45
Beef roast	315	Lettuce	5
Bologna	180	Milk	120
Broccoli	40	Orange	60
Carrot	30	Pickle, dill	5
Cheese	115	Popcorn	55
Chicken	140	Wheat bread	65

Critical Thinking

What happens to the calories in the food you eat?

Summary

There are two main kinds of energy, but energy can come in many different forms. Energy interacts with matter. This causes certain changes in matter.

Lesson 15.1

Energy is the ability to do work, produce heat, or, in science, to make things move. Energy has no mass, but energy is present in all things. Potential energy is energy stored in matter. Kinetic energy comes from movement. Energy cannot be destroyed or created, but it can change forms.

Lesson 15.2

Some forms of energy are heat energy, light energy, electrical energy, chemical energy, nuclear energy, and mechanical energy.

Lesson 15.3

Changes in matter can be either physical or chemical. A physical change affects only the state, shape, or volume of matter. A chemical change affects the chemical makeup of the substance.

Vocabulary Review

Match each definition with a term from the list.

chemical energy

electrical energy

heat energy

kinetic energy

light energy

nuclear fission

nuclear fusion

potential energy

1. Energy that comes from movement

2. Energy in the form of electrons moving through a substance

3. The joining together of two or more atomic nuclei

4. Energy in the form of moving molecules

5. Energy stored in molecules

6. Energy that is stored

7. The breakup of the nucleus of an atom

8. Energy in the form of moving waves of light

Chapter Quiz

Write your answers on a separate sheet of paper.

1. How much mass does energy have?

2. What is stored energy? What is energy of motion? Give an example of each.

3. What are six forms of energy? Give an example of each.

4. What nuclear process takes place in a nuclear reactor?

5. Can you use up energy? Explain your answer.

6. What happens to a liquid if you add enough heat to it?

7. What causes matter to change?

8. What is one way to make a physical change in a wooden chair?

9. What is one way to make a chemical change in a wooden chair?

10. How do you know a chemical change takes place when a log burns?

Test Tip
Reread the summaries for each chapter before the quiz. They usually cover the main points and tie the pieces of the chapter together.

Research Project

When you turn on a light switch, you are using electricity that has been changed from some other type of energy. This change takes place in a power plant. Three main types of power plants are hydroelectric, coal-burning, and nuclear. Choose a type of power plant and research it. Draw a diagram or flow chart to show how the "source energy" is changed to "electric energy."

Sharply curved bobsled tracks must be tilted to keep the sled on the track. What do you think might happen if the track were not tilted as steeply?

Learning Objectives

- Describe the effects of gravity, friction, and centripetal force.

- Explain the difference between weight and mass.

- Describe how inertia affects an object's motion.

- LAB ACTIVITY: Observe the relationship between the weight of an object and friction.

- ON-THE-JOB SCIENCE: Relate motion and inertia to stopping distances of vehicles.

Words to Know

force	any push or pull on an object
gravity	the force of attraction between any two objects that have mass
weight	the measure of the force of gravity on an object
friction	a force that slows motion or prevents it
lubricant	a substance that reduces friction between the moving parts of machines
centripetal force	a force that causes objects in motion to move in a curved path
inertia	the tendency of an object to stay at rest or in motion unless it is acted upon by a force
motion	a change in the position or place of an object

Words to Know

force	any push or pull on an object
gravity	the force of attraction between any two objects that have mass
weight	the measure of the force of gravity on an object
friction	a force that slows motion or prevents it
lubricant	a substance that reduces friction between the moving parts of machines
centripetal force	a force that causes objects in motion to move in a curved path

Physics and Everyday Life

Remember
Physics is the scientific study of energy and how it interacts with matter.

Physics has a lot to teach us about our everyday lives. For example, knowing physics can make someone a better athlete. Physics explains why it is important to follow through when hitting a baseball. It explains why it is harder to stop a big football player than a small one.

In many of your everyday activities, you exert a **force** on something. A force is any push or pull on an object. When you throw a baseball or hit a baseball with a bat, you push it away from you. When you drag a sled, you pull it behind you. Your body pushes on a chair as you sit in it. A dog tugging on a leash pulls its owner behind it. These are all examples of force.

In many sports, you want to hit the ball as hard as possible. This means you try to give the ball as much force as you can. In golf, a ball hit hard means the ball goes farther. In tennis, a ball hit hard means the other player has to move faster to return the shot.

The longer you exert a force on something, the greater the effect of that force will be. That is why a coach will tell a player to "follow through" on a swing or stroke. By following through, the bat, racquet, or club is on the ball longer. The player exerts a force for a longer period of time. That makes the ball go faster and farther. In this chapter, you will learn about different kinds of forces and their effects on objects.

✓ **What happens when a force is exerted on something?**

Gravity

All objects that have mass are attracted to each other. This force of attraction between any two objects that have mass is called **gravity.** The more mass an object has, the greater the force of its gravity. The Earth is a very massive object. So, its force of gravity is very great.

Gravity is the force that holds us on the ground. It pulls all matter toward the center of the Earth. The sun and moon also have a gravitational effect on the Earth. The sun's gravity keeps the Earth traveling around the sun. The moon's gravity pulls on the Earth's oceans, causing tides.

Imagine the Earth without gravity. If you let go of an apple, it would not fall. It would just float away. In fact, you would also float away. There would be nothing holding you to the ground.

The force of gravity depends on the distance between two objects. The farther apart two things are from each other, the less gravitational pull they have on each other.

✓ **What two things affect the force of gravity between two objects?**

Science Fact

Sir Isaac Newton was the first person to explain what gravity is. After seeing an apple fall, he realized that the force that makes the apple fall is the same force that keeps the moon traveling around the sun.

Weight

The measure of the force of gravity on an object is its **weight.** The stronger the pull, the greater the weight is. Weight is different from mass. Mass is the amount of matter in an object. An object's mass will stay the same wherever the object is. However, the weight of an object can change. This is because the amount of gravitational pull on an object can change. For example, the moon is less massive than the Earth. If you were on the moon, there would be less gravitational pull on you than if you were on Earth. You would weigh one-sixth as much on the moon as you do on Earth.

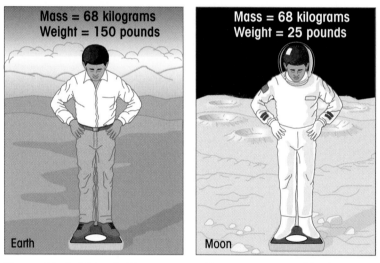

Mass = 68 kilograms
Weight = 150 pounds

Earth

Mass = 68 kilograms
Weight = 25 pounds

Moon

Figure 16-1 *Mass is the same on the moon as on Earth, but weight is only one-sixth as much on the moon.*

The force of gravity is slightly weaker near the equator than it is at the North and South poles. This is because the Earth bulges. It is bigger at the equator. An object on the equator is farther from the Earth's center. Therefore, it will weigh slightly less than an object near one of the poles.

✓ **How is weight different from mass?**

Friction

Some riders wish their skateboard rides would never end. They would like to push off once and never have to push again. This would be possible if it were not for **friction.** Friction is a force that slows motion or prevents motion. Three types of friction are *rolling friction, sliding friction,* and *fluid friction.*

Rolling Friction

When you drive a car, you must overcome rolling friction. The car wheels roll over the road. The road slows down the rolling of the wheels. The rougher the surface, the greater the friction is. The smoother the surface, the less the friction is. For example, ice is very slippery. When a car travels on ice, there is much less friction than there is on a dry road. This is why cars often have trouble stopping on ice.

Sliding Friction

If you try to slide across a polished floor in sneakers, you will come to a stop very quickly. However, when you slide in socks, sliding friction will stop you after a few feet. There is greater sliding friction with sneakers than with socks.

Fluid Friction

When you row a boat, you must overcome the fluid friction in water. The boat pushes against the water. The water slows the boat's motion. A flying airplane must overcome the same type of friction in the air.

To begin this marathon, these racers must overcome rolling friction.

The more friction, the more force a boat needs to exert to get started. The fastest boats only skim the water. Less contact with the water means less friction.

Friction explains why many things break down or wear out. The friction of a fingernail scraping against a wall will eventually wear off the paint on the wall. The friction of moving parts in a car engine will wear down the parts. After a time, you will have to replace some parts.

A **lubricant** is a substance that reduces friction between the moving parts of machines. Oil, grease, and graphite are all lubricants. These substances are much more slippery than metal.

In the 1600s, the Italian scientist Galileo Galilei studied falling objects. He found that light objects fall at the same speed as heavy objects unless friction in the air causes the lighter object to fall more slowly. You can try Galileo's experiment. Drop a tennis ball and a baseball from the same height and at the same time. Which of these hits the ground first? Now drop a feather and a stone. What happens this time?

✓ **What are three types of friction?**

Centripetal Force

One law of physics says that all moving objects travel in a straight path. However, an outside force can change that path. **Centripetal force** is an example of such a force. It causes objects in motion to move in a curved path.

When you drive a car fast around a curve, you get pressed against the car door. Your body naturally wants to continue forward in the direction it was going. The car door is acting as a centripetal force, keeping you in the path of the curve.

Centripetal force keeps the roller-coaster cars on the track.

The tracks of many amusement park rides are examples of centripetal force. The tracks keep the cars from going out in a straight line. Centripetal force also keeps the bobsled shown on page 230 moving in a curved path.

You can demonstrate centripetal force yourself. Tie a ball to the end of a rope. Hold onto the rope and swing the ball in a circle. This is centripetal force in action. Holding the rope creates the centripetal force that keeps the ball in its circular path.

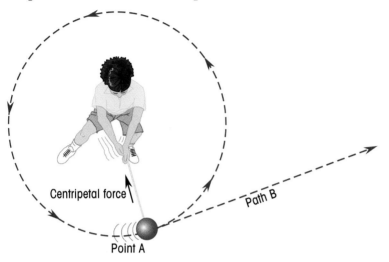

Figure 16-2 *Centripetal force keeps the ball going in circles. If you released the rope at Point A, the ball would follow Path B. It would go straight.*

✓ **How does centripetal force affect an object in motion?**

Lesson Review

1. Does an astronaut weigh more, less, or the same on the moon as on Earth? Why?

2. What force causes a skateboarder on a flat sidewalk to come to a stop?

3. What force keeps a ball on a string moving in a circular path?

4. **CRITICAL THINKING** What would cause the gravitational pull between two objects to change? How would it change?

Words to Know

inertia	the tendency of an object to stay at rest or in motion unless it is acted upon by a force
motion	a change in the position or place of an object

The Law of Inertia

Sir Isaac Newton

The English scientist Sir Isaac Newton was born in 1642. Newton was one of the greatest scientists of all time. He figured out many physical laws, including the law of **inertia.** Inertia is the tendency of an object to stay at rest or in motion unless it is acted upon by a force. **Motion** is a change in the position or place of an object. Rest is a complete lack of motion.

An object at rest will stay at rest forever unless a force moves it. An object in motion will stay in motion forever unless a force stops it.

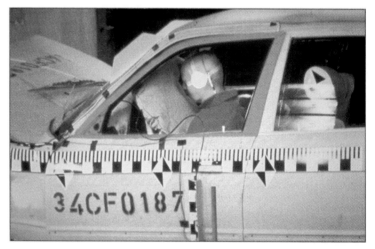

When the car stops suddenly, inertia makes this dummy keep moving forward. Seat belts and air bags supply the forces needed to stop the dummy's forward motion.

Inertia is a property of all matter. The greater the mass of an object, the greater the inertia is. A big football player running down a field has greater inertia than a small player. It will take a stronger force to stop the bigger player.

✓ **What does the law of inertia say about an object?**

Lesson Review

1. Who figured out the law of inertia?

2. What will stop an object in motion?

3. CRITICAL THINKING Why does it take a stronger force to stop a bus than it does to stop a small car?

On the Cutting Edge

TECHNOLOGY IN THEME PARKS

At many theme parks, technology is used to create new and different rides. At one park in Florida, visitors walk through a tunnel of swirling water. Forty high-powered jets shoot water at 100 miles (160 kilometers) per hour up and around the curved walls of the tunnel. The water is held against the sides of the tunnel by centripetal force and the inertia of the water. You can actually put your hand into the water stream to feel the force of the moving water.

Centripetal force and inertia hold the water against the tunnel walls.

Another new ride will combine a Ferris wheel and a roller coaster. The Ferris wheel cab will be attached to a loop of roller-coaster track. As the Ferris wheel spins, gravity will pull the cabs around the loops for a more thrilling ride.

CRITICAL THINKING What force must be overcome to keep the water on the tunnel ceiling from crashing down on visitors?

LAB ACTIVITY
Weight and Friction

BACKGROUND
Different surfaces cause different amounts of friction. The force needed to move an object depends on the object and the surface it moves across.

PURPOSE
You will measure and compare the amount of force needed to move objects across different surfaces.

MATERIALS
paper, pen, 18-inch piece of string, book, large paper clip, large metal washers, masking tape, waxed paper, sandpaper, long pencils

WHAT TO DO
1. Copy the chart to the right.
2. Tie the ends of the string to make a loop. Put the loop over the front cover of the book.
3. Place the book on a table about 4 inches from the edge. Let the loop of the string hang over the edge of the table.
4. Straighten the paper clip to form an S-shape. Hang the paper clip from the string.
5. Put a washer on the paper clip. Add washers one at a time until the book begins to move. Record the number of washers needed to move the book.
6. Tape waxed paper to the table top. Repeat Steps 3 to 5.
7. Tape sandpaper to the table top. Repeat Steps 3 to 5.
8. Repeat Steps 3 to 5, placing some pencils under the book.

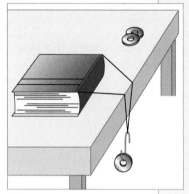

You need to add washers, one at a time, until the book starts to move.

Surface	Number of Washers
Table top	
Waxed paper	
Sandpaper	
Pencils	

DRAW CONCLUSIONS
- How do the amounts of friction caused by the different surfaces compare?
- What can you conclude about how surface friction affects the force needed to move something?

ON-THE-JOB SCIENCE
Truck Driver

Connie Alfaro is a long-distance truck driver. Her 18-wheeler carries things between Chicago and New York. She might carry food, medical supplies, or furniture. Connie drives her truck on highways. She knows that the huge mass of her truck gives it a lot of inertia at 55 or 60 miles an hour. She must think about the truck's mass, its speed, and the weather to drive safely. She knows the faster she goes, the longer it takes to stop the truck. If she must stop suddenly, she must allow herself enough room to stop safely.

Connie must think about her truck's mass and speed to stop safely.

Study the chart and answer the questions.

Stopping Distances for Vehicles on Dry Roads		
Speed (miles per hour)	Car Stopping Distance	Truck Stopping Distance
40	125 feet	200 feet
50	185 feet	305 feet
60	240 feet	430 feet

1. At 50 miles per hour, how far will a car travel before it is able to stop?

2. At 50 miles per hour, how far will a truck travel before it is able to stop?

3. Why does a truck take a greater distance to stop than a car does?

Critical Thinking

Connie will make four stops on her trip from Chicago to New York. At each stop, she will pick up a load of furniture to deliver to New York. The truck's speed and the weather conditions are the same at each stop. At which stop will her stopping distance be the longest? Why?

Summary A force is any push or pull on an object. Forces affect our movements every day.

Lesson 16.1 Gravity is a force that pulls all matter toward the center of the Earth. The amount of gravitational pull on an object can change its weight. Friction is a force that resists motion. Centripetal force causes objects in motion to move in a curved path.

Lesson 16.2 Motion causes a change in the position or place of an object. Inertia is responsible for the tendency of an object to stay at rest or in motion, unless acted on by a force.

Vocabulary Review

Complete each sentence with a term from the list.

centripetal force

force

friction

gravity

inertia

lubricant

motion

weight

1. A _____ must be exerted on an object at rest to cause it to move.

2. The force that causes a ball to fall to the ground is _____.

3. A change in the position or place of an object is _____.

4. The measure of the force of gravity on your body is your _____.

5. The force that slows motion or prevents it is _____.

6. The force that causes objects in motion to move in a curved path is _____.

7. The tendency of an object at rest to stay at rest unless it is acted upon by a force is _____.

8. A substance that reduces friction between the moving parts of machines is a _____.

Chapter Quiz

Write your answers on a separate sheet of paper.

1. What is one example of a pulling force?

2. What is one example of a pushing force?

3. What force causes rivers to run downhill?

4. What is the difference between weight and mass?

5. What force are people using when they put sand or gravel on icy roads in the winter?

6. What type of friction must you overcome when you ice skate?

7. What force keeps a roller-coaster car on the track?

8. When you wear a seat belt, you are being protected from possible harm by what force?

9. What has greater inertia, a large car or a small car moving at the same speed? Why?

10. If someone is playing in a baseball game, what are three forces or laws of motion that could affect the game?

Test Tip

As you read quiz questions, look for key words, such as *force*, *inertia*, and *motion*. Try to remember where these appeared in the chapter to help you answer the questions.

Research Project

Research the work of Sir Isaac Newton in a reference book or on the Internet. Describe his three laws of motion. Then write an example of each of his three laws in everyday life.

This crane is a very powerful machine. It uses a device called a pulley. What do you think the pulley does?

Learning Objectives

- Define a machine in relation to doing work.
- Explain how effort force and resistance force affect an object's movement.
- Identify the six simple machines.
- Compare compound machines with simple machines.
- LAB ACTIVITY: Explore how a lever makes work easier.
- SCIENCE IN YOUR LIFE: Show how kitchen tools are based on simple machines.

Words to Know

machine	a tool or device that makes work easier to do
work	what happens when a force moves something through a distance
effort force	a force that is applied when doing work
resistance force	a force that must be overcome when doing work
load	an object to be moved
mechanical advantage	a measure of how helpful a machine is
lever	a simple machine made of a bar or rod that turns on a support
fulcrum	the support on which a lever turns
pulley	a wheel with grooves in its rim through which a rope or chain can run
inclined plane	a slanted surface used for raising objects to another level
wedge	a simple machine made of two inclined planes, back to back
screw	an inclined plane that is wrapped around a nail
wheel and axle	a wheel attached to a rod called an axle; as the axle turns, the wheel also turns

Words to Know

machine	a tool or device that makes work easier to do
work	what happens when a force moves something through a distance
effort force	a force that is applied when doing work
resistance force	a force that must be overcome when doing work
load	an object to be moved
mechanical advantage	a measure of how helpful a machine is

What Is a Machine?

A **machine** is a tool or device that makes work easier to do. In science, **work** is what happens when a force moves something through a distance. In all machines, force and distance are connected.

A machine makes work easier in three ways. First, a machine can increase the amount of force put into a task. Second, a machine can change the direction of the force. Third, a machine can change the speed of the force.

Machines are used to do all kinds of work. Some kinds of work would be impossible or very difficult to do without machines. You could not open a can with your bare hands or cut the lawn in an afternoon's time without a lawn mower. You could not safely get from the United States to Europe without an airplane or a ship.

There are many different kinds of machines. Some have lots of parts. Some have only one or two parts. However, all machines are really made from one or more of the six different *simple machines*.

Science Fact

Granville T. Woods, a 19th century African American, invented electrical machines in his machine shop. Woods sold some of his inventions to Bell Telephone System, General Electric, Westinghouse, and Thomas Edison.

A simple machine is a machine that changes the size or direction of an applied force. Most simple machines produce work with one movement. In this chapter, you will learn about the six simple machines and how they help people do work.

✓ How do machines make work easier?

Effort and Resistance

There are two forces involved in work. One is the **effort force**, which is the force that is applied when doing work. The other is the **resistance force**, which is the force that must be overcome when doing work. The **load** is the object to be moved.

Suppose you had to pick up a heavy sack of grain. The sack of grain is the load. Your lifting is the effort force. Gravity holding the bag down is the resistance force. Now suppose you want to drag the load across the ground. Your pulling is the effort force. Friction on the ground is the resistance force.

Mechanical advantage is a measure of how helpful a machine is. The mechanical advantage of a machine is a number. It is based on the number of times a machine multiplies an effort force.

For example, suppose you are using a crowbar to pry old kitchen cabinets from the wall. You slip one end of the crowbar behind the cabinets and push against the other end. The crowbar has a mechanical advantage of 4. This means the force produced by the crowbar is 4 times greater than the effort force you applied to your end of the crowbar. You only had to apply one-fourth of the force needed to remove the cabinets from the wall. However, you had to push your end of the crowbar 4 times farther than the other end moved.

✓ What two forces are involved in work?

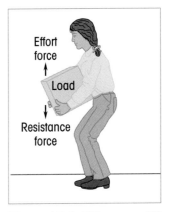

Figure 17-1 *When you lift something, the resistance force is gravity.*

Lesson Review

1. What is the purpose of a machine?

2. When you lift a box, what is the effort force? What is the resistance force?

3. **CRITICAL THINKING** Is a machine more useful if its mechanical advantage is higher or lower? Why?

Great Moments in Science

A PERPETUAL MOTION MACHINE

In 1874, an American scientist named John Worrell Keely announced a new discovery. He claimed to have built a machine that would run forever without needing outside energy.

Keely raised more than a million dollars to improve his machine. He claimed he would soon be able to have the machine run trains and do factory work.

Keely worked on his machine for 20 years. When he died, his home was searched. A pump was found under the floorboards. He had used it to power his "perpetual motion machine." The machine was a fake. Today, scientists know that perpetual motion machines are impossible to build. All machines must have energy to work.

CRITICAL THINKING What are some kinds of energy sources that machines need in order to work?

John Worrell Keely claimed he had built a perpetual motion machine.

17·2 Simple and Compound Machines

Words to Know

lever	a simple machine made of a bar or rod that turns on a support
fulcrum	the support on which a lever turns
pulley	a wheel with grooves in its rim through which a rope or chain can run
inclined plane	a slanted surface used for raising objects to another level
wedge	a simple machine made of two inclined planes, back to back
screw	an inclined plane that is wrapped around a nail
wheel and axle	a wheel attached to a rod called an axle; as the axle turns, the wheel also turns

The Six Simple Machines

The six simple machines are levers, pulleys, inclined planes, wedges, screws, and wheels and axles. Each type of simple machine has some mechanical advantage. This means it increases the effort force.

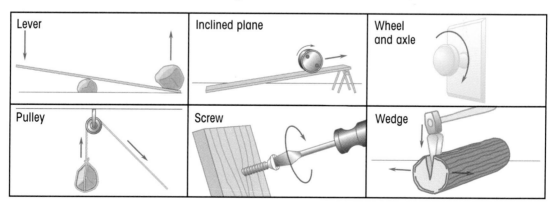

Figure 17-2 *Here are the six different kinds of simple machines.*

✓ **What are the six simple machines?**

Figure 17-3 *This screwdriver is being used as a lever.*

Levers

A **lever** is a simple machine made of a bar or rod that turns on a support. The **fulcrum** is the support on which a lever turns. Some examples of machines that have or act as levers are seesaws, wheelbarrows, nutcrackers, brooms, bottle openers, scissors, screwdrivers, shovels, and crowbars.

There are three types, or classes, of levers. In a Class 1 lever, the fulcrum is between the effort force and the resistance force. A seesaw is an example of a Class 1 lever.

In a Class 2 lever, the resistance force is between the effort force and the fulcrum. A wheelbarrow is an example of a Class 2 lever. The wheel of the wheelbarrow is the fulcrum. The wheel is the support on which the lever sits. The resistance force is in the wheelbarrow. The effort force is in your arms. A nutcracker is another example of a Class 2 lever.

In a Class 3 lever, the effort force is between the resistance force and the fulcrum. A broom is an example of a Class 3 lever. The fulcrum is where your hand is at the top of the broom. The resistance force is the floor. The effort force is you pushing the broom handle. Some other examples of Class 3 levers are tongs, fishing poles, fly swatters, tweezers, and baseball bats.

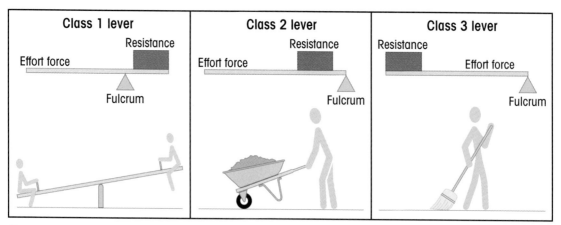

Figure 17-4 *Here are examples of the three classes of levers.*

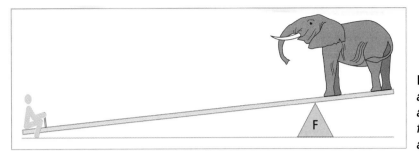

Figure 17-5 *If you have a long enough lever and a strong enough fulcrum, you can lift almost anything.*

Think of the bar of a Class 1 lever as having two parts: the resistance arm and the effort arm. The resistance arm is between the fulcrum and the resistance force. The effort arm is between the fulcrum and the effort force.

By having a long effort arm, the work is spread over a greater distance. By increasing the distance over which the work is spread, you increase the mechanical advantage. So, the longer the effort arm, the greater the mechanical advantage is.

✓ **How are the three classes of levers different?**

Pulleys

A **pulley** is a wheel with grooves in its rim through which a rope or chain can run. A groove is a long cut. The rope or chain fits into the grooves. The load is tied to one end of the rope or chain. The effort force pulls on the other end. Pulleys are used on flagpoles, sails, clotheslines, and elevators.

Suppose you want to lift a bag of cement onto a platform. Lifting the bag by hand would be very difficult. You would be fighting gravity. Instead, you can attach a rope to the load. Then you wind that rope around a pulley hanging above you. The pulley changes the direction of the effort force to help you. Now all you have to do is pull *down* on the free end of the rope. Of course, you are still fighting gravity. But the gravity pulling your body down will help you pull the rope.

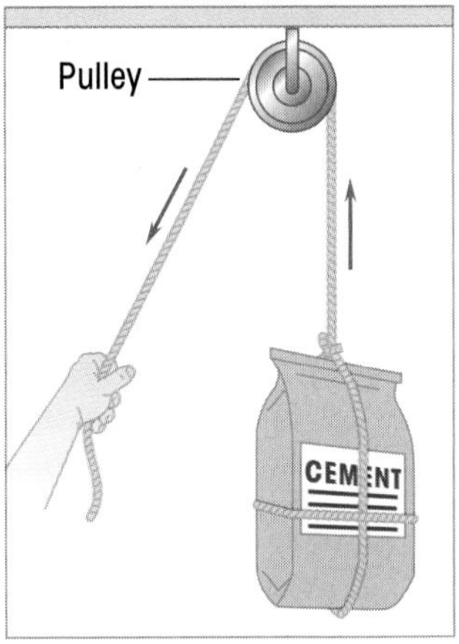

✓ **How does a pulley help you lift a load?**

Pulley

Figure 17-6 *A pulley changes the direction of the effort force.*

Inclined Planes, Wedges, and Screws

If someone gave you the choice of climbing straight up the face of a cliff or climbing up a gradual road, which way would you take? You would probably take the gradual road because it is an **inclined plane.**

Inclined Planes

An inclined plane is a slanted surface used for raising objects to another level. Inclined planes make the work of going up easier. The work is spread out over a greater distance. Mountain roads and ramps are both inclined planes.

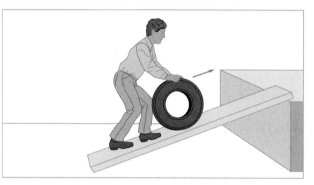

Figure 17-7 *It is easier to raise an object using an inclined plane than to pick it up.*

Wedges

A **wedge** is a simple machine made of two inclined planes, back to back. The wedge is thicker at one edge. Wedges are used to pry things apart. Knives, axes, needles, can openers, and razor blades are all wedges.

Screws

A **screw** is an inclined plane that is wrapped around a nail. Screws are very useful machines. Their mechanical advantage is high. When you turn a screw, a small effort force overcomes a large resistance force.

✓ **How do inclined planes make the work of going up easier?**

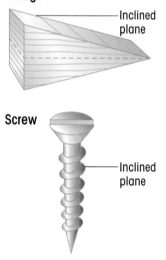

Wedge

— Inclined plane

Screw

— Inclined plane

Figure 17-8 *A wedge and a screw are types of inclined planes.*

Wheels and Axles

To turn a car, you turn its steering wheel. You only turn it a few inches, yet this makes the car turn many feet. Car steering wheels are based on a simple machine called a **wheel and axle**. A wheel and axle is a wheel attached to a rod called an axle. The axle increases the force applied to the wheel. Pencil sharpeners are examples of wheels and axles.

Doorknobs are also wheels and axles. The knob is the wheel. The long piece attached to the knob, called the shaft, is the axle. See if you can get permission to remove the knob from a door. Then try to turn the shaft with your fingers. It will be difficult. Now put the knob back on. Since it is much bigger than the shaft, you can turn it easily. It turns the shaft for you and helps open the door.

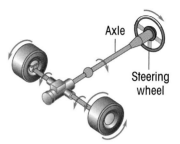

Figure 17-9 *Each set of wheels on a car is attached to an axle.*

✓ **What part causes an axle to turn easily?**

A Closer Look

THE GREAT PYRAMID AT GIZA

No one knows for sure what simple machines were used to build the Great Pyramid at Giza in Egypt. Each of its 2 million blocks weighs over 2 tons. Some of the blocks are 18 feet (5.5 meters) wide and more than 7 feet (over 2 meters) high. How did people move these blocks without trucks and cranes?

They must have used giant levers to lift up the blocks and inclined planes to reach the top of the pyramid. Perhaps ropes dragged the blocks up the inclined planes or a pulley system was used. No one knows for sure.

The Great Pyramid at Giza was built about 4,500 years ago.

CRITICAL THINKING What simple machine could have been used to shape the blocks?

What Are Compound Machines?

Remember
The six simple machines are the lever, pulley, inclined plane, wheel and axle, wedge, and screw.

A *compound machine* is made of two or more simple machines. Think of a pencil sharpener. The handle is a wheel and axle. The blades that cut the pencil are wedges. Another example is the can opener. A can opener has a lever to force the blade into the can. The blade itself is a wedge. There is also a wheel and axle to turn the opener around the rim of the can.

Most machines are compound machines. Compound machines can do more difficult jobs than simple machines. Scissors, bicycles, cars, CD players, and lawn mowers are all examples of compound machines.

Most simple machines run on people power. Compound machines often use fuels such as gas or oil. Many run on electricity.

A bicycle is a compound machine made of several simple machines.

✓ **How is a compound machine different from a simple machine?**

Lesson Review

1. What are two examples of levers in your classroom?

2. A wedge and a screw are two types of another simple machine. What is it?

3. What is one example of a compound machine in your classroom? What simple machines does it include?

4. CRITICAL THINKING Some furniture movers use wooden platforms on wheels. How does this help?

On the Cutting Edge

ROBOTS AT WORK

It might be nice to have compound machines known as robots doing chores in our homes. However, most of them are too clumsy to perform ordinary household tasks. Most robots today are used in factories. Robots often perform jobs that are too boring or too dangerous for humans to do.

Robots are very good at putting large products such as cars together. They can handle dangerous materials, spray finishes on items, and inspect parts. They can also cut and polish things.

Scientists today are trying to make tiny robots to do more delicate jobs in factories. These robots would put together small products such as cameras. The tiny robots would fit in a factory the size of a table top.

CRITICAL THINKING What are some possible disadvantages of using robots in factories?

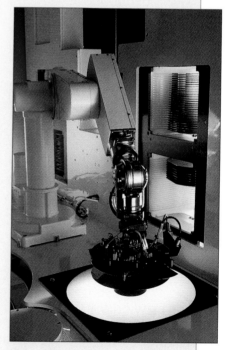

This robotic arm is making computer chips.

LAB ACTIVITY
Working With Levers

BACKGROUND
A lever is just a bar and a fulcrum. But the place you put the fulcrum makes a big difference in how useful the lever is.

PURPOSE
You will find out how the position of the fulcrum affects how a lever works.

MATERIALS
paper, pen, tape, pencil, flat stick, metric ruler, 2 checkers

WHAT TO DO
1. Copy the chart to the right.
2. Tape a pencil to a flat surface as shown in the picture.
3. Divide the flat stick into four equal parts. Mark three of the parts 1, 2, 3 as shown.
4. Put the flat stick on the pencil so that the Line 1 mark is over the pencil.
5. Place the two checkers as shown.
6. Push gently on the other end of the stick.
7. Measure and record how high the checkers were lifted.
8. Repeat Steps 4–7 with the fulcrum at Lines 2 and 3.
9. Compare the forces used for all three lines. Record your answers in the chart.

DRAW CONCLUSIONS
- What can you conclude about how the position of the fulcrum affects how a lever works?

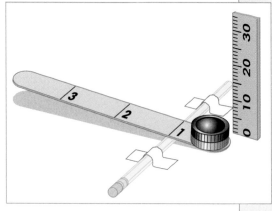

Set up your experiment as shown above.

Fulcrum	Line 1	Line 2	Line 3
Height from desk top to end of stick			
Force (easiest, harder, hardest)			

Did you know that there are more simple machines in the kitchen than in any other room in a home? If you look at a kitchen tool catalog, you will see a great many gadgets. Some of the items have been around for a long time, while others are new inventions.

Here are some tools listed in a kitchen tool catalog:

	Pastry Brush This lets you spread milk, egg yolk, and cream.
	Apple Corer This cores fruit easily.
	Pizza Cutter This makes a clean cut through the crust and topping.
	Tongs These let you safely lift, turn, and carry food.
	Pastry Scraper This helps you pry rolled dough off a work surface.
	Slotted Spoon This lets you drain foods cooked in liquids.

Based on the information in the chart above, answer these questions.

1. Which tools are levers?

2. Which tool has a wheel and axle?

3. Which tools have wedges?

4. Which tool is a compound machine? Explain.

Critical Thinking

What four kitchen tools that are simple machines can you add to the list? Describe each tool.

Summary

Work is moving something through a distance, using force. A machine makes work easier by changing the speed, direction, or amount of force.

Lesson 17.1

There are two forces involved in work. Effort force is the force applied to do the work. Resistance force is the force that must be overcome if the work is to be done. The load is the object that work moves. Mechanical advantage is the number of times a machine multiplies an effort force.

Lesson 17.2

The six simple machines are the lever, pulley, wheel and axle, inclined plane, screw, and wedge. Compound machines are made of two or more simple machines put together.

Vocabulary Review

Match each definition with a term from the list.

lever

work

pulley

fulcrum

inclined plane

mechanical advantage

wedge

load

1. A slanted surface used for raising objects to another level

2. A simple machine made of two inclined planes

3. A simple machine made of a bar or rod that turns on a support

4. A measure of how helpful a machine is

5. An object to be moved

6. What happens when a force moves something through a distance

7. A support on which a lever turns

8. A wheel with grooves in its rim through which a rope or chain can run

Chapter Quiz

Write your answers on a separate sheet of paper.

1. How does a machine make work easier?

2. What is the force that must be defeated in work?

3. What force is put into a machine to do work?

4. Where is the fulcrum in a Class 1 lever?

5. Where would you place the fulcrum of a lever to lift a heavy load most easily?

6. What simple machine lets you raise a load by pulling down on a rope?

7. What two simple machines are types of inclined planes?

8. What kind of simple machine is a doorknob?

9. What kind of machines are most machines?

10. A pencil sharpener is a compound machine. What two simple machines is it made up of?

Test Tip
To prepare for a test, be sure you can do all the Learning Objectives given at the beginning of the chapter.

Research Project

Most machines were invented to make everyday tasks easier. Research information about three of these machines in encyclopedias or on the Internet. Make a chart that shows the following information about each machine: description, job, inventor's name, date invented, and use.

Unit 4 Review

Choose the letter for the correct answer to each question.

Use the diagram for Questions 1 to 3.

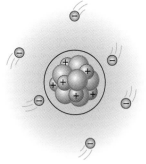

1. How many particles of each type are in this atom's nucleus?
   A. 6 protons, 6 electrons
   B. 6 electrons, 6 neutrons
   C. 6 elements, 6 neutrons
   D. 6 protons, 6 neutrons

2. Which statement is true of this atom?
   A. It has no charge.
   B. It has more electrons than protons.
   C. It is made of two elements.
   D. Its protons have a negative charge.

3. What forms if the atom shown above combines chemically with an oxygen atom?
   A. a mixture
   B. a nucleus
   C. a compound
   D. a proton

4. What type of energy does a ball have as it rolls down a hill?
   A. potential energy
   B. nuclear energy
   C. kinetic energy
   D. light energy

5. Which of the following shows a physical change in matter?
   A. a frozen pan of water
   B. a burned piece of wood
   C. a cooked pot of vegetables
   D. a rusted piece of iron

6. What force do you apply to lift a book?
   A. centripetal force
   B. effort force
   C. gravity force
   D. resistance force

7. Which type of simple machine are wheelbarrows and seesaws?
   A. a pulley
   B. an inclined plane
   C. a screw
   D. a lever

Critical Thinking

How do gravity and friction affect the speed of a roller-coaster car?

Different forms of energy make this video game exciting and fun to play.

A video game is powered by electricity. The machine uses the electricity to produce flashing colors of light and the sounds of voices.

Use the chart to answer the following questions.

1. How does light travel from the video screen to the player's eyes?

2. How does electricity move through the wires of a video machine?

3. What kind of energy is produced by the video game's voices?

Form of Energy	How It Travels
Light	In waves
Sound	In waves
Electricity	Through wires as a flow of electrons

You can feel the heat from a campfire. You can see the light of its orange-yellow flames. You can hear the sound of the crackling wood. What do you think heat, light, and sound all have in common?

Learning Objectives

- Describe how heat and temperature are related.
- Identify ways that heat moves.
- Identify the features of a wave.
- List four things that light may do when it strikes an object.
- Explain where colors come from.
- Explain how sounds are produced.
- **LAB ACTIVITY:** Show how different colors of light can be combined.
- **ON-THE-JOB SCIENCE:** Interpret codes that are scanned by lasers.

Words to Know

conduction	the way heat is passed along by molecules of matter that bump into one another
insulator	matter that does not conduct heat well
convection	the transfer of heat within a gas or a liquid by the movement of warmer particles
vacuum	any place where there is no matter
radiation	energy that travels in waves
wavelength	the distance from the crest, or top, of one wave to the crest of the next wave
amplitude	the height of a wave
frequency	the number of wave cycles that pass through a point in one second
reflection	the bouncing of light off an object
refraction	the bending of light rays as they pass from one substance into another
spectrum	the band of colors that make up white light
prism	a triangular-shaped, three-dimensional object made of clear glass that breaks up white light into its different colors

Words to Know

conduction	the way heat is passed along by molecules of matter that bump into one another
insulator	matter that does not conduct heat well
convection	the transfer of heat within a gas or a liquid by the movement of warmer particles
vacuum	any place where there is no matter
radiation	energy that travels in waves

Heat and Temperature

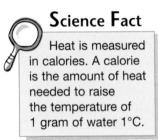

Science Fact

Heat is measured in calories. A calorie is the amount of heat needed to raise the temperature of 1 gram of water 1°C.

Heat and temperature are related, but they are not the same. You feel heat energy while you are standing in sunlight. You feel it next to a fire. You feel your own heat energy when you sleep under blankets. There is heat energy in everything, even in the oceans.

Heat is a form of kinetic energy. Remember that all matter is made up of moving atoms and molecules. The moving particles all have kinetic energy.

However, no two particles in a substance have exactly the same amount of kinetic energy. Heat is the *total* kinetic energy of the particles in a substance. Temperature is the measure of the *average* kinetic energy of the particles in a substance.

If you add heat energy to a substance, its particles move faster. They become hotter. You raise the average kinetic energy and temperature of the substance. If you remove heat from a substance, the particles in the substance move slower. You lower its temperature.

A small cup of hot soup and a large pot of hot soup have the same temperature. This is because the *average* kinetic energy of the particles in both containers of soup is the same. However, remember that heat is the *total* kinetic energy of the particles in a substance. There are many more particles of soup in the large pot than in the small cup. Therefore, the large pot of soup has a higher total kinetic energy, or more heat, than the smaller cup.

The difference between heat and temperature explains why the Pacific Ocean has more heat than a cup of hot soup. The soup has a higher temperature, or average kinetic energy. However, the ocean is so huge that it has a tremendous number of particles. Its total kinetic energy, or heat, is much greater than that of the cup of hot soup.

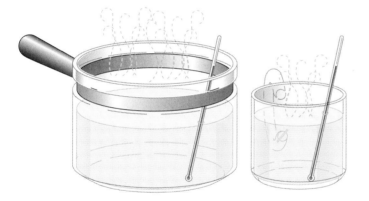

Figure 18-1 *The temperatures of the pot and cup are the same. The pot has twice as much soup. So, there is twice as much heat energy in the pot as in the cup.*

Heat always moves from a warmer place to a cooler place. That is why you become cold when you step outdoors on a cold day. The heat moves out from your body into the cold air. That is also why you can warm up a piece of cold pizza in the oven. The oven's heat moves into the cold pizza.

✔ **How is heat different from temperature?**

Heat and Solids

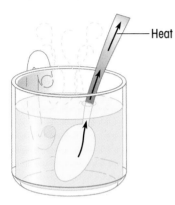

Heat

Figure 18-2 *Heat from the cup of soup moves up the spoon by conduction.*

Suppose you put a spoon into a cup of hot soup. The top of the spoon does not touch the soup at all. Yet it will soon be hot. This is because of a process that moves the heat along. This process is called **conduction.**

In conduction, heat is passed along by molecules of matter that bump into one another. The soup heats the bottom of the spoon. The hot molecules on the bottom of the spoon bump into other molecules in the spoon. This warms them up. In turn, these molecules warm up the next closest molecules up the spoon. The heat moves up to the handle of the spoon.

Some kinds of matter are good conductors. Heat moves quickly through these substances. Metals are good conductors. Copper, for example, is a very good conductor. Some kinds of matter are very poor conductors. Heat moves through poor conductors very slowly. Paper, wood, rubber, glass, and plastic do not conduct heat well. A poor conductor of heat is called an **insulator.**

There are many examples of conductors and insulators around your home. Cooking pans often have copper bottoms to conduct the heat. They also have plastic handles that stay cool to the touch. People insulate their homes to keep the warm air in during the winter and hot air out during the summer.

✓ **What is the difference between a good conductor and a poor conductor?**

Figure 18-3 *A potholder is an insulator.*

Heating Liquids and Gases

In conduction, heat moves through solids when molecules bump into one another. In liquids and gases, the heat is usually moved along by a process called **convection.** Convection is the passing of heat within a gas or a liquid by the movement of warmer particles.

Think of a space heater in a room. The heater warms the air around it. This causes the kinetic energy of the molecules in the air to increase. As the molecules move faster, they spread out. The air becomes less dense. This less dense, warm air then rises to the ceiling. The warm air pushes the cooler air down toward the heater. In turn, this cooler air gets heated and rises. This circular movement of air is called a *convection current*.

Most weather is caused by convection currents in the air around the Earth. There are also convection currents in the oceans called density currents. These are caused by warm water rising and pushing down cool water.

Convection current

Warm water

Cold water

Figure 18-4 *In convection, warm water rises and pushes the cooler, denser water down.*

✓ **How does a convection current form in air?**

Heat and Space

Both conduction and convection move heat energy through matter. In some places, however, there is no matter. A **vacuum** is any place where there is no matter.

Conduction and convection cannot move heat through a vacuum. However, the energy from the sun can travel through a vacuum. It travels in waves. Energy that travels in waves is called **radiation.** When the light from the sun strikes the Earth, a lot of it changes to heat energy.

✓ **What kind of energy can travel through a vacuum?**

Lesson Review

1. What happens to a substance if heat is added to its particles?

2. What is the measure of the average kinetic energy of the particles in a substance called?

3. Why can conduction and convection not move energy through a vacuum?

4. CRITICAL THINKING A bathtub of water and a sink of water both have the same temperature. Which has more heat? Explain.

Great Moments in Science

THE MERCURY THERMOMETER

People have used thermometers since the 1500s. A thermometer measures the temperature of a substance. Early thermometers were sealed tubes that contained water and alcohol. The liquid in the tube rose as the temperature of the substance being measured rose.

The problem with these thermometers was that the water and the alcohol did not rise evenly. The thermometers were not very accurate. In 1714, the German scientist Gabriel Daniel Fahrenheit invented something much more accurate. It was the mercury thermometer. The mercury in the tube rises evenly as the temperature rises.

Fahrenheit also developed the Fahrenheit temperature scale. Most people in the United States use the Fahrenheit scale. On this scale, the freezing point of water is 32°. The boiling point of water is 212°.

CRITICAL THINKING How was Fahrenheit's invention important to science?

Words to Know

wavelength	the distance from the crest, or top, of one wave to the crest of the next wave
amplitude	the height of a wave
frequency	the number of wave cycles that pass through a point in one second
reflection	the bouncing of light off an object
refraction	the bending of light rays as they pass from one substance into another
spectrum	the band of colors that make up white light
prism	a triangular-shaped, three-dimensional object made of clear glass that breaks up white light into its different colors

Energy in Waves

Waves carry energy from one place to another. These waves move in repeated patterns. If you could see waves of energy, they would look something like ocean waves. TV and radio signals move through space in waves. Light and sound move in waves, too.

The top of a wave is called the *crest*. The bottom of a wave is called the *trough*. Every wave has three features that can be used to describe the wave. These features are wavelength, amplitude, and frequency. A **wavelength** is the distance from the crest, or top, of one wave to the crest of the next wave. The height of a wave is called its **amplitude**.

The greater a wave's amplitude, or height, the more energy it has. So, a sound wave with a big amplitude will make a loud sound. A light wave with a big amplitude will make a bright light.

The **frequency** of a wave is the number of wave cycles that pass through a point in one second. Wave frequency is the rate of a wave's movement.

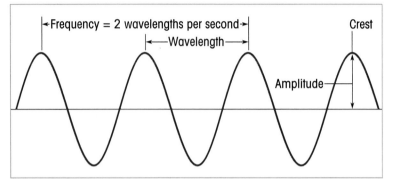

Figure 18-5 *The three basic features of a wave are its wavelength, amplitude, and frequency.*

✓ **What are three features of a wave?**

What Is Light?

Light energy travels in waves. Light waves always travel in straight lines. These straight lines of light are called *rays*. When a group of rays all travel in the same direction, they are called a *beam*.

Light travels through a vacuum at about 186,000 miles (almost 300,000 kilometers) per second. However, air slows down light waves. Liquids slow them down even more, and solids even more.

Light travels in many different wavelengths. Some wavelengths we can see. What we see is called *visible light*. Some wavelengths are too short for us to see. These wavelengths are called *ultraviolet light*. Some wavelengths are too long for us to see. These wavelengths are called *infrared light*.

✓ **What are three different kinds of light? What makes them different from each other?**

Light and Objects

Light can do one of four things when it strikes an object.

1. It can pass straight through the object.
2. It can get absorbed into the object.
3. It can bounce off the object.
4. It can be bent by the object.

A substance or an object is *transparent* if light passes through it. Some things that are transparent are air, clear glass, clear plastic, and colorless liquids such as water. A *translucent* object allows some light to pass through it. Frosted glass, stained glass, and most paper are translucent. An object that blocks light completely is *opaque*. An opaque object makes a shadow where the light is being blocked.

Objects that are opaque absorb most of the light that hits them. The light does not pass through the objects. Light energy that is absorbed is changed into heat energy. Dark colors and rough surfaces absorb a lot of light.

When light bounces off an object, **reflection** occurs. All substances reflect some light. Mirrors and objects with shiny surfaces reflect almost all the light that strikes them. The light reflecting off objects sends images to your eyes. That is how you see the objects.

It you dip a pole into clear water, it appears to bend. The pole looks like it bends just at the point where it enters the water. Of course, the pole does not really bend. The water bends the light rays. This bending of light rays when they pass from one substance to another is called **refraction.**

Refraction is caused by a change in the speed of light as the light passes from one substance into another. When light strikes the water, the light slows down. Then it bends away from the surface of the water.

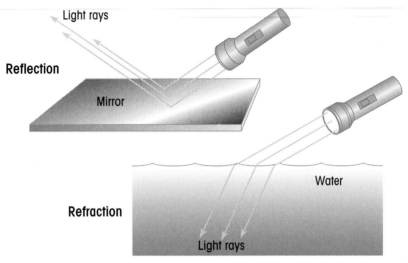

Figure 18-6 *This picture shows the reflection and refraction of light.*

✓ **What four things might light waves do when they strike an object?**

Where Does Color Come From?

White light, such as sunlight, is made up of several different wavelengths. These different wavelengths are the different colors we see. Red, orange, yellow, green, blue, indigo (violet-blue), and violet are the seven visible colors in white light.

These are the same colors in a rainbow. Rainbows are caused by sunlight passing through drops of water. The drops of water refract the white light. The different wavelengths of the white light bend different amounts, so they separate into a band of seven different colors. This band is called a **spectrum.** It is made up of red, orange, yellow, green, blue, indigo, and violet. All these colors together make up white light.

You can create a spectrum yourself by letting sunlight shine through a prism. A **prism** is a triangular-shaped, three-dimensional object made of clear glass that breaks up white light into its different colors.

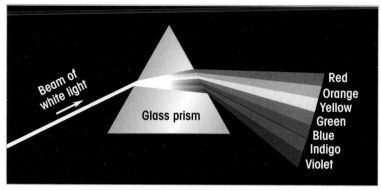

Figure 18-7 *A prism refracts white light and separates it into a spectrum.*

You know that objects absorb light, reflect light, refract light, or let light pass straight through them. The color of an object is determined by the color of light that the object reflects.

Suppose you were looking at a red sweater. Light strikes the sweater. The sweater absorbs all the colors in white light except red. It absorbs orange, yellow, green, blue, indigo, and violet. Only the red band of light bounces off the sweater and enters your eyes. You see red.

A pure black object absorbs all the light striking it. A pure white object reflects all the light striking it.

✓ **What is white light made up of?**

Lesson Review

1. What are three forms of energy that move in waves?

2. What happens when light strikes an object?

3. What happens to light when it passes through a prism?

4. **CRITICAL THINKING** What colors of light are absorbed by a yellow hat?

18·3 Sound

Using the Science of Sound

Until the middle 1800s, Native Americans of the Great Plains hunted buffalo. To find the herds, a hunter would press his ear to the ground. Why?

Sound travels better through solids than through the air. The hunters could not hear the stampede of hooves in the air. However, they could sometimes hear it in the ground. Using the science of sound, Native Americans found buffalo for food and clothing.

✓ **Does sound travel better through solids or through the air?**

What Is Sound?

Sound is another form of energy that moves in waves. Sound waves travel about a million times slower than light waves.

Sounds are made by matter that vibrates. When you shout across a room to a friend, the folds of tissue in your throat, called vocal cords, vibrate.

When your vocal cords vibrate, they cause surrounding air molecules to vibrate. The vibrating air forms sound waves. Eventually, the sound waves reach your friend's ear. They cause tiny bones in the ear to vibrate. As a result, your friend hears your voice.

Try humming while holding your fingers at your throat. You can feel your vocal cords vibrate. Musical instruments also make sounds by vibrating.

Unlike light, sound cannot travel in a vacuum. Sound travels fastest through solids. It moves slowest through gases.

Science Fact

Sound travels well underwater. Whales can hear one another from hundreds of miles away.

Remember
Vibrations are quick back-and-forth movements of air.

The loudness of sound is determined by the amplitude of the sound waves. If you hit a drum hard, you will cause it to vibrate in big waves. You will make a loud sound. If you just tap the drum, you will cause only tiny waves. You will make a quiet sound.

✓ **How are sounds made?**

Lesson Review

1. What can sound waves not travel through?

2. What happens when the amplitude of a sound wave is increased?

3. **CRITICAL THINKING** What produces sound when you pluck a guitar string?

On the Cutting Edge

SONAR

Like light waves, sound waves can reflect off objects. Scientists use reflected sound waves to locate objects underwater, using sonar. A short sound wave is sent out from the bottom of a ship by using a device called a transducer.

In 1985, scientists used sonar to locate the wreckage of the ship *Titanic*. The *Titanic* sank in the Atlantic Ocean in 1912 after hitting an iceberg. To find the *Titanic*, the scientists sent sound waves into the ocean. They measured how long it took the sound waves to strike the wreckage and then return. Because sound waves travel in water at a certain speed, the scientists could figure out how far down the *Titanic* was located.

The wreckage of the Titanic *was found by using sonar.*

CRITICAL THINKING How can scientists use sonar to map the ocean floor?

LAB ACTIVITY
Combining Colors of Light

BACKGROUND
White light is made up of seven colors: red, orange, yellow, green, blue, indigo, and violet. You can combine red light, green light, and blue light to produce other colors of light.

PURPOSE
You will combine different colors of light and observe the colors that are produced.

MATERIALS
paper; pencil; 3 flashlights; red, green, and blue cellophane; transparent tape; white wall

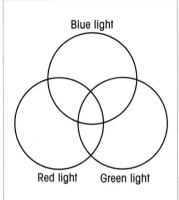

Blue light

Red light   Green light

WHAT TO DO
1. Copy the chart to the right.
2. Work in groups of three. Cover the front of each flashlight with one of the cellophane sheets. Use tape to hold the cellophane in place. Darken the room.
3. Each member of the group turns on one of the flashlights and shines the light near the same spot on a white wall. The lights should form three overlapping circles on the wall, as shown in the picture.
4. In the chart, record the color of light that is produced where the red light and green light overlap. Then do the same for red light and blue light and for blue light and green light. Finally, record the color that is produced where all three colors of light overlap.

Color Used	Color Produced
Red and green	
Red and blue	
Blue and green	
Red, blue, and green	

DRAW CONCLUSIONS
- How many different colors of light must be combined to produce white light?

- What can you conclude about these three colors?

ON-THE-JOB SCIENCE
Store Manager

Maurice is the manager of a grocery store. He has many responsibilities. He hires people and makes sure that they do their job well. He orders items, or merchandise, for the store. He also records the prices of the merchandise. To do this, Maurice uses light and the *bar codes* printed on the merchandise packages.

Maurice checks the computer for the price of bananas. The customer had seen a different price displayed.

A bar code is a series of thick and thin lines with numbers printed below them. The manager inputs the information on the bar codes into a computer. Then a specific price is given to each bar code and recorded in the computer.

When a customer buys an item, the checkout person uses a *scanner* to find out the item's price. The scanner is a machine. It produces a beam of light that reads the patterns on the item's bar code. This beam of light is a laser. The scanner sends the information it reads to a computer. The computer then checks the item's price. The price is then sent to the cash register.

Compare bar codes A and B. Notice the numbers for the product, company, and price.

1. Are bar codes A and B for the same kind of product? How do you know?

2. Are bar codes A and B from the same company? How do you know?

Critical Thinking

What must a store manager do to change the price of an item?

Price
$12.95

A   01295

9 780327 35284

Product code   Company code

Price
$19.95

B   01995

9 780527 56836

Product code   Company code

> **Summary** Heat, light, and sound are all forms of energy. They travel by the movement of particles or in waves.

> **Lesson 18.1** In solids, heat moves by conduction. In liquids and gases, heat moves by convection. Heat cannot travel in a vacuum. Rays of sunlight can. They turn into heat energy when they strike the Earth.

> **Lesson 18.2** A wave has a certain wavelength, amplitude, and frequency. The color of visible light depends on its wavelength. The color of an object is determined by the wavelength of light that is reflected from the object.

> **Lesson 18.3** Sound is produced when matter vibrates. A person hears sound when sound waves enter the ears.

Vocabulary Review

prism

vacuum

insulator

frequency

spectrum

conduction

refraction

radiation

Complete each sentence with a term from the list.

1. Glass is an _____ because it does not conduct heat well.

2. The colors that make up white light form a _____.

3. There is no matter in a _____.

4. Heat moves through a spoon by _____.

5. When white light passes through a _____, it separates into colors.

6. Energy that can move through a vacuum is _____.

7. The bending of light rays is _____.

8. The number of wave cycles that pass through a point in one second is a wave's _____.

Chapter Quiz

Write your answers on a separate sheet of paper.

1. How are heat and temperature related?

2. How does heat move by conduction?

3. In convection, why does warm air rise?

4. What three features can be used to describe a wave?

5. What does increasing the amplitude of a light wave do?

6. What is the difference between reflection and refraction?

7. In what way does green light differ from red light?

8. What determines the color of an object?

9. What does the vibrating of matter produce?

10. What determines the loudness of a sound?

Test Tip
Make sure you understand what a test question is asking. Read a question twice before answering.

Research Project

One of the characteristics of sound is its strength, or intensity. Sound intensity is measured in units called *decibels*. Research the decibel levels of at least four different sounds, such as a whisper and a jet taking off. Find out which decibel levels are harmful to human hearing. Make a chart that shows what you learned.

Chapter 19

Electricity and Magnetism

A bolt of lightning cuts across the sky during a thunderstorm. A severe storm may produce hundreds of lightning bolts. How do you think lightning is like turning on a light switch?

Learning Objectives

- Show the relationship between electrons and electricity.
- Explain what causes static electricity.
- Describe what happens when lightning occurs.
- Explain how batteries and generators work.
- Compare electrical conductors and insulators.
- Describe an electrical circuit.
- Describe magnetism and magnetic fields.
- LAB ACTIVITY: Identify materials that are conductors and insulators.
- SCIENCE IN YOUR LIFE: Compare how much electricity different appliances use.

Words to Know

electricity	a form of energy caused by the movement of electrons
static electricity	the electricity caused when objects with opposite charges are attracted to each other
discharge	the throwing off of static electricity
electrical conductor	a material that electricity travels through easily
electrical insulator	a material that electricity does not travel through easily
battery	a device that changes chemical energy into electrical energy
generator	a machine that changes some other kind of energy into electrical energy
circuit	an unbroken, circular path that an electrical current flows through; includes a source of energy, such as a battery
fuse	a weak link in an electrical circuit; made of metal wire that has a low melting point
magnet	a solid substance that attracts iron or steel
magnetic field	the area around a magnet in which a magnetic force is active

Words to Know

electricity	a form of energy caused by the movement of electrons
static electricity	the electricity caused when objects with opposite charges are attracted to each other
discharge	the throwing off of static electricity

What Is Electricity?

Imagine living without TV, radio, hair dryers, computers, washing machines, light bulbs, or telephones. Only a short time ago, people did not have any of these things. That is because all of these tools run on **electricity**. Electricity is a form of energy caused by the movement of electrons. Until about 100 years ago, people did not know how to control electricity.

In Chapter 14, you learned that every atom has a nucleus. Inside the nucleus of an atom are protons, which have a positive (+) charge. Circling the nucleus are electrons, which have a negative (−) charge. Most of the time, atoms have the same number of protons as electrons. These atoms are *neutral*. This means that they have no charge at all.

Electrons, though, can be separated from their atoms. For example, suppose you rub a balloon on a wool sweater. Electrons from the atoms in the sweater rub off onto the atoms in the balloon. The sweater will now have fewer electrons than protons. It will have a positive charge. The balloon will have more electrons than protons. It will have a negative charge.

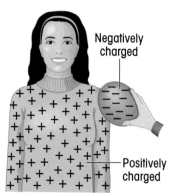

Negatively charged

Positively charged

Figure 19-1 *Electrons are rubbed off the sweater and onto the balloon. The balloon becomes negatively charged.*

If you hold the balloon to the wall, it will stick there. The negative charge in the balloon will be attracted to the positive charge in the wall.

The loss or gain of electrons creates an electrical charge. Electricity is produced in the process.

✓ **What causes electricity?**

Static Electricity

Have you ever heard crackling as you brushed your hair? Or felt a small shock when you touched something metal? You may have noticed how clothes that have been in a dryer stick together. Sometimes they make a crackling sound when you pull them apart. All these things are caused by electricity.

Negatively charged objects have extra electrons. When two objects are both negatively charged, they *repel* one another. This means that they push each other away or try to move apart.

Objects that have too few electrons are positively charged. Two positively charged objects will also repel each other.

Objects that have opposite charges *attract* each other. This is what causes the crackling sounds when you take clothes out of a dryer. It is what causes clothes such as socks to stick to jeans. **Static electricity** holds them together. Static electricity is the electricity caused when objects with opposite charges are attracted to each other.

Most charged objects do not keep their charges for long. Negatively charged objects try to give up their extra electrons. Positively charged objects take on needed electrons to become neutral again.

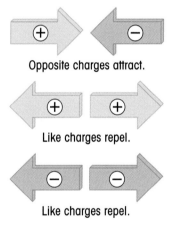

Opposite charges attract.

Like charges repel.

Like charges repel.

Figure 19-2 *Opposite charges attract, and like charges repel.*

Think again of your laundry. If you pulled socks and jeans apart in the dark, you might see little sparks. You might hear a crackling noise. The sparks and noise are the **discharge**, or throwing off, of static electricity. The socks and jeans are returning to their neutral states.

✓ How is static electricity caused?

Lightning

Lightning is a huge electrical discharge. It is really just a giant spark between a cloud and the ground. This discharge can also take place between two clouds with opposite charges or within the same cloud.

Here is how lightning can occur. First, a cloud builds up a lot of electrons. It gets a large negative charge. Then the cloud becomes attracted to something with a positive charge, such as a treetop. Suddenly, the extra electrons in the cloud "jump" to the treetop. This creates a lot of light and heat. The light is the bolt of lightning. The heat warms the air and causes it to expand very quickly. This quick expansion causes the loud boom called *thunder*.

✓ What causes lightning?

Figure 19-3 *Lightning occurs when extra electrons in a cloud move through the air to the positively charged treetop.*

Lesson Review

1. Which part of the atom moves in electricity?

2. Why do clothes stick to each other when you take them out of a dryer?

3. How does lightning cause thunder?

4. CRITICAL THINKING Suppose you rubbed two balloons on a wool sweater. Would the balloons attract or repel each other? Why?

BENJAMIN FRANKLIN AND LIGHTNING

Benjamin Franklin was a great American statesman and scientist of the 1700s. He played an important role in forming the United States. He was also one of the first scientists to experiment with electricity.

Franklin believed that lightning was a form of electricity. He came up with an experiment to test this idea. In 1752, he tied a key to the string of a kite. Franklin let the key hang near the ground. He then flew his kite during a thunderstorm. A bolt of lightning struck the kite. Electricity traveled down the string toward the ground. Franklin put his hand near the key and felt a spark. This showed that lightning is an electrical discharge.

Franklin also invented the lightning rod. Lightning rods are long metal poles that are often placed on the tops of buildings. They are designed to attract lightning. The charge from the lightning passes from the rod to a grounding wire and safely into the ground.

Many of the electrical terms we use today were first used by Franklin. For example, he was the first to use the terms *positive* and *negative* to describe opposite charges.

CRITICAL THINKING How is a lightning rod like the kite that Franklin flew during a thunderstorm?

Benjamin Franklin experimented with electricity.

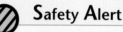 **Safety Alert**

NEVER TRY FRANKLIN'S EXPERIMENT YOURSELF! It was very dangerous. The charge from the lightning could have killed Franklin. It did kill some of the other scientists who tried the experiment.

Words to Know

electrical conductor	a material that electricity travels through easily
electrical insulator	a material that electricity does not travel through easily
battery	a device that changes chemical energy into electrical energy
generator	a machine that changes some other kind of energy into electrical energy

For safety reasons, electrical wiring is almost always covered with plastic or rubber.

You already learned that heat moves through some materials better than others. The same is true for electricity. A material that electricity travels through easily is called an **electrical conductor.**

Metals are excellent conductors. Metal wire is often used to conduct electricity. Many other substances can conduct electricity. Even your body can conduct electricity.

An **electrical insulator** is a material that electricity does not travel through easily. Rubber and plastic are good electrical insulators. The rubber coating on the wire leading from your TV to the plug is an insulator. It protects you from the electricity running through the electrical conductor inside.

To get electrons to move through a conductor, people often use a **battery.** A battery is a device that changes chemical energy into electrical energy.

One kind of battery is a *wet cell*. A wet cell, such as a car battery, is actually made up of a series of wet cells. Each cell contains two kinds of metal plates and an acid solution. Chemical reactions between the plates and the acid cause electrons to build up at the cell's negative pole. When the negative and positive poles are connected, electrons flow. This is an electrical current.

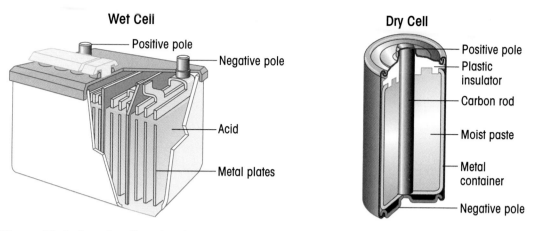

Wet Cell
- Positive pole
- Negative pole
- Acid
- Metal plates

Dry Cell
- Positive pole
- Plastic insulator
- Carbon rod
- Moist paste
- Metal container
- Negative pole

Figure 19-4 *A wet cell and a dry cell are two kinds of batteries.*

Another kind of battery is a *dry cell*. Most batteries you use for flashlights, smoke alarms, and CD players are dry cells. A dry cell uses a paste instead of an acid solution. A chemical reaction between the metal case and the paste causes electrons to build up on the metal, making it negative. The rod in the middle of the cell becomes positive. Current flows when the two poles are connected, such as by a wire or other conductor.

A **generator** is sometimes used instead of a battery to start the flow of electrons. A generator is a machine that changes some other kind of energy into electrical energy. Some generators turn mechanical energy into electrical energy. Other generators turn heat energy into electrical energy.

✓ **What do batteries and generators do?**

Lesson Review

1. What makes metal a good electrical conductor?

2. How are wet cells and dry cells similar? How are they different?

3. CRITICAL THINKING Why might it be helpful to own a small generator?

Words to Know

circuit	an unbroken, circular path that an electrical current flows through; includes a source of energy, such as a battery
fuse	a weak link in an electrical circuit; made of metal wire that has a low melting point

Many things in your home are powered by electricity. Lamps, dishwashers, computers, and TVs are a few examples. However, the electricity to power these appliances must be controlled. You would not want electrical charges shooting around your home.

Remember
Electricity is the flow of electrons through a substance.

The trick to making electricity useful is getting it to flow in a certain direction. Electricians set up paths that electrical currents flow through. These paths are circular. They flow in a circle and come back to the place where they start without being broken anywhere along the way. Such a path is called a **circuit.** A circuit always includes a source of energy, such as a battery.

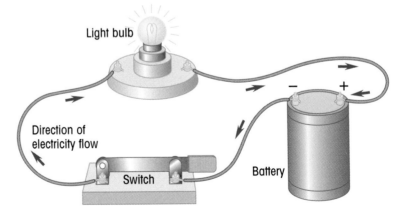

Figure 19-5 *This closed electrical circuit connects a battery to a light.*

Look at the picture on page 288 of a closed electrical circuit. It connects a battery to a light. The battery produces the electricity, which flows through the wires. As it passes through the light bulb, the electricity heats a piece of material called a *filament*. The filament gets so hot it glows. This produces light. The electricity continues along the circuit back into the battery.

Some of the electricity used to light the filament turns into heat energy. That heat energy is lost from the circuit. Before long, the battery will run out of energy.

Some circuits have switches. If the switch is turned off, the circuit is *open*. This means that a gap is formed in the circuit. The electricity cannot flow. If the switch is turned on, the circuit is *closed*. Now the electricity can flow.

A fuse has a metal filament.

When too many electrical appliances are put on one circuit, it can become *overloaded*. Too much electricity is running through the wire. An overloaded circuit can cause the wire to get too hot and start a fire.

Fuses are used to prevent overloaded circuits from causing fires. A **fuse** is a weak link in an electrical circuit. It is made of metal wire that has a low melting point. When too much electricity flows through the wire, the fuse melts. When the fuse melts, the circuit is broken, and the flow of electricity stops.

✓ **How are closed circuits different from open circuits?**

Science Fact

Most new homes are protected by circuit breakers instead of fuses. A circuit breaker has a switch that turns off when too much electricity flows through the circuit.

Lesson Review

1. What shape do all circuits have?

2. What does a switch do?

3. CRITICAL THINKING Why is it a bad idea to replace a melted fuse with a piece of wire that will not melt easily?

Words to Know

magnet	a solid substance that attracts iron or steel
magnetic field	the area around a magnet in which a magnetic force is active

What Is a Magnet?

More than 2,000 years ago, the Greeks discovered that certain stones had special properties. These stones, called *lodestones*, naturally attracted each other. They also attracted iron. Any stone, piece of metal, or other solid substance that attracts iron or steel is called a **magnet.** You might use magnets to stick notes onto your refrigerator. Some people use them at their desks to hold all their paper clips together. *Magnetism* is the state of being magnetized.

All matter is magnetic. However, only the elements iron, nickel, and cobalt have strong magnetism.

✓ **Which three elements have strong magnetism?**

Magnetic Poles and Fields

Each end of a magnet is called a *pole*. If you hang a bar magnet on a string and let it swing freely, one end of the magnet will point toward the north. The other end will point toward the south.

A compass helps you see what direction you are facing. The needle is a magnet that points toward the North and South poles.

Magnetic poles act like electrical charges do. Poles that are the same are called *like* poles. Like poles repel each other. Opposite poles attract each other. The magnetic force is strongest at the poles. However, it can be felt all around the magnet. The area in which a magnetic force is active is called the **magnetic field.**

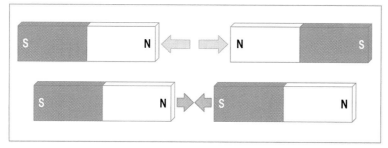

Figure 19-6 *Like poles repel, and opposite poles attract.*

Electrons are like tiny magnets. They spin around the nucleus of an atom in no particular order. So, their magnetic pull is in all different directions. When a piece of metal becomes magnetized, the electrons line up. The tiny magnetic fields turn so that all the north poles face north. Because the magnetic pull is all in one direction, it is a lot stronger.

You can stir up the tiny magnetic fields of a magnet's electrons by hammering or heating the object. This causes the object to lose its magnetism.

✓ **Where is a magnet's force active?**

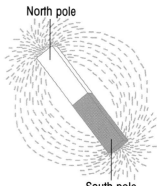

Figure 19-7 *The iron filings sprinkled around this magnet show its magnetic field.*

Lesson Review

1. What are lodestones?

2. If you let a bar magnet swing freely, where do the ends point?

3. What happens to the electrons in a piece of metal when it becomes magnetized?

4. **CRITICAL THINKING** Why won't a compass work when you hold it near a strong magnet?

LAB ACTIVITY
Identifying Conductors and Insulators

BACKGROUND
Electricity travels easily through conductors but not easily through insulators. You can tell if something is a conductor or an insulator by using a simple circuit.

PURPOSE
You will test four objects to find out if they are conductors or insulators.

MATERIALS
paper, pen, 6-volt battery, 3 wires with ends stripped, flashlight bulb in base holder, wooden block, 2 metal screw hooks, objects to be tested

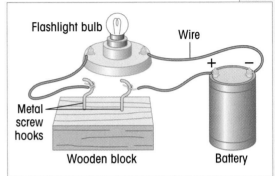

Use this setup for testing conductors and insulators

WHAT TO DO
1. Copy the chart to the right. Add one row to the chart for each object you will test. A sample is given.
2. Connect the circuit as shown in the diagram. First, screw the hooks into the wood. Then connect the wires by wrapping the bare ends around the screw hooks, battery poles, and metal parts of the bulb holder.

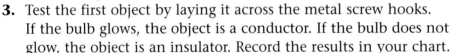

Object Tested	Conductor	Insulator
Metal spoon	Yes	No

3. Test the first object by laying it across the metal screw hooks. If the bulb glows, the object is a conductor. If the bulb does not glow, the object is an insulator. Record the results in your chart.
4. Repeat Step 3 for each of the other objects to be tested.

DRAW CONCLUSIONS
- Which of the objects you tested were conductors? Which were insulators?
- How can you determine whether an object is a conductor or an insulator?

SCIENCE IN YOUR LIFE
Using Electricity

Sarah's electric bill seems to get higher every month. She wants to see how her family can use less electricity.

First, Sarah went to the library to find out how much electricity each appliance in her home uses when it is on. The chart below shows some of this information. Electricity use is measured in kilowatt-hours (kWh). Next, she figured out how often each appliance is used in an average month. Finally, she multiplied the numbers in the second and third columns to find out how much electricity each appliance uses in a month.

A meter on the outside of a building records how much electricity is used in the building.

Appliance	kWh per Use	Use per Month	kWh per Month
Refrigerator	5 per day	30 days	150
Washing machine	2.5 per load	10 loads	
Stove	2 per meal	60 meals	
Dishwasher	1 per load	30 loads	
TV	0.3 per hour	180 hours	

Answer these questions.

1. How much electricity does each appliance use per month? Remember, multiply the numbers in the second and third columns for each appliance. The first one is done for you.

2. List the appliances, in order, from the one that uses the most electricity per month to the one that uses the least.

Critical Thinking

How might Sarah's family use less electricity? Give examples.

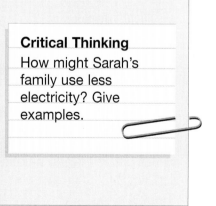

Chapter

19 ▷ Review

Summary Energy in the form of electricity and magnetism is used in nature and to run machines that do work.

Lesson 19.1 Electricity is caused by the movement of electrons. Lightning is a large discharge of static electricity.

Lesson 19.2 Electricity flows well through electrical conductors. This flow is called a current.

Lesson 19.3 Electricity can be made to flow in a circular path called a circuit. People use electrical circuits to power appliances.

Lesson 19.4 A magnet attracts iron or steel. When electrons line up in a substance, they create a strong magnetic field.

Vocabulary Review

Match each definition with a term from the list.

static electricity

discharge

electrical conductor

electrical insulator

battery

generator

fuse

magnetic field

1. A material that electricity travels through easily

2. A device that changes chemical energy into electrical energy

3. The area of magnetic force around a magnet

4. The throwing off of static electricity

5. The electricity caused when objects with opposite charges are attracted to each other

6. A material that electricity does not travel through easily

7. A machine that changes some other kind of energy into electrical energy

8. A weak link in an electrical circuit

Chapter Quiz

Write your answers on a separate sheet of paper.

1. What is the relationship between electricity and electrons?

2. What type of charge does an object have if it has more electrons than protons?

3. What state does an object return to when it discharges static electricity?

4. Which part of the atom moves in a bolt of lightning?

5. Why are wires made out of metals instead of rubber?

6. What causes current to flow in a dry cell?

7. What does a generator turn mechanical energy or heat energy into?

8. How does an electrical circuit work?

9. What characteristic do the metals iron, nickel, and cobalt share?

10. Where is the magnetic force strongest around a magnet?

Research Project

The Earth is a giant magnet. It has magnetic poles just like those on a small magnet. Research the Earth's magnetism. Write down at least three facts about it. Then draw and label a diagram showing the Earth's magnetic field and where the magnetic poles are located.

Chapter 20 ▷ Energy Resources

These windmills at Tehachapi Pass in California use the energy of the wind to produce electricity. Would windmills be good to use where you live? Why or why not?

Learning Objectives

- Identify five different sources of energy.
- Describe how people use different energy sources.
- Explain the benefits and problems of using different energy sources.
- LAB ACTIVITY: Compare how different surfaces absorb solar energy.
- ON-THE-JOB SCIENCE: Read and interpret gauges in a nuclear power plant.

Words to Know

nuclear reactor	a device that splits atoms to release energy
radioactive	giving off radiation, or harmful rays
solar collector	a device with a dark surface that absorbs sunlight and changes it into heat energy
hydroelectric energy	the electrical energy from moving water
turbine	a machine with blades that can be turned; used to run an electric generator
geothermal energy	the heat contained in rock deep inside the Earth
geyser	a hot spring that shoots steam and hot water into the air

Power of the Past

We get energy from many sources. An explosion releases a lot of energy. Ocean waves and strong winds are full of energy, too. The sun has an almost unlimited supply of energy. Even tiny atoms hold huge amounts of energy.

You already know a lot about energy. You know the forms it can take: heat, sound, light, electricity, chemical forms, and mechanical forms.

You learned that burning fossil fuels releases energy. Coal, oil, and natural gas are fossil fuels. Over 80 percent of all the energy used in the United States comes from burning fossil fuels. Fossil fuels are used to run cars, heat homes, and provide power for factories. Many plastics also come from fossil fuels.

✓ **Where does most of the energy that Americans use come from?**

Problems With Fossil Fuels

There are two serious problems with burning fossil fuels for energy. First, there is only so much fossil fuel in existence. Fossil fuels take millions of years and just the right conditions to form. People cannot make more. When fossil fuels run out, they are gone for good. Another problem with fossil fuels is that they cause air pollution when they burn. Their waste products are poisonous and very harmful to the environment.

People can help with these problems. The less often fossil fuels are used, the longer the supply will last. Gasoline can be saved by riding a bike, walking, or taking a bus instead of a car. These ways of getting around also help to keep the air cleaner.

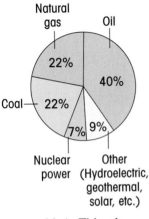

Natural gas 22%
Oil 40%
Coal 22%
Nuclear power 7%
Other (Hydroelectric, geothermal, solar, etc.) 9%

Figure 20-1 *This pie chart shows energy use in the United States.*

Remember
A fossil fuel is a fuel made of organisms that died millions of years ago.

Insulation in homes helps, too. Using insulation means less energy is needed to heat the homes.

✓ **What are two problems with fossil fuels?**

Lesson Review

1. What percent of energy used in the United States comes from fossil fuels?

2. How do people use fossil fuels?

3. How can people use less of fossil fuels?

4. CRITICAL THINKING How can recycling products made from plastic help us use less of fossil fuels?

On the Cutting Edge

ELECTRIC CARS

One of the problems with using gasoline in cars is that it causes air pollution. Scientists are looking for ways to cut down on air pollution. One way is for people to drive electric cars.

Electric cars run on rechargeable batteries instead of gasoline. They can travel about 100 miles (160 kilometers) before their batteries need to be recharged. It takes about 3 hours to recharge the battery. Unlike cars that use gasoline, electric cars do not pollute the air. They also produce less noise.

An electric car runs on a rechargeable battery.

CRITICAL THINKING What is an advantage and a disadvantage of using an electric car?

Words to Know

nuclear reactor	a device that splits atoms to release energy
radioactive	giving off radiation, or harmful rays
solar collector	a device with a dark surface that absorbs sunlight and changes it into heat energy
hydroelectric energy	the electrical energy from moving water
turbine	a machine with blades that can be turned; used to run an electric generator
geothermal energy	the heat contained in rock deep inside the Earth
geyser	a hot spring that shoots steam and hot water into the air

Nuclear Energy

You learned earlier that scientists know how to split the nucleus of an atom. This process is nuclear fission. It releases a tremendous amount of energy.

Nuclear Fission

Nuclear power plants use nuclear reactors. A **nuclear reactor** is a device that splits atoms to release energy. In a nuclear reactor, millions of atomic nuclei are split every second. This process releases a great deal of heat. The heat is used to change water into steam. The steam is then used to power electric generators. The generators change the heat energy into electricity.

Remember
Radiation is energy that comes from the sun or is released by the breakdown of atomic nuclei.

However, nuclear fission has some serious problems. For one thing, the fission process produces **radioactive** wastes. Radioactive means giving off radiation, or harmful rays.

Radioactive wastes give off large amounts of rays that can be very dangerous to living things. These wastes may remain dangerous for millions of years. No one is sure what to do with them. If the wastes are buried, they may pollute the groundwater and soil. Scientists are looking for places where nuclear wastes can be buried safely. These sites must be dry so that the containers of wastes do not come into contact with water. Also, there can be no earthquakes near the burial sites. An earthquake could damage and break open the containers.

Accidents inside nuclear power plants are a problem. Harmful substances have leaked out of a few power plants. Many people think nuclear energy is not worth the risks.

Nuclear Fusion

Scientists are looking for ways to use the energy released by nuclear fusion. Nuclear fusion is the process the sun uses to release heat and light energy.

Nuclear fusion is a very clean process. The fuel used in nuclear fusion is hydrogen. Hydrogen is easy to get from seawater. The wastes from nuclear fusion are water and other safe substances. However, scientists still do not know how to control the nuclear fusion process.

Remember
Nuclear fusion joins atoms together. Energy is released in this process, just as it is when atoms are split apart.

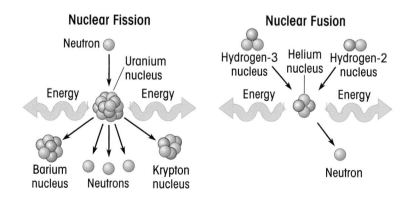

Figure 20-2 *In nuclear fission, one large nucleus splits to form two smaller nuclei. In nuclear fusion, small nuclei join to form a larger nucleus.*

✓ **What are the problems with using nuclear fission and nuclear fusion to produce electricity?**

Solar Energy

Remember
Solar energy is energy given off by the sun. It reaches us mostly in the form of light energy.

You have probably at some time sat in a car in the sunshine. You may have started to feel warm. Sunlight hitting your car was turned into heat energy and trapped inside. This is how a **solar collector** works. A solar collector is a device with a dark surface that absorbs sunlight and changes it into heat energy.

Figure 20-3 *The solar collectors on a house face the direction that gets the most sunlight.*

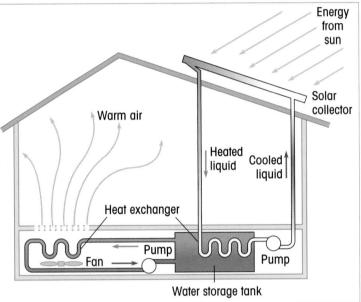

Here is how a solar collector heats a house:

1. Sunlight strikes the solar collector on the house. The solar collector changes the sunlight into heat energy.

2. The heat warms the water in the solar collector.

3. The heated water is pumped into the house through a pipe.

4. A fan blows air across the warm pipe, warming the air in the house.

Solar energy can also be used to produce electricity. A *solar cell* changes sunlight into electricity. However, this technology can be very expensive.

Another problem with solar energy is that the sun's light is spread out over wide areas. Scientists must find better ways to collect and store it.

Energy from the sun is clean, there is a lot of it, and it is free. Scientists hope that solar energy will provide much of the world's energy in the future.

✓ **What does a solar collector do?**

Hydroelectric Energy

Hydroelectric energy is electrical energy from moving water. A dam traps the water in a river. The water behind the dam is released a little at a time, often by opening its flood gates. The moving water strikes a **turbine.** A turbine is a machine with blades that can be turned. When the moving water hits the turbine, it turns the blades. This motion runs an electric generator, which changes the mechanical energy of the blades into electrical energy.

Dams provide energy to many cities. People do not want to dam up too many rivers, though. Dams can affect fish and other wildlife found in or near rivers by changing the ecology of the area.

Hydroelectric energy from dams is used to turn turbines and to store water for future use.

✓ **How is moving water used to power an electric generator?**

Geothermal Energy

The heat contained in rock deep inside the Earth is called **geothermal energy.** This heat is produced by radioactivity and the movements of rock below the surface of the Earth. Geothermal energy heats rock and any water that trickles through cracks in the rock. Sometimes the heat is released in geysers and hot springs. A **geyser** is a hot spring that shoots steam and hot water into the air.

Geysers carry geothermal energy up from under the ground.

Scientists have learned how to use geothermal energy to heat homes and produce electricity. Wells are drilled into the ground. Hot water is pumped out to heat buildings. If the rock is hot enough, steam rises to the surface and is used to run an electric generator. There are only a few places on Earth where hot rock is close enough to the surface to make drilling worthwhile. These places include Iceland, New Zealand, and parts of Italy, Japan, and California.

✓ **What causes geothermal energy?**

Winds and Tides

People have used the energy of the wind for many centuries. All over the world, windmills pump water, grind grain, and make electrical energy. Of course, windmills work best where there is a lot of wind. The picture on page 296 shows a wind farm in a windy mountain pass. Rows of windmills operate electric generators.

There is a lot of energy in ocean waves and tides. Power plants can use the energy in waves and tides to produce electrical energy. However, such power plants have to be built near oceans. Even there, conditions must be just right for setting up a power plant.

✓ **How is the energy in wind and in waves and tides used?**

Lesson Review

Match each energy source with its problem.

Energy Source	Problem
1. fossil fuels	**a.** produces radioactive wastes
2. nuclear fission	**b.** hard to store its energy
3. sun	**c.** needs many windy days
4. hydroelectric	**d.** heated rock too deep
5. geothermal	**e.** limited amounts
6. wind	**f.** harmful to river wildlife
7. nuclear fusion	**g.** cannot yet be controlled

8. CRITICAL THINKING What are two advantages of using wind energy?

A Closer Look

ENERGY FROM GARBAGE

Every year, people in the United States produce millions of tons of garbage. Most of the garbage is buried in areas called *landfills*. However, instead of being buried, some food and paper wastes are being burned to release their stored energy. The wastes are burned in electric power plants. The energy that is released is used to heat water and produce steam. The steam powers electric generators.

Some power plants burn garbage to make steam and produce electricity.

The garbage in landfills is also a source of energy. The buried garbage produces a gas called methane. The methane is taken from the landfill and mixed with natural gas, which is a fossil fuel. Mixing the two fuels helps the supply of natural gas last longer.

CRITICAL THINKING Burning garbage and burning fossil fuels both pollute the air. What is the advantage of burning garbage instead of fossil fuels?

LAB ACTIVITY
Absorbing Solar Energy

BACKGROUND
Solar collectors are placed on the roofs of houses to absorb the sun's energy and change it into heat energy. The collectors have a dark surface.

PURPOSE
You will compare how well different-color surfaces absorb the sun's energy and change it into heat energy.

MATERIALS
paper; pencil; 4 thermometers; 1 sheet each of black, white, red, and yellow construction paper; clock or watch

WHAT TO DO
1. Copy the chart below.

	Color of Paper			
	Black	White	Red	Yellow
Temperature Reading				

2. Place four thermometers in sunlight.
3. Cover each thermometer with a different color sheet of construction paper.
4. Leave the thermometers in the sunlight for 15 minutes.
5. After 15 minutes have passed, record in the chart the temperature reading of each thermometer.

DRAW CONCLUSIONS
- Which paper absorbed the most solar energy? How do you know?

- Why do you think solar collectors on a house have a dark surface?

> **Safety Alert**
> Be careful when working with glass thermometers to avoid breaking them.

ON-THE-JOB SCIENCE
Nuclear Reactor Operator

Julio works in a nuclear power plant. He is a nuclear reactor operator. He spends most of his time in the control room. Here, he keeps close watch on the many gauges. They show that all the parts of the power plant are working right.

Some of the gauges measure the amount of fission occurring in the reactor. This is the reactor power. Other gauges measure the temperature of the water that cools the reactor. Julio checks the amount of steam flow in the steam generator. He also checks the amount of electricity produced at the power plant. If there is a problem, he shuts down the reactor.

Julio sometimes trains other nuclear reactor operators.

These three gauges show different temperatures of the reactor coolant system. For this reactor, the temperature ranges from 530°F at 0 percent power to 570°F at 100 percent power.

Reactor Coolant System: Temperature (°F)

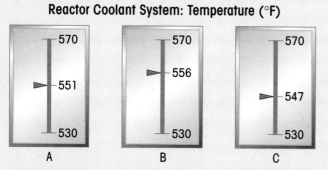

A   B   C

Use the gauges above to answer the questions.

1. What is the correct order of the gauges from the lowest power to the highest power?
2. Which gauge shows the reactor operating at about 50 percent?
3. Which gauge shows the reactor operating at about 65 percent?

Critical Thinking

Draw two temperature gauges. One should show that the reactor is at 0 percent power. The other should show that the reactor is at 100 percent power.

Summary ▷ People use various sources of energy. These include fossil fuels, nuclear fission, the sun, moving water, hot rocks deep underground, wind, ocean waves, and tides.

Lesson 20.1 ▷ Fossil fuels are the most commonly used source of energy. However, there are limited amounts of fossil fuels on Earth. Another problem is that fossil fuels cause air pollution.

Lesson 20.2 ▷ Nuclear fission and nuclear fusion both release energy from the nuclei of atoms. Solar energy is energy from the sun. Hydroelectric energy uses moving water as its energy source. Geothermal energy is energy from hot rocks underground.

Vocabulary Review

Write *true* or *false* for each sentence. If the sentence is false, replace the underlined term to make the sentence true.

1. A <u>turbine</u> has blades that can be turned.

2. A <u>nuclear reactor</u> splits atoms to obtain energy.

3. The energy from hot rocks deep inside the Earth is called <u>solar energy</u>.

4. A <u>radioactive</u> substance gives off harmful rays.

5. A <u>windmill</u> has a dark surface that absorbs sunlight and changes it into heat energy.

6. A <u>fossil fuel</u> is a hot spring that shoots steam and hot water into the air.

7. <u>Hydroelectric energy</u> comes from moving water.

Chapter Quiz

Write your answers on a separate sheet of paper.

1. What three fossil fuels are good sources of energy?

2. How do people get energy from fossil fuels?

3. How is using fossil fuels harmful to the environment?

4. What two processes release energy from the nuclei of atoms?

5. Which one of the two processes in Question 4 above produces radioactive wastes?

6. Why is solar energy a good energy source to use?

7. How do we get hydroelectric energy?

8. How is geothermal energy changed to electricity?

9. What are three ways in which people use wind energy?

10. What is the problem with using the energy of ocean waves and tides to produce electricity?

Test Tip

Before taking a chapter test, use the summary questions and the questions in each Lesson Review to help you review the chapter.

Research Project

Research how one of the following energy sources is changed to electricity: hydroelectric energy, geothermal energy, wind, ocean tides, and waves. Find out where in the world that energy source is used. Write a report. Then make a diagram and a map that shows what you learned.

Unit 5 **Review**

Choose the letter for the correct answer to each question.

Use the diagram to help you answer Questions 1 to 3.

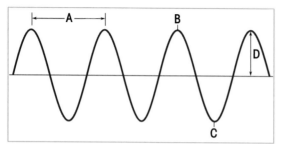

Light waves

1. What does the letter B on the diagram show?

A. trough

B. crest

C. wavelength

D. amplitude

2. How would the light change if D was increased?

A. change color

B. become brighter

C. move faster

D. become dimmer

3. What letter shows the wavelength of the light waves?

A. A

B. B

C. C

D. D

4. Which objects attract each other?

A. two negatively charged objects

B. two positively charged objects

C. two objects with opposite charges

D. two objects with no charges

5. When does electricity flow through a circuit?

A. when the circuit is open

B. when the circuit's fuse melts

C. when the circuit is broken

D. when the circuit's switch is closed

6. Which of the following produce harmful substances?

A. solar energy and nuclear fusion

B. geothermal energy and wind energy

C. fossil fuels and nuclear fission

D. wind energy and nuclear fusion

7. Which of the following comes from moving water?

A. oil

B. hydroelectric energy

C. nuclear fission

D. geothermal energy

Critical Thinking

Redraw the pie chart on page 298 to show how you would like energy sources to be used in the United States 20 years from now. Explain your choices.

Unit 6 ▷ Earth Science: Part I

A spacecraft high above the Earth took this photograph of a part of Florida. Technicians used a computer to add false colors and to increase detail. Scientists use these photos to study different features of the Earth.

Use the photo and the chart to answer these questions.

1. What color shows where forests are located?

2. What colors shows where most people live?

3. What are the black rounded shapes?

Color Key for Photo	
Color	**What It Shows**
Red	Farmland
Pink/purple	Buildings, parking lots, streets
Green	Trees
Black/dark blue	Water

This is a photograph of the Earth taken from space. What features of the Earth can you recognize from this photograph?

Learning Objectives

- Explain how the Earth moves through the solar system.
- Explain the theory of how and when the Earth was formed.
- Describe the features of the Earth.
- Identify the Earth's three layers.
- Compare rotation and revolution.
- Identify what causes the seasons.
- Explain longitude, latitude, and time zones.
- LAB ACTIVITY: Explore how the Earth's tilt causes the seasons.
- SCIENCE IN YOUR LIFE: Demonstrate how to use topographic maps.

Words to Know

solar system	the sun and all the planets and other objects that circle around it
orbit	a closed, curved path
continent	a large landmass
equator	an imaginary line that circles the Earth halfway between the North and South poles
core	the layer at the center of the Earth
mantle	the middle layer of the Earth
crust	the outer layer of the Earth
axis	an imaginary line that runs from one pole, through the center of the Earth, to the other pole
globe	a sphere, or ball, that has a map of the Earth on its surface
line of latitude	a line that circles a globe; runs east to west
line of longitude	a line that circles a globe; runs north to south
prime meridian	the 0-degree line of longitude

Words to Know

solar system	the sun and all the planets and other objects that circle around it
orbit	a closed, curved path

The Earth's Place in Space

Science Fact

The word *solar* means "sun." The solar system is the system of planets revolving around the sun.

The Earth is a planet in the **solar system**. The solar system is made up of the sun and all the planets and other objects that circle around it. The Earth moves in its own closed, curved path around the sun. This kind of path is called an **orbit**. The Earth is like a spaceship on a voyage around the sun.

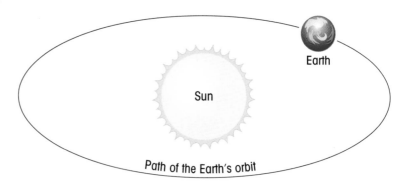

Earth

Sun

Path of the Earth's orbit

Figure 21-1 *The Earth's orbit is an oval, not a perfect circle.*

The Earth stays in orbit because of the strong pull of gravity from the sun. This pull keeps all the planets and objects of the solar system in their own orbits.

✓ **How does the Earth move around the sun?**

How the Earth Was Formed

Most scientists think that the Earth formed about 4.5 billion years ago. They think that the Earth and the rest of the solar system started off as a huge cloud of gas and dust. Over time, gravity drew the gas and dust particles together. Eventually, they formed the planets and the sun. The Earth is the third planet from the sun.

Remember
Gravity is the force of attraction between any two objects that have mass.

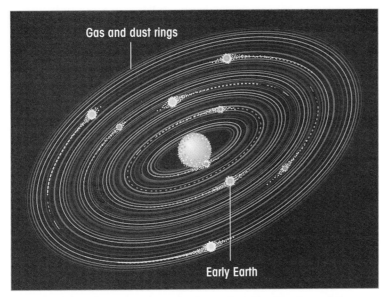

Gas and dust rings

Early Earth

Figure 21-2 *Most scientists believe that the Earth and the rest of the solar system were formed from gas and dust.*

✓ **How do most scientists think the Earth was formed?**

Lesson Review

1. What is the solar system made up of?

2. How long ago do scientists think the Earth was formed?

3. What is the third planet from the sun?

4. CRITICAL THINKING Why don't the Earth and the other planets bump into one another as they move around the sun?

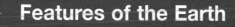

Words to Know

continent	a large landmass
equator	an imaginary line that circles the Earth halfway between the North and South poles
core	the layer at the center of the Earth
mantle	the middle layer of the Earth
crust	the thin, outer layer of the Earth
axis	an imaginary line that runs from one pole, through the center of the Earth, to the other pole

The Earth's Surface

Science Fact

The color of ocean water varies from dark gray to blue and green. The color is caused partly because of microscopic organisms near the surface.

Water

Seventy percent of the Earth's surface is covered with water. Water covers so much of our planet that it is sometimes called the "water planet." This is why the Earth appears blue from space.

There are four oceans, or seas, on Earth: the Arctic Ocean, the Atlantic Ocean, the Indian Ocean, and the Pacific Ocean. All of the oceans are made of salt water, and they are all connected. There are also rivers, streams, lakes, ponds, and large masses of ice on Earth. These are mostly made of fresh water.

Land

A **continent** is a large landmass. The Earth has seven continents: Africa, Antarctica, Asia, Australia, Europe, North America, and South America. Mountains, plains, deserts, and islands are found on or near the surface of the continents.

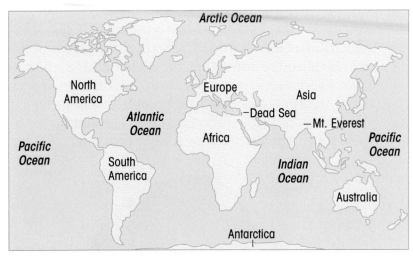

Figure 21-3 *The Earth has seven continents and four oceans.*

The highest point on Earth is at the top of Mount Everest. This mountain rises to a height of 29,028 feet (8,848 meters) above sea level. Mount Everest is on the border between Nepal and Tibet in Asia.

The lowest point of land on Earth's surface is the shore of the Dead Sea. It is 1,310 feet (almost 400 meters) below sea level. The Dead Sea is found between Israel and Jordan in the Middle East.

The Poles and the Equator

The northernmost part of the Earth is called the *North Pole*. The southernmost part is called the *South Pole*. An imaginary line circles the Earth halfway between the North and South poles. This line is called the **equator.**

The Earth is shaped like a ball. This ball shape is called a *sphere*. However, the Earth is not a perfect sphere. It is slightly squashed at the poles, and it bulges at the equator. A *diameter* is a straight line drawn through the center of a circle or a sphere. The Earth's diameter at the equator is 7,926 miles (12,753 kilometers). The diameter of the Earth from pole to pole is 7,899 miles (12,709 kilometers).

Science Fact

The circumference of the Earth, or distance around the Earth at the equator, is 24,901 miles (40,075 kilometers).

✓ **What covers most of the Earth's surface?**

Layers of the Earth

The Earth has three layers. The layer at the center of the Earth is called the **core.** The core is about 2,173 miles (3,500 kilometers) across. Scientists think that the inner part of the core is made of solid nickel and iron. The outer part is probably nickel and iron also, but in a liquid form. The Earth's core is very, very hot.

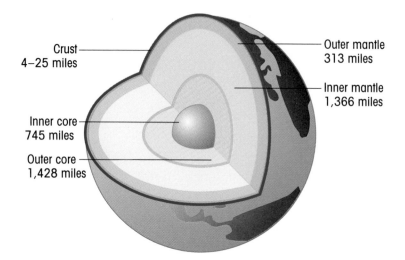

Crust
4–25 miles

Inner core
745 miles

Outer core
1,428 miles

Outer mantle
313 miles

Inner mantle
1,366 miles

Figure 21-4 *The Earth has three layers: the core, the mantle, and the crust.*

The middle layer of the Earth is called the **mantle.** The mantle is about 1,700 miles (2,720 kilometers) thick. Most of it is made up of solid rock. The outer 93 miles (150 kilometers) of the mantle is more like thick molasses. It moves very slowly. The mantle is made of silicon, oxygen, aluminum, iron, and magnesium.

Remember
Silicon, oxygen, aluminum, iron, and magnesium are elements. An element is a basic material out of which matter is made.

The outer layer of the Earth is the **crust.** The crust is very thin. In some places, it is only about 4 miles (6 kilometers) thick. In other places, it is about 25 miles (40 kilometers) thick. The continents and ocean floor are part of the Earth's crust, which is like a hard shell around the mantle.

✓ **What are the three layers of the Earth?**

Movements of the Earth

The Earth moves in two ways. First, it orbits the sun. One full orbit around the sun is called a *revolution*. The Earth takes $365\frac{1}{4}$ days to revolve around the sun. That is one year.

Remember
An orbit is a closed, curved path.

As the Earth orbits the sun, it also spins like a top on its **axis.** The Earth's axis is an imaginary line. It runs from one pole, through the center of the Earth, to the other pole. The Earth makes one complete turn, or *rotation*, on its axis once a day, or every 24 hours.

The spinning of the Earth causes the cycle of day and night. The areas on Earth facing the sun have daylight. When those same areas are facing away from the sun, the light is blocked. So, that side of the Earth experiences night.

The Earth spins on its axis from west to east. This explains why the sun appears to rise in the east and to set in the west.

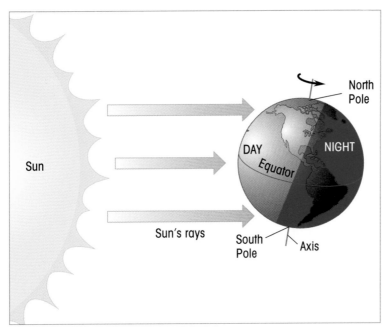

Figure 21-5 *The Earth revolves around the sun and rotates on its axis.*

✓ **What are the two ways the Earth moves in space?**

The Seasons

The four seasons result because the Earth is tilted on its axis. While one hemisphere is tilted toward the sun, the other is tilted away. As the Earth orbits the sun, the direction of the tilt changes. The number of daylight hours also changes. These differences cause the change of seasons.

It is winter in the hemisphere tilted away from the sun. This is because the sun's rays strike the Earth at more of an angle. There are also fewer hours of daylight. It is summer in the hemisphere tilted toward the sun. Here the sun's rays strike the Earth at less of an angle. There are also more hours of daylight.

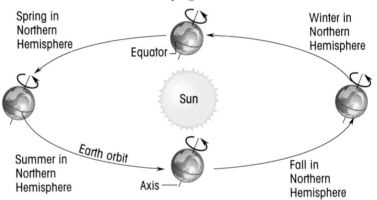

Spring in Northern Hemisphere

Equator

Winter in Northern Hemisphere

Sun

Earth orbit

Summer in Northern Hemisphere

Axis

Fall in Northern Hemisphere

Figure 21-6 *This diagram shows the Earth's position at the beginning of each of the four seasons in the Northern Hemisphere.*

✓ **What causes seasons on Earth?**

Lesson Review

1. What are the names of the seven continents?

2. How are the core, mantle, and crust different from each another?

3. What causes day and night?

4. **CRITICAL THINKING** How would conditions on Earth be different if the Earth were not tilted on its axis?

Words to Know

globe	a sphere, or ball, that has a map of the Earth on its surface
line of latitude	a line that circles a globe; runs east to west
line of longitude	a line that circles a globe; runs north to south
prime meridian	the 0-degree line of longitude

Lines of Latitude and Longitude

A **globe** is a sphere, or ball, that has a map of the Earth on its surface. Globes have lines running around them from east to west and north to south. These lines help people find different places and features on Earth.

A line that runs east to west is called a **line of latitude.** The equator is a line of latitude. A line that runs north to south is called a **line of longitude.** Lines of longitude run from the North Pole to the South Pole.

Lines of latitude and longitude are assigned numbers called *degrees*. Lines of latitude are measured in degrees north and south of the equator. The equator is at 0 degrees. It lies halfway between the poles. The North Pole is 90 degrees north latitude. The South Pole is 90 degrees south latitude.

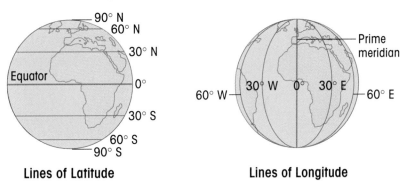

Figure 21-7 *All globes show lines of latitude and longitude.*

Lines of Latitude

Lines of Longitude

The 0-degree line of longitude is called the **prime meridian.** It runs through Greenwich, England. The other lines of longitude are measured in degrees east and west of the prime meridian. Directly opposite the prime meridian is the 180-degree line of longitude.

✔ **Why do globes have lines of latitude and longitude?**

Time Zones Around the World

There are 24 time zones that have been set up around the world. A time zone is an area in which the same time is used. Each zone covers about 15 degrees of longitude. The time zones are like this because the Earth rotates 15 degrees of longitude in 1 hour.

The boundaries of the time zones are not always straight lines. They are drawn so that most states and small countries fit into one time zone.

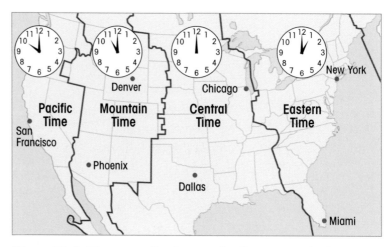

Figure 21-8 *These are the four major time zones in the United States.*

Most of the United States is divided into four time zones. These are called the Pacific, Mountain, Central, and Eastern time zones. Alaska and Hawaii are west of the Pacific zone, so they fall into different time zones.

Each time zone is one hour different from the ones on either side. If you travel east, you lose one hour as you cross into each new time zone. Going west, you gain one hour as you cross into each new time zone.

Suppose it is 7:00 A.M. in New York. New York is in the Eastern time zone. At that same moment, it would be 6:00 A.M. in Chicago (Central time zone), 5:00 A.M. in Salt Lake City (Mountain time zone), and 4:00 A.M. in Los Angeles (Pacific time zone).

✔ **Why are there 24 time zones in the world?**

Lesson Review

1. What is the difference between the prime meridian and the equator?

2. About how many degrees are covered by each time zone?

3. CRITICAL THINKING If it is 3:00 P.M. in the Eastern time zone, what time is it in the Mountain time zone?

Great Moments in Science

SETTING UP THE TIME ZONES
People used to set their clocks by the time the sun was highest in the sky at that place. So, the time from town to town was often different by a few minutes. This was very confusing for travelers.

In 1883, railroad companies made their railroad schedules simpler by creating four standard time zones in the United States. The next year, the International Meridian Conference set up the 24 worldwide time zones that we use today.

CRITICAL THINKING How might it be confusing not to have time zones? Give an example.

In 1883, railroad companies created standard time zones in the United States.

LAB ACTIVITY
Making a Model of the Seasons

BACKGROUND
A globe is a model of the Earth. It can help us understand things such as seasons, rotation, and tilt.

PURPOSE
You will use a globe to see what causes the seasons.

MATERIALS
paper, pencil, 60-watt bulb and socket, globe

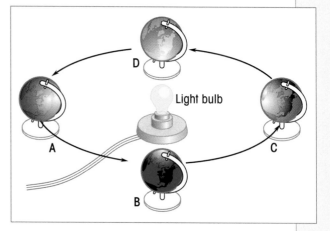

Light bulb

WHAT TO DO

1. Set the bulb and socket on a table. The bulb represents the sun. Copy the chart to the right.

2. Position the globe as shown in **A** in the diagram. The globe should be about a foot from the bulb. Turn on the bulb. Record what part of the globe is tilted away from the light. Record what season would occur in the northern part of the Earth in this position.

Position	Part of Globe Tilted Away From Light	Season
A		
C		

3. Position the globe as shown in **C**. Keep the same distance between the globe and bulb. Record what part of the globe is tilted away from the light in this position. Record what season would occur in the southern part of the Earth in this position.

4. Position the globe in position **B** and then **D**. What part of the globe is tilted away from the light in this position?

DRAW CONCLUSIONS

• Do the seasons change at the equator? Why or why not?

• What would happen to the seasons if the Earth were tilted more than it is?

SCIENCE IN YOUR LIFE
Topographic Maps

If you wanted to explore a natural area, it would be helpful to have a *topographic map*. Topographic maps show the shape and elevation of the Earth's surface. *Elevation* is how far above or below sea level a place is.

Topographic maps use *contour lines*. A contour line connects all points at the same elevation. The number shows feet above sea level. The drawing above shows an island and how that island looks on a topographic map. Notice how the imaginary contour lines on the island match up with the contour lines on the map. Points located on the 0-foot contour line are at sea level. Points on the 10-foot contour line are 10 feet above sea level. When contour lines are close together, that shows steep slopes. A series of closed loops shows a hill or mountain. Contour lines that form a V show a valley. The V points uphill.

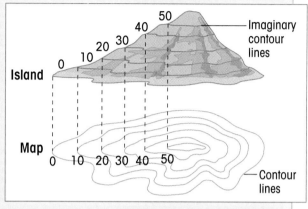

This shows how an island's different elevations would look on a topographic map.

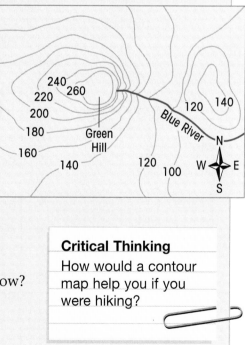

Use the topographic map to the right to answer these questions.

1. How many hills are on the map?

2. Would it be easier to walk up Green Hill from the west or from the east? Why?

3. In which direction does the Blue River flow?

Critical Thinking

How would a contour map help you if you were hiking?

Summary

The Earth is a planet in the solar system. It has four oceans and seven continents. It also has two poles. It is not a perfect sphere. It bulges at the equator.

Lesson 21.1

The Earth revolves around the sun. Most scientists believe the Earth was formed about 4.5 billion years ago.

Lesson 21.2

About 70 percent of the Earth is covered with water. The rest is land. The Earth's three layers are the core, the mantle, and the crust. The seasons are caused by the tilt of the Earth. The Earth takes one year to revolve around the sun and one day to rotate on its axis.

Lesson 21.3

Lines of latitude and longitude help people locate places on Earth. There are 24 time zones. Each time zone is 1 hour different from the ones next to it.

Vocabulary Review

Complete each sentence with a term from the list.

continents

crust

line of latitude

solar system

prime meridian

mantle

orbit

axis

1. The _____ includes the sun and all the planets.
2. The Earth moves in a closed, curved path called an _____.
3. The Earth has seven large landmasses called _____.
4. The _____ is the middle layer of the Earth.
5. The ocean floor is part of the Earth's _____.
6. The Earth's _____ is an imaginary line that runs from one pole through the Earth's center to the other pole.
7. A line that runs east to west on a globe is a _____.
8. The _____ is the 0-degree line of longitude.

Chapter Quiz

Write your answers on a separate sheet of paper.

1. What is the scientific theory for the formation of the Earth? About how long ago did the Earth form?

2. Why is the Earth sometimes called the "water planet"?

3. What are the three layers of the Earth? On which layer do you live?

4. How long does it take for the Earth to make one complete revolution around the sun?

5. What is the difference between the Earth's rotation and its revolution?

6. Where is the equator located?

7. In what direction do lines of latitude run?

8. In what direction do lines of longitude run?

9. What is a time zone? What are the four major time zones in the United States?

10. If you cross time zones traveling east, how does time change?

Test Tip
Make sure you understand what each test question is asking. Read a question at least twice before you answer it.

Research Project

Doing exercise and using topographic maps are combined in a sport called orienteering. This sport has become quite popular both in the United States and around the world. Do some research to find out about orienteering. Answer these questions: What equipment is needed for orienteering? Who can participate? Are there orienteering clubs in your area?

Mount St. Helens in the state of Washington blew up in May of 1980. The force of the explosion ripped off the top of the volcano. The sky turned black in the middle of the day. What material do you think turned the sky black?

Learning Objectives

- Describe the theory of plate tectonics.
- Explain how trenches and mountains are formed.
- Compare and contrast earthquakes and volcanoes.
- Identify the three main types of rock in the Earth's crust and describe how they are formed.
- Describe the processes of weathering and erosion.
- LAB ACTIVITY: Compare the contents of different types of soil.
- ON-THE-JOB SCIENCE: Relate rock identification to the work of a geologist.

Words to Know

earthquake	a sudden, violent shaking of the Earth
geologist	a scientist who studies rocks to learn about the history and structure of the Earth
plate tectonics	the scientific theory that the Earth's crust is made up of plates that slowly shift position
trench	a deep, long valley in the ocean floor
magma	melted rock formed in the Earth's mantle
volcano	an opening in the Earth's surface that releases magma from the mantle
lava	magma that has reached the Earth's surface
igneous rock	a type of rock formed from magma
sedimentary rock	a type of rock formed by the pressing together of smaller particles of rock or the remains of living things
metamorphic rock	a type of rock formed when igneous or sedimentary rock changes under very high temperatures or pressure
weathering	a process that breaks down rocks and minerals
soil	rocks on the Earth's surface broken down by weathering to very tiny pieces that mix with the nutrients from living and once-living things
erosion	the wearing away of rock and soil
glacier	a large, slow-moving field of ice

Words to Know

earthquake	a sudden, violent shaking of the Earth
geologist	a scientist who studies rocks to learn about the history and structure of the Earth
plate tectonics	the scientific theory that the Earth's crust is made up of plates that slowly shift position
trench	a deep, long valley in the ocean floor
magma	melted rock formed in the Earth's mantle
volcano	an opening in the Earth's surface that releases magma from the mantle
lava	magma that has reached the Earth's surface

Drifting Continents

The Earth's crust moves. Most of the time, we do not feel the movements. An **earthquake** is a sudden, violent shaking of the Earth. In California, there is at least one earthquake every week. Earthquakes are caused by a shifting of pieces of the Earth's crust.

Most earthquakes are so small that only scientists notice them. However, every 50 to 100 years or so, a big one comes along and does a lot of damage.

A **geologist** is a scientist who studies rocks to learn about the history and structure of the Earth. Geologists also study the movements of the Earth's crust and what causes them.

Most geologists think that all the continents were once part of one big supercontinent called *Pangaea*. About 200 million years ago, pieces of land began breaking free from Pangaea. These landmasses came together and separated many times. Eventually they drifted to the positions they are in today.

Plate tectonics is the scientific theory that states that the Earth's crust is made up of plates that slowly shift position. A plate is a large piece of the Earth's crust. The movement of these plates causes earthquakes.

Remember
A theory is a guess about something based on evidence.

Some of the plates are very big, but there are smaller plates, too. A plate can include a landmass, such as a continent, as well as a section of the ocean floor. The plates are moving all the time. However, they move very slowly. Most of the United States is on the North American plate, which is drifting westward.

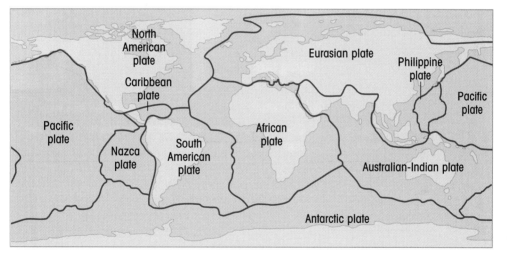

Figure 22-1 *This map shows the main plates of the Earth's crust.*

Continental drift is the theory that the Earth's large landmasses are carried along, or drift, because of the movement of the plates. Geologists think they know why these pieces of the Earth's crust are moving. It is because the crust floats on the hot, softer rock of the mantle. The plates are carried along in the flow.

Remember
The outer part of the Earth's mantle is like thick molasses. It flows very slowly.

✔ **How do continents drift across the Earth's surface?**

Trenches and Mountains

The plates of the Earth's crust may bump into each other, or collide. As they collide, one plate may be forced under the other. This plate gets pushed down into the hot mantle, where the crust melts. When one plate gets pushed down under another beneath the sea, a **trench** forms between them. A trench is a deep, long valley in the ocean floor.

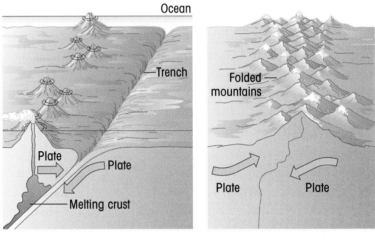

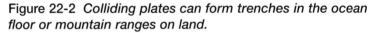

Ocean Trench　　　　**Underwater Mountain**

Figure 22-2 *Colliding plates can form trenches in the ocean floor or mountain ranges on land.*

Sometimes two colliding plates pile up against each other on land. This is how some mountain ranges are formed.

Mountains build up very, very slowly. Over millions of years, the plates push against each other. As they push, the land gets shoved upward, making mountains. The Alps in Europe were formed this way. So were the Andes in South America and the Himalayas in Asia. Mount Everest, in the Himalayas, is 29,028 feet (8,848 meters) above sea level. It is the highest point on Earth.

✓ **What two kinds of landforms develop when plates collide? How do they develop?**

Earthquakes

Sometimes, instead of two plates pushing into each other, they slide past each other. This is true of the Pacific and North American plates. They meet along the western coast of North America. The Pacific plate moves about 2 inches (5 centimeters) each year in a northwest direction.

Many earthquakes occur along this coast. Each time there is a sudden slip between the plates, an earthquake occurs.

Two huge pieces of the Earth's crust may rub against each other. The plates do not slip by each other smoothly. Friction holds the upper layers of the crust together. However, the plates continue to move deeper down. Pressure builds up on the surface. Finally, when the strain becomes too great, the plates slip. The sudden movement sends shock waves through the Earth. An earthquake is the result.

The Pacific and North American plates meet in California at the San Andreas fault.

✓ **How do moving plates cause earthquakes?**

Great Moments in Science

PUTTING THE PUZZLE TOGETHER

A German scientist named Alfred Wegener was looking at a map of the world in 1912. He noticed that the continents looked like jigsaw puzzle pieces that fit together. He thought that at one time these pieces were part of one big continent, which he called Pangaea. This was the beginning of the theory of continental drift. Wegener's discovery was used to develop the theory of plate tectonics.

Wegener called the supercontinent Pangaea.

CRITICAL THINKING How does the theory of plate tectonics explain Wegener's discovery?

Volcanoes

Sometimes, when plates move, openings form in the crust. Melted rock, called **magma,** squeezes up from the Earth's mantle. An opening in the Earth's surface that releases magma from the mantle is called a **volcano.** The word *volcano* is also used to describe the mountain that builds up around the opening.

Volcanoes can form on dry land or on the ocean floor. The magma comes up through openings called *vents.* Magma that has reached the Earth's surface is called **lava.** As the lava cools, it hardens into rock. Over time, the lava builds up and creates a mountain.

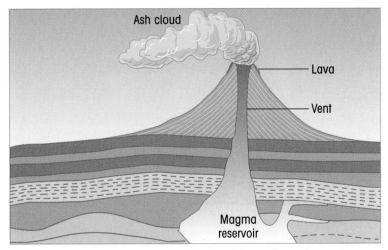

Figure 22-3 *Magma reaches the Earth's surface through vents in volcanoes.*

When volcanoes occur on the ocean floor, they can create islands. The Hawaiian Islands were formed this way. There are many earthquakes and volcanoes around the edge of the Pacific plate. In fact, there are so many volcanoes in this area that it is called the "Ring of Fire."

Some volcanoes erupt violently. Lava, ash, and hot gas explode high into the air. Other volcanoes erupt more gently. The lava flows quietly onto the surface.

✓ **How does a volcano form?**

Lesson Review

Write *true* or *false* for each sentence. If the sentence is false, replace the underlined term to make the sentence true.

1. Most <u>geologists</u> think that all the continents were $\mathcal{T}$ once attached.

2. When two plates collide, they can form <u>trenches</u> or mountains.

3. The Earth's plates float on the <u>crust</u>.

4. **CRITICAL THINKING** Why does an earthquake near a volcano warn that the volcano may erupt soon?

A Closer Look

POMPEII

In 79 A.D., Pompeii was a lively seaside town in what is today called Italy. A volcano named Mount Vesuvius towered over the city. But the people did not fear it. No one had ever seen Vesuvius erupt. It had sat quietly for 800 years. Its slopes were covered with trees and vines. Farmers worked the rich soils around it.

A thick layer of ash formed molds around the people of Pompeii when they died.

That August, however, Vesuvius erupted suddenly and with great violence. A cloud of hot ash and gas rolled down the slopes of the volcano. Thousands of people were killed as they tried to escape the city. Tons of hot ash and cinders fell on the city for three days. The ash hardened almost instantly around the dead bodies. Today, in Pompeii, you can see the shapes of the people who were taken by surprise when the ash rained down.

CRITICAL THINKING Why did the eruption of Mount Vesuvius kill so many people?

Words to Know

igneous rock	a type of rock formed from magma
sedimentary rock	a type of rock formed by the pressing together of smaller particles of rock or the remains of living things
metamorphic rock	a type of rock formed when igneous or sedimentary rock changes under very high temperatures or pressure
weathering	a process that breaks down rocks and minerals
soil	rocks on the Earth's surface broken down by weathering to very tiny pieces that mix with the nutrients from living and once-living things
erosion	the wearing away of rock and soil
glacier	a large, slow-moving field of ice

Kinds of Rock

Obsidian is a smooth, shiny igneous rock. It looks like glass. Long ago, people made tools from obsidian.

The Earth's crust is made of rock. Maybe you collect or once collected rocks. If so, you know that there are many different kinds. Some of the physical properties of rocks are color, shape, hardness, and texture.

There are three basic kinds of rock. These are igneous, sedimentary, and metamorphic rock.

Igneous Rock

Igneous rock is a type of rock formed from magma. The magma is forced up from the mantle or lower crust. When it reaches the surface, the magma hardens into rock. Some kinds of igneous rock are *obsidian*, *basalt*, and *granite*. Igneous rocks make up about 95 percent of the Earth's crust.

Sedimentary Rock

Sedimentary rock is a type of rock formed by the pressing together of smaller particles of rock or the remains of living things. It takes a very long time for sedimentary rock to form. Beds of clay, sand, or gravel may harden to make sedimentary rock. *Shale* is a kind of sedimentary rock made of hardened clay. *Sandstone* is a kind of sedimentary rock made of sand. *Coal* is a sedimentary rock formed from plant fossils. *Limestone* is a common sedimentary rock. Some limestone forms from the shells and bones of tiny animals in the sea. Sedimentary rocks are the most common rocks on the Earth's surface.

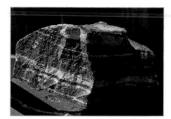

Sandstone is made of sand grains cemented together by minerals.

Metamorphic Rock

The third kind of rock is called **metamorphic rock.** Metamorphic rock is a type of rock formed from sedimentary or igneous rock that changes under high temperatures or pressure. When igneous or sedimentary rocks become extremely hot, they change chemically. They *metamorphize.* Two kinds of metamorphic rock are *marble* and *slate.*

Marble is a metamorphic rock that is used for buildings and monuments. It comes mostly from quarries such as this one.

✓ **What are the three kinds of rock, and how do they form?**

Building Rocks From Minerals

All rocks are made of minerals. There are at least 2,000 different kinds of minerals. Each one has a unique chemical makeup. Many minerals are pure elements. However, most are combinations of elements. Some examples of minerals are talc, gold, quartz, and bauxite.

Talc is ground into talcum powder. Quartz is made into glass. Gold is used for jewelry. Bauxite is used for aluminum baseball bats.

✓ **What are rocks made of?**

Weathering

Weathering is a process that breaks down rocks and minerals. Running water, ice, rain, plants, animals, and chemicals all help to weather rocks and minerals.

For example, as a river flows, it washes away little bits of rock from the riverbed. These bits of rock are swept downstream. As they move, they bump into other rocks and tumble along the bottom. Slowly, they break into smaller and smaller pieces.

Ice also causes rocks to weather. Rocks have many cracks. Water fills the cracks in the rocks. When the water freezes, it expands. The freezing water, or ice, acts like a wedge to break the rock into smaller pieces.

Rain causes weathering, too. Raindrops beat on rocks like millions of little hammers. Eventually, the rocks wear down. Rain also causes weathering by mixing with gases in the air to make a weak acid. This acid dissolves certain minerals in rocks. Over time, the rocks crumble. Even plants help weather rocks. Some plants start growing in the cracks of rocks. As the roots grow, they push on the rocks and help break them apart.

Soil is an important product of weathering. Soil is made up of rocks on the Earth's surface broken down by weathering to very tiny pieces that mix with the nutrients from living and once-living things. A layer of soil takes thousands of years to form.

✓ **How does weathering create soil?**

Erosion

Erosion is the wearing away of rock and soil. Like weathering, a river can cause erosion. Very slowly, a river valley can be carved out of rock by moving water. Valleys that are cut by rivers are V-shaped. Wind can also erode soil by blowing the rich top layer away.

A **glacier** is a large, slow-moving field of ice. Glaciers cause erosion, too. As they move, they clear out everything in their paths. Valleys cut by glaciers are U-shaped.

Glaciers carve out valleys as they flow downhill.

✓ **What are two ways rock and soil are eroded?**

Lesson Review

1. What are four physical properties of rocks? color, shape hardness + texture

2. What are three things that cause weathering? running H₂O, ice, rain

3. How do glaciers cause erosion? as move, clear out paths

4. **CRITICAL THINKING** How would the Earth's surface look different if there were no weathering or erosion?

LAB ACTIVITY
Recognizing Types of Soil

BACKGROUND
Soil comes in many different types. Some soils are dark. Others are light. Some have large grains and are dry. Some have tiny grains that hold moisture better. Very rich soils contain live plants or animals or pieces of dead plants and animals. They add nutrients to the soil.

PURPOSE
You will describe what is in different samples of soil and determine which are good for growing plants.

MATERIALS
paper, pen, 2 different soil samples, hand lens, toothpick

WHAT TO DO
1. Copy the chart to the right.
2. Work with a partner. Put two soil samples on separate sheets of paper.
3. Use a hand lens to observe the first sample close up. Use the toothpick to separate the soil grains and other particles to observe them better. Record your observations in the chart.
4. Repeat Step 3 with the second soil sample.

Safety Alert

Wear goggles while doing this activity and wash your hands afterward.

	Sample 1	Sample 2
Color		
Size of grains		
Shape of grains		
Live animals or plants?		
Dead animals or animal parts?		
Dead plants or plant parts?		
Other observations		

DRAW CONCLUSIONS
- Which soil would be better for growing plants? Why?

- Which soil would hold moisture better?

ON-THE-JOB SCIENCE
Geologist

Maria Ramirez is a geologist. She studies rocks. In high school, Maria liked earth science, math, and chemistry. She went to college and earned a master's degree in geology.

Maria spends a lot of time outdoors. She uses maps and special tools to collect rock samples. Maria studies the samples in a lab. She finds out which minerals a rock contains. Then she studies the properties of the minerals.

Besides noting the mineral's color, Maria tests the hardness of the mineral. On a scale of 1 to 10, 10 is the hardest. She also finds out if the mineral is made up of crystals. A crystal has many sides. The research helps her find possible uses for the rocks and minerals she identifies.

Maria has just collected five new mineral samples. She made this chart.

Maria is a geologist.

Critical Thinking

How can observing the properties of rocks and minerals help geologists find uses for rocks and minerals?

Mineral	Color	Hardness	Other Properties
Sample 1	Bright yellow	2.5	Shiny
Sample 2	Clear	10.0	8-sided crystals
Sample 3	Bright yellow	6.5	Shiny
Sample 4	Black	6.0	12-sided crystals, magnetic
Sample 5	Black	6.0	12-sided crystals

Use the chart to answer the questions.

1. Which of the minerals is hardest? softest?

2. How can Maria tell Samples 1 and 3 apart?

3. Samples 4 and 5 are very similar. What can Maria do to tell them apart?

Summary

The Earth's crust is made up of a number of rock plates that fit together. Plate movements cause earthquakes and volcanic eruptions. Other processes wear down the rock into soil.

Lesson 22.1

Plate tectonics is the theory that the Earth's crust is made up of moving plates that can cause earthquakes. They also help form mountains and ocean trenches. Volcanoes erupt when magma squeezes up through openings between plates.

Lesson 22.2

The three main kinds of rock are igneous, sedimentary, and metamorphic. Rocks are made of minerals. Weathering breaks down rocks and minerals. Soil is a product of weathering. Erosion carries away soil and rock.

Vocabulary Review

Write *true* or *false* for each sentence. If the sentence is false, replace the underlined term to make the sentence true.

1. A <u>geologist</u> is a scientist who studies rocks to learn about the Earth's history and structure.

2. A <u>trench</u> is a deep, long valley in the ocean floor.

3. Magma is called <u>lava</u> once it reaches the Earth's surface.

4. <u>Igneous rock</u> forms from many different rock particles that are pressed together.

5. <u>Metamorphic rock</u> forms when igneous or sedimentary rock changes under high temperatures or pressure.

6. <u>Erosion</u> breaks down rocks and minerals.

7. The wearing away of rock and soil is called <u>weathering</u>.

8. A <u>glacier</u> is an opening in the Earth's surface that releases magma from the mantle.

Chapter Quiz

Write your answers on a separate sheet of paper.

1. What does the theory of plate tectonics say?

2. What forms when two plates collide under the sea and one plate gets pushed down under the other?

3. What forms when two plates collide and pile up on each other?

4. What causes earthquakes?

5. How are earthquakes and volcanoes similar?

6. What are the three basic kinds of rock?

7. What are the building blocks of rocks?

8. How does weathering change rocks?

9. How do rivers form river valleys?

10. What happens during erosion?

Test Tip

If you do not know the full answer to a question, write down what you do know. As you answer the rest of the questions, you might find clues to help you answer the questions you did not know.

Research Project

Choose a natural feature in or near your community. It could be a mountain, canyon, river, beach, lake, plain, swamp, or glacier. Describe and draw it or take a picture of it. Do research to find its age, size, and anything special about it. Include ways your community uses the feature. If it has changed in recent years, describe how. Share what you find in a short oral report to your class.

Chapter **23** The Earth's Atmosphere

On most days, you can look up into the sky and see clouds. They do not always look like the ones shown in the photo. How would you describe other kinds of clouds that you have seen?

Learning Objectives

- Identify the layers of the atmosphere.
- Explain air pressure.
- Describe how winds are formed.
- Explain how convection currents work.
- Compare different types of precipitation.
- List the different cloud forms.
- LAB ACTIVITY: Observe how a cloud forms.
- SCIENCE IN YOUR LIFE: Use a chart to find wind chill temperatures.

Words to Know

atmosphere	the air that surrounds the Earth or another body in space
troposphere	the layer nearest the Earth in the atmosphere, where we live and where most weather takes place
stratosphere	the second layer in the atmosphere
ozone	a thin layer of gas found in the stratosphere that filters out much of the harmful radiation from the sun
mesosphere	the third layer in the atmosphere
ionosphere	the fourth layer in the atmosphere, where there are many electrically charged particles
thermosphere	the outermost layer in the atmosphere
air pressure	the weight of the gases pressing down on the Earth
barometer	an instrument that measures air pressure
humidity	the amount of water vapor in the air at any given time
precipitation	any form of water that falls from the air
dew point	the temperature at which water vapor turns into liquid water
cirrus cloud	a high-altitude cloud made of ice crystals
stratus cloud	a low-lying gray cloud that covers a wide area
cumulus cloud	a big, puffy low-altitude cloud that usually signals good weather

Words to Know

atmosphere	the air that surrounds the Earth or another body in space
troposphere	the layer nearest the Earth in the atmosphere, where we live and where most weather takes place
stratosphere	the second layer in the atmosphere
ozone	a thin layer of gas found in the stratosphere that filters out much of the harmful radiation from the sun
mesosphere	the third layer in the atmosphere
ionosphere	the fourth layer in the atmosphere, where there are many electrically charged particles
thermosphere	the outermost layer in the atmosphere

What Is the Atmosphere?

Take a deep breath. You just filled your lungs with air. The air that surrounds the Earth or another body in space is called the **atmosphere.** The pull of gravity holds the atmosphere to the Earth. The atmosphere travels with the Earth as it moves through space.

Some people do not think of the air as anything at all. However, air is matter. Air has mass, even though you cannot see it. Air is made up mostly of gases, including the gas water vapor. There is also a certain amount of fine dust always floating in the air. Sometimes the air is heavy, and sometimes it is light. Air is also affected by gravity and heat from the sun.

The Earth's atmosphere is about 78 percent nitrogen. Oxygen makes up about 21 percent. There are also small amounts of water vapor, argon, carbon dioxide, and other gases in the atmosphere.

The higher up you go in the atmosphere, the thinner the air is. Mountain climbers gasp for air on top of high mountains. Climbers need to breathe in more air to get enough oxygen. People who climb the highest peaks in the world carry oxygen in tanks with them.

The atmosphere does not suddenly end. It becomes thinner and thinner as you go farther from the Earth. At about 600 miles (960 kilometers), there is almost no atmosphere left.

✓ **What two gases make up most of the atmosphere?**

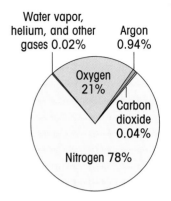

Figure 23-1 *This chart shows what the atmosphere is made up of.*

Layers in the Atmosphere

Scientists often divide the atmosphere into five layers. Some of these layers overlap.

Troposphere

The layer nearest the Earth is called the **troposphere.** This is the layer in which we live and where most weather takes place. Planes fly in the troposphere.

The troposphere is warmest near the Earth. It is cooler farther away from the Earth. The air is most dense near the bottom of the troposphere. Here, air molecules are packed close together by the weight of the air above.

Stratosphere

The second layer is called the **stratosphere.** Within the stratosphere is a thin layer of the gas **ozone.** Ozone is a form of oxygen. This layer is very important to living things. Ozone filters out much of the harmful radiation from the sun.

Air pollution may be breaking down the ozone layer. Without protection from ozone, more ultraviolet light can get through to the Earth's surface. Ultraviolet light, which is invisible, is the cause of sunburn and some skin cancers. Scientists say an increase in this radiation could cause an increase in skin cancer in humans.

Mesosphere and Ionosphere

The third layer in the atmosphere around the Earth is called the **mesosphere**. The fourth layer is called the **ionosphere**. The ionosphere actually begins in the mesosphere and goes upward through the fifth layer. The ionosphere contains many electrically charged particles. These particles are important in radio communications. They reflect radio signals.

Thermosphere

The outermost layer is called the **thermosphere**. The air in the thermosphere is very thin.

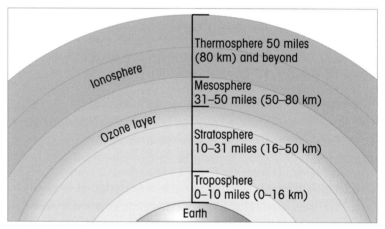

Thermosphere 50 miles (80 km) and beyond

Mesosphere 31–50 miles (50–80 km)

Stratosphere 10–31 miles (16–50 km)

Troposphere 0–10 miles (0–16 km)

Earth

Ionosphere

Ozone layer

Figure 23-2 *These are the layers of the atmosphere.*

✓ How many layers are in the atmosphere, and what are they called?

Lesson Review

1. What substances make up the atmosphere?

2. About how far does the atmosphere go above the surface of the Earth?

3. What layer of the atmosphere helps radio communication? Explain how.

4. **CRITICAL THINKING** Suppose the Earth had much less gravity. How would that change the atmosphere?

Words to Know

air pressure   the weight of the gases pressing down on the Earth

barometer   an instrument that measures air pressure

Air Has Weight

Science Fact

Barometers are used to help predict the weather. A change in barometric pressure usually means a change in the weather.

Gravity keeps the Earth's atmosphere from flying off into space. Gravity is strongest near the Earth's surface. Therefore, the atmosphere closest to the Earth is pulled the most by gravity. This causes the air molecules to pack together more tightly. So, the air close to the Earth's surface is heavier, or denser. The air farther away is less dense, or lighter.

Air pressure is the weight of the gases pressing down on the Earth. Air pressure changes all the time. A **barometer** is an instrument that measures air pressure.

✓ **Why is the air close to the Earth's surface very dense?**

Air Has Heat

Energy from the sun reaches the Earth as radiation. Once radiation strikes the ground, it changes to heat energy. Then the ground radiates the heat back into the atmosphere. At that point, water vapor and other gases in the air absorb some of the warmth.

Clouds often block the sun's energy. They also reflect sunlight back into the outer atmosphere. At night, though, clouds around the Earth act as a blanket. They trap the heat and keep it from escaping into space.

✓ **How do clouds affect sunlight striking the Earth?**

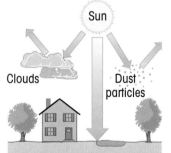

Figure 23-3 *Energy from the sun warms the surface of the Earth. The Earth's surface warms the atmosphere.*

Air Can Move

Wind is moving air. Remember that heat causes the molecules in all matter to move. The warmer air is, the faster it moves and the more the molecules spread out. In other words, heat causes matter to become less dense. When air becomes less dense, it moves up, or rises. Colder air sweeps into the empty space left by the warmer air. This action sets up a circular motion of air called a *convection current.*

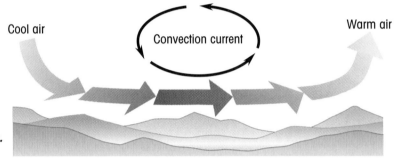

Figure 23-4 *Convection currents result from the uneven heating of the atmosphere. Warm air rises. Cool air takes its place.*

The Earth's Wind Systems

Convection currents form large wind systems. Warm air at the equator rises and moves toward the poles. Cooler air flows toward the equator from the north and south to replace the rising warm air. This causes a huge convection current. However, the rotation of the Earth breaks up this big wind into a number of smaller, circular winds. This picture shows some of the Earth's large wind systems.

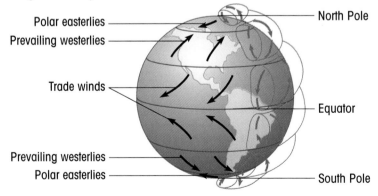

Figure 23-5 *Convection currents cause most of the large wind systems on Earth.*

Local Winds

As you just read, the Earth has several major wind systems. However, the Earth's surface features, such as mountains, valleys, and big bodies of water, create local winds. Local winds are smaller wind systems. For example, cold mountain breezes blow down mountain slopes at night. Warm valley breezes blow up mountain slopes on sunny days.

Winds over the land and water also change between day and night. Land heats up faster than oceans or large lakes. So, during the day, the air over land becomes warmer than the air over large bodies of water. When the warm air over the land rises, the cold air over the ocean or lake rushes in. This kind of wind is called a *sea breeze*.

At night, the opposite happens. The land cools off faster than the ocean. So, the air over land gets cooler than the air over the ocean. The ocean air rises and the land air rushes out. This creates a *land breeze*.

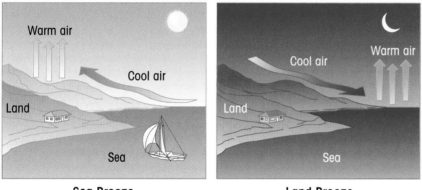

Sea Breeze   Land Breeze

Figure 23-6 *Sea breezes and land breezes are local winds.*

Local winds are always named for the direction from which they come. So a *westerly* is blowing from the west. It blows toward the east. A *north wind* is blowing from the north. It blows toward the south.

✓ **What causes most of the Earth's winds?**

Lesson Review

1. What are three properties of air?

2. How does sunlight heat the air?

3. What is a convection current?

4. **CRITICAL THINKING** On a hot day, why is it often cooler near the shore of an ocean than farther inland?

A Closer Look

JET STREAMS

Have you ever tried to ride a bicycle against the wind? If so, you probably had to work hard to overcome the moving air. Airplanes also have to use more energy to overcome very strong moving streams of air. That is why the routes many airplanes take are designed with the *jet streams* in mind. Jet streams are narrow rivers of fast-moving air.

Two major jet streams flow from west to east across the Earth. The winds of the jet streams move at an average of 35 miles (56 kilometers) per hour in the summer. In the winter, the winds move at an average of 75 miles (120 kilometers) per hour. Airplanes that are moving eastward try to fly along a jet stream. The powerful winds push the airplane through the atmosphere. The airplane gains speed and uses less fuel.

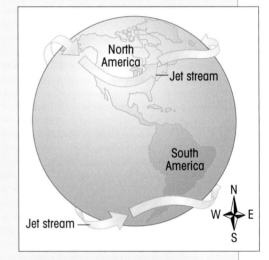

Jet streams flow in wavelike patterns from west to east.

CRITICAL THINKING Why do you think pilots flying west try to avoid the jet streams?

Water and Air

Words to Know

humidity	the amount of water vapor in the air at any given time
precipitation	any form of water that falls from the air
dew point	the temperature at which water vapor turns into liquid water
cirrus cloud	a high-altitude cloud made of ice crystals
stratus cloud	a low-lying gray cloud that covers a wide area
cumulus cloud	a big, puffy low-altitude cloud that usually signals good weather

Precipitation

Remember
When water evaporates, it turns from a liquid into a gas.

There is always some water in the air. Water enters the air by evaporating off the ground, lakes, oceans, rivers, plants, and animals. The amount of water in the air at any given time is the level of **humidity**. When the humidity is high, water may fall from the air. **Precipitation** is any form of water that falls from the air. The form the water takes depends partly on the temperature of the air.

Rain
Liquid water falls as rain. Warming can change rain into the gas water vapor. Cooling can turn water vapor back into a liquid. The temperature at which water vapor turns back into a liquid is called the **dew point.** If air is cooled below the dew point, some of the water vapor in the air forms tiny droplets of water. These droplets collect to make clouds. Fog is a low-lying layer of cloud. When the droplets become large enough and heavy enough, they fall as rain.

Sleet, Snow, and Hail
If the temperature in a cloud is below freezing, the water vapor may form ice crystals. These then fall as snow.

Sleet is rain that freezes as it falls through a layer of cold air near the ground. Hail is made up of lumps of ice. These lumps form as winds toss ice crystals up and down in a rain cloud. Each time the crystals move up, water freezes around them. Heavy lumps of ice form and fall to the ground. Hail usually occurs during strong thunderstorms.

✓ **What are three frozen forms of precipitation?**

How Clouds Form

Clouds form whenever water droplets or ice particles collect in the atmosphere. A lot of moisture in the air and cold temperatures help clouds to form.

There are three main kinds of clouds. A **cirrus cloud** is a high-altitude cloud made of ice crystals. *Cirrus* means "curled." Cirrus clouds are thin and feathery. They are usually bright white.

A **stratus cloud** is a low-lying gray cloud that covers a wide area. Stratus clouds are made of water droplets. *Stratus* means "spread out." Stratus clouds form broad, flat layers. They float low in the sky and usually appear as an unbroken cloud cover. Stratus clouds are often a sign of rainy weather.

Cirrus clouds usually contain ice crystals because the surrounding air is very cold.

Stratus clouds often look like a blanket in the sky.

A **cumulus cloud** is a big, puffy low-altitude cloud that usually signals good weather. Cumulus clouds are made of water droplets. *Cumulus* means "heaped up." A *thunderhead* is a special kind of cumulus cloud. Thunderheads usually bring storms.

✓ **What do the three main kinds of clouds look like?**

Lesson Review

1. How does water enter the air?

2. What causes rain?

3. How do clouds form?

4. CRITICAL THINKING Sometimes water drops fall through the air without ever reaching the ground. What happens to them?

Cumulus clouds can grow very tall.

On the Cutting Edge

CLOUD SEEDING

Some places never get a steady supply of rain. Months can go by without rain. This causes problems for plants and animals in the area.

Sometimes rain can be brought to a dry place through a process called *cloud seeding*. An airplane flies into clouds with tops colder than 23 degrees Fahrenheit (°F). The airplane drops tiny crystals of a chemical called silver iodide onto the clouds. Water vapor in the clouds condenses around the crystals. Droplets form. If the droplets reach a certain size, they fall to the ground as rain. Sometimes cloud seeding is used to clear away fog over airports. Cloud seeding is not always successful. However, in some situations, it is worth trying.

An airplane drops crystals of silver iodide to try to make rain.

CRITICAL THINKING In what situations would cloud seeding be worth trying?

LAB ACTIVITY
Making a Cloud

BACKGROUND
Cooling can cause water vapor to condense into liquid water. But the vapor needs a surface to condense onto. Water vapor condenses onto tiny particles of dust in the air. This forms the droplets that make up clouds.

PURPOSE
You will observe how particles in the air help clouds to form.

  Safety Alert

Always keep hair and clothing away from an open flame.

MATERIALS
paper, pencil, safety goggles, jar with lid, pitcher of warm water, aluminum foil tray, ice, matches, wooden splint

WHAT TO DO
1. Put on your safety goggles.
2. Fill the jar with warm water. Put the lid on and let the jar stand for 2 minutes.
3. Empty the jar and replace the cover. Immediately place a tray of ice cubes on the lid. Observe the jar for 1 minute. Record your observations.
4. Rinse the jar and repeat Step 2.
5. Ask your teacher to use a match to light the splint. Blow out the splint immediately.
6. Hold the smoldering splint inside the jar so that some smoke enters it.
7. Replace the lid and cover it with the tray of ice cubes. Observe the jar again for 1 minute and record your observations.

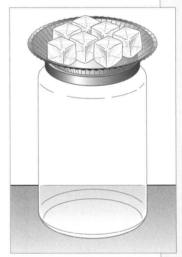

Step 3

DRAW CONCLUSIONS
- Did you see a thicker cloud in Step 3 or in Step 7?
- What caused the thicker cloud to form?
- What three things are needed for clouds to form?

SCIENCE IN YOUR LIFE
Wind Chill Temperature

A cold day feels a lot colder if there is a strong wind. To dress for the weather on a cold day, you need to know more than air temperature. You also need to know the *wind chill temperature*. The faster the wind blows, the quicker your body will lose heat. So, the faster the wind blows, the colder you will feel.

Wind Chill Temperatures

Actual Temperature	Wind Speed (miles per hour)				
	5	10	15	20	25
50°F	48°	40°	36°	32°	30°
40°F	37°	28°	22°	18°	16°
30°F	27°	16°	9°	4°	0°
20°F	16°	4°	−5°	−10°	−15°
10°F	6°	−9°	−18°	−25°	−29°
0°F	−5°	−21°	−36°	−39°	−44°
−10°F	−15°	−33°	−45°	−53°	−59°
−20°F	−26°	−46°	−58°	−67°	−74°
−30°F	−36°	−58°	−72°	−82°	−87°

The chart shows wind chill temperatures. The first column lists the actual air temperatures. The other columns show how air at that temperature feels when it is moving at a certain speed. For example, look at the third row. It shows wind chill temperatures when the actual air temperature is 30°F. When the air is moving 5 miles per hour, the air feels as if is 27°F. When the air is moving 25 miles per hour, the air feels as if it is 0°F. So, when you go outside, you should dress for the wind chill temperature, not the actual temperature.

Use the chart to answer these questions.

1. What is the wind chill temperature if the actual temperature is 20°F with a wind of 15 miles per hour?

2. If the wind is 25 miles per hour and the wind chill temperature is −44°F, what is the actual temperature?

3. What would you wear to go outside if the actual temperature was 40°F with a wind of 10 miles per hour? Why?

Critical Thinking

It is 50°F outside. The weather forecast calls for winds to increase from 5 miles per hour to 25 miles per hour. How would you explain to friends going outside that it will be colder than they think?

23 > Review

Summary The Earth's atmosphere is divided into layers. It also has properties such as air pressure, winds, and clouds that affect our daily life.

Lesson 23.1 The atmosphere is a mixture of gases, including water vapor. The atmosphere has five layers.

Lesson 23.2 Air pressure is the weight of gases pressing down on the Earth. Warm air rises. Cold air sweeps in to fill the space. This sets up a convection current. Convection currents cause most winds. There are also local winds caused by the Earth's surface features.

Lesson 23.3 There is always some moisture in the air. Precipitation is any kind of moisture that falls to the ground. Rain, snow, hail, and sleet are forms of precipitation. Clouds are made of water droplets or ice.

Vocabulary Review

Complete each sentence with a term from the list.

air pressure

atmosphere

barometer

dew point

humidity

precipitation

stratosphere

troposphere

1. Water vapor turns to liquid water at the _____.
2. Ozone is a thin layer of gas found in the _____.
3. The weight of gases pressing down on the Earth is _____.
4. A _____ is used to measure air pressure.
5. Any water that falls from the air is _____.
6. Air that surrounds the Earth makes up the _____.
7. Water in the air is called _____.
8. We live in the layer of the atmosphere called the _____.

Chapter Quiz

Write your answers on a separate sheet of paper.

Test Tip
Review the pictures and captions in the chapter. Try explaining to a friend what each picture shows.

1. What are the layers of the atmosphere, starting from the nearest to the Earth?

2. What causes air pressure?

3. What happens when sunlight hits clouds?

4. How does uneven heating of the atmosphere cause winds?

5. What are three surface features that can cause local winds?

6. What kind of wind occurs when the warm air over land rises and the cold air over the ocean rushes in?

7. What happens to air cooled below the dew point?

8. How are sleet, snow, and hail different from each other?

9. What are the three main groups of clouds?

10. What kind of cloud is a thunderhead?

Research Project

The Beaufort scale is a scale of wind speed. Do research and write a report on the Beaufort scale. The report should describe the scale and explain how it is used. Use the Beaufort scale to estimate the wind speed near your home each day for a week. Include this information in your report.

Tornadoes are the Earth's most violent windstorms. A tornado may last only a few minutes. However, in that time, it can completely destroy buildings. What other problems might tornadoes cause?

Learning Objectives

- Compare and contrast weather and climate.
- Describe how air masses and fronts affect weather.
- Explain how air pressure affects weather.
- Identify different kinds of violent storms.
- Identify the three main types of climate.
- LAB ACTIVITY: Observe the movements of cold fronts and warm fronts.
- ON-THE-JOB SCIENCE: Relate gathering weather data to weather forecasting.

Words to Know

weather	the condition of the atmosphere at a certain time and place
climate	the average weather in a region over many years
air mass	a huge body of air that moves from place to place
front	the place where two air masses of different temperatures meet
occluded front	the front that forms when a cold front overtakes a warm front
meteorology	the scientific study of the Earth's atmosphere and weather
cumulonimbus cloud	a tall, thick, white cumulus cloud that is dark at the bottom; also known as a thunderhead
cyclone	an area of low air pressure with circling winds
hurricane	a stormy cyclone with high winds that forms over the Atlantic Ocean
typhoon	a stormy cyclone with high winds that forms over the Pacific Ocean
tornado	a cyclone that extends down from a cumulonimbus cloud and forms a funnel-shaped cloud

Words to Know

weather	the condition of the atmosphere at a certain time and place
climate	the average weather in a region over many years
air mass	a huge body of air that moves from place to place
front	the place where two air masses of different temperatures meet
occluded front	the front that forms when a cold front overtakes a warm front
meteorology	the scientific study of the Earth's atmosphere and weather

What Are Weather and Climate?

Remember
Air pressure is the weight of the atmosphere pressing down on the Earth's surface. Humidity is the amount of water vapor in the air. Precipitation is any form of water that falls to the Earth's surface from clouds.

Some people live where palm trees grow. They enjoy warm **weather** all year long. Other people live where it snows throughout most of the year. They usually have cold weather. Weather is the condition of the atmosphere at a certain time and place. **Climate** is the average weather in a region over many years.

Weather and climate affect people's lives in many ways. Weather affects what people wear and what activities they can do outside. Climate affects outdoor jobs such as farming, construction, and tourism. Many people choose where to live depending on the climate.

✓ **How are weather and climate different?**

Air Masses

Temperature, air pressure, humidity, wind speed, clouds, and precipitation are all part of what makes up weather. However, the weather in an area changes because of air masses. An **air mass** is a huge body of air that moves from place to place.

Air masses can cover land or ocean areas. They can have high or low humidity. They can be cold or hot. An air mass over the North Pole is very cold. An air mass over the equator is very warm. As an air mass travels over an area, it can change the area's temperature or humidity.

Air masses can meet, but they do not mix together. The place where two air masses of different temperatures meet is called a **front.** Clouds and precipitation, such as rain and snow, often form at fronts.

When a warm air mass moves into a cold air mass, a *warm front* forms. As the warm air rises over the cold air, the warm air cools. As it cools, water vapor condenses and forms precipitation. There is usually rain or snow along a warm front. After a warm front passes, the temperature rises.

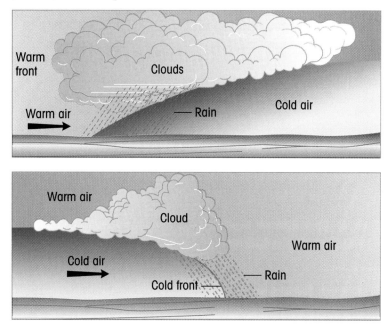

Figure 24-1 *A warm front forms when a warm air mass meets and rises over a cold air mass.*

Figure 24-2 *A cold front forms when a cold air mass meets and moves under a warm air mass.*

When a cold air mass moves against a warm air mass, a *cold front* forms. The cold air pushes forward. This forces the warm air up over the cold air. The rising warm air quickly cools, causing short but heavy rain or snow showers. Temperatures drop as the cold front passes.

Cold fronts move much faster than warm fronts. Sometimes a cold front overtakes a warm front. This is called an **occluded front.** An occluded front produces calmer weather than a cold front or a warm front.

✓ **What is the difference between a warm front and a cold front?**

Weather Forecasting

Weather forecasting is based on **meteorology,** the scientific study of the Earth's atmosphere and weather. Information used for weather forecasts comes from many places. Weather stations have instruments that measure air pressure, humidity, wind speed and direction, air temperature, and the amount of precipitation.

Weather information also comes from satellites, weather balloons, ocean floats, airplanes that carry instruments, and radar. Computers collect and process the data. The computers then make models of possible weather patterns.

Meteorologists use computers to put the information on maps. They update the maps several times each day. Other meteorologists study the maps and computer models. Computers may also help meteorologists analyze the data.

Weather station

✓ **How do weather stations help meteorologists forecast the weather?**

Lesson Review

1. What happens when a cold air mass passes?

2. What are three ways meteorologists gather weather data?

3. **CRITICAL THINKING** How would our lives be different if there were no weather forecasts?

Words to Know

cumulonimbus cloud	a tall, thick, white cumulus cloud that is dark at the bottom; also known as a thunderhead
cyclone	an area of low air pressure with circling winds
hurricane	a stormy cyclone with high winds that forms over the Atlantic Ocean
typhoon	a stormy cyclone with high winds that forms over the Pacific Ocean
tornado	a cyclone that extends down from a cumulonimbus cloud and forms a funnel-shaped cloud

Thunderstorms can produce heavy rainfall.

Thunderstorms

A thunderstorm is a short, violent storm with rain, lightning, and thunder. It happens when warm, moist air rises quickly. The air may be forced upward by a mountain or a cold front. The warm, humid air cools quickly as it rises. This turns the moisture in the air into rain.

Thunderstorms may also occur on hot summer afternoons, when the Earth's surface heats moist air. As the warm air rises and then cools, it forms cumulus clouds. More warm air, called an *updraft*, blows up through the clouds. The updraft turns the cumulus cloud into a **cumulonimbus cloud.** Cumulonimbus clouds are tall, thick, white cumulus clouds with dark bases. You may also know them as thunderheads.

Electric charges build up in thunderheads. When these electric charges are thrown off, or *discharged*, they cause lightning. The heat from the lightning suddenly expands the air. This causes the sound of thunder.

If you are outdoors during a thunderstorm, look for shelter. If you cannot find shelter, lie down or crouch in a low spot, such as a ditch. Do not look for shelter under a tree. The tree might be hit by lightning, or the wind might break off branches.

✓ **What causes thunderstorms?**

Highs and Lows

If you watch weather reports on TV, you probably have heard about *highs* and *lows*. A high is an area where the air pressure is very high. A low is an area where the air pressure is very low.

Wind is moving air. It forms when air moves from high-pressure areas to low-pressure areas. Usually winds blow out from the center of a high toward a low.

Most of the time, high air pressure means clear weather. Low air pressure means rainy or stormy weather. Almost all storms are caused by lows.

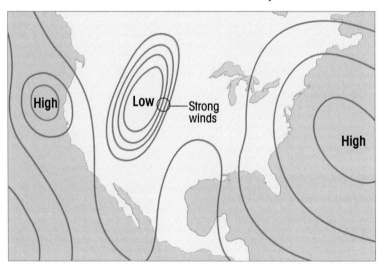

Figure 24-3 *The blue lines on this weather map show the differences in air pressure. The closer the lines are to each other, the stronger the wind in that area is.*

✓ **What causes wind?**

Low Pressure Storms

A **cyclone** is an area of low air pressure. It has circling winds. The low pressure is caused by warm air rising. Winds blow toward the opening left by the rising air. As the winds blow, they circle around the center of the low. Cyclones travel as they spin around. They move across land at a rate of 500 to 1,000 miles (800 to 1,600 kilometers) a day.

A **hurricane** is a stormy cyclone with high winds. It forms over the Atlantic Ocean near the equator. A hurricane gets energy from warm ocean water. As a hurricane moves into colder northern waters or over land, it usually weakens. However, it can do a lot of damage along the coast and cause flooding inland.

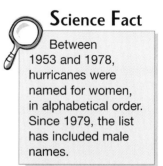

Science Fact

Between 1953 and 1978, hurricanes were named for women, in alphabetical order. Since 1979, the list has included male names.

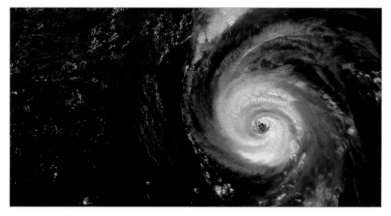

This satellite photo shows a hurricane moving toward the United States.

A storm has to have winds of at least 74 miles (119 kilometers) per hour to be a hurricane. However, hurricane winds of more than 130 miles (208 kilometers) per hour are common. A stormy cyclone with high winds that forms over the Pacific Ocean has a different name. It is called a **typhoon**.

A **tornado** is a cyclone that extends down from a cumulonimbus cloud and forms a funnel-shaped cloud. The spinning winds sometimes reach speeds of 300 miles (480 kilometers) per hour.

Safety Alert

Always stay inside if there is a tornado warning. It is best to go to the basement. If there is no basement, stay on the ground floor. Keep away from windows. Crawl under a stairway or heavy table and cover your head.

The swirling winds of a tornado can destroy everything in its path.

Tornadoes do not cover as much ground as most cyclones. However, they are much more violent. Most of the tornadoes on Earth occur in the Great Plains and the Mississippi Valley of the United States.

✓ **What are four low-pressure storms, and how are they formed?**

Lesson Review

1. Why does lightning form in thunderstorms?

2. What kind of weather does high air pressure bring? What does low air pressure bring?

3. **CRITICAL THINKING** Why do hurricanes get weaker over cold water and land?

A Closer Look

MORE ABOUT HURRICANES

Hurricanes produce strong winds. They also produce heavy rain and *storm surges*. A storm surge is a rise in sea level that is caused by winds pushing seas onto the shore. About 90 percent of hurricane deaths are caused by flooding, not by wind.

The Saffir-Simpson Scale		
Category	Wind Speed (miles per hour)	Damage
1	74–95	Minor
2	96–110	Moderate
3	111–130	Extensive
4	131–155	Extreme
5	more than 155	Catastrophic

The Saffir-Simpson scale measures the wind speed of hurricanes. The category number tells the strength and amount of damage they can cause.

Hurricanes are violent storms, except at their centers. The center of a hurricane is called its *eye*. The eye is usually about 20 miles (32 kilometers) across. There are no winds in the eye. The air pressure in the eye is extremely low. The sun might even shine in the eye of a hurricane.

CRITICAL THINKING Why do people sometimes think a hurricane has ended when the eye passes over?

What Affects Climate?

Many things affect an area's climate, such as latitude, mountains, water, and ocean currents.

Latitude

Regions near the equator get a lot of sunlight. The rays of the sun strike the Earth most directly at the equator. Near the poles, the rays spread out over a much larger area. This makes the rays weaker. The sun's rays also lose some of their energy as they pass through the denser atmosphere near the poles.

Mountains

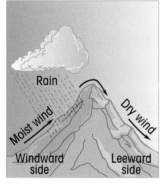

Mountains can affect climate. They stop the flow of moist winds. The land on the side of a mountain facing the wind gets a lot of rainfall. This happens because winds drive clouds over the mountains. As the clouds rise, they cool and drop rain or snow. After crossing the mountain, the winds are drier. Often a desert is on the *leeward* side of a mountain, which is the side away from the wind.

Figure 24-4 *Warm air rises and drops its rain on the windward side of mountains.*

Water

Large bodies of water affect climate, too. This is because water absorbs and holds heat well. Places near water have milder temperatures all year than places inland.

Ocean Currents

Ocean currents also affect climate. For example, the warm Gulf Stream current flows across the northern Atlantic Ocean toward Europe. This current warms the winter air over northwestern Europe.

✓ **What are four things that affect climate?**

Types of Climate

The three main types of climate zones are *tropical*, *polar*, and *temperate*. Tropical climate zones are very warm and have no true winter season. These climates often have heavy rainfall. Hawaii has a tropical climate.

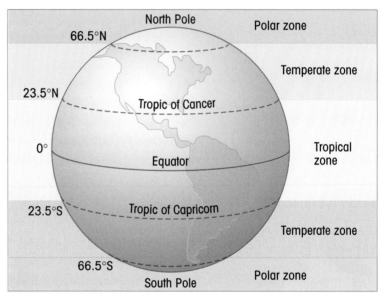

Figure 24-5 *The Earth has three main types of climate. They are tropical, polar, and temperate.*

Polar climates have no true summer season. They have only a little precipitation. This is usually in the form of fine, dry snow. This is because the air is too cold to hold much water. Northern Alaska has a polar climate.

Temperate climates are warmer than polar climates. They are also cooler than tropical climates. Summers are warm. Winters are cold. The precipitation varies. Most of the United States has a temperate climate.

Any kind of climate can be dangerous for people. People can get frostbite from being out in the cold and wind too long. Exposure to too much sun can cause sunburn. High heat and humidity can cause heat stroke.

✓ **What are the three main types of climates? How are they different?**

Lesson Review

1. How can mountains affect climate?

2. How are seasons in polar climates different from seasons in tropical climates?

3. **CRITICAL THINKING** Which climate would require the greatest variety of clothing? Why?

Great Moments in Science

BENJAMIN BANNEKER AND THE *FARMER'S ALMANAC*

Benjamin Banneker was an African-American scientist and inventor who lived at the time of the American Revolution. Most African Americans were slaves at that time. Banneker was a free man who owned his own farm.

Banneker was excellent at math. The new president, George Washington, had heard of his skill. Banneker was invited to help do a land survey of the new country's capital in Washington, D.C.

In Banneker's time, most families had an almanac. An almanac is a book of dates, information, and weather forecasts. Since most Americans were farmers, this book was very important. Banneker decided to create his own almanac.

Banneker farmed by day and studied the sky at night. He used a compass and ruler to measure the movements of the sun and moon. He calculated exactly when the tides would come in and how high they would be. He used a telescope to study the rising and setting of the stars and planets. Then he forecast the weather for the coming year based on what he saw and calculated.

Benjamin Banneker (1731–1806) was one of the first African-American scientists. The picture above shows him on a postage stamp.

Banneker's almanac was a great success. Farmers all over the new United States used it. By 1797, at least 28 different versions of Banneker's *Farmer's Almanac* had been printed.

CRITICAL THINKING Why would an almanac be important to farmers?

LAB ACTIVITY
Observing Fronts

BACKGROUND

If you watch the weather, you can tell when a cold front or warm front has passed. A cold front often brings a short, heavy burst of rain or snow. Then the temperature drops. A warm front often brings a longer period of lighter precipitation. Then the temperature rises.

PURPOSE

You will observe the weather for three days to identify the passing of fronts.

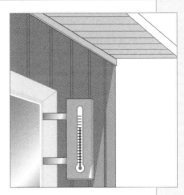

Measure the outdoor temperature in the shade.

MATERIALS

paper, pen, outdoor thermometer

WHAT TO DO

1. Make three copies of the chart to the right.
2. Set up a thermometer outside where you can take readings. Put it in a protected area that is not in direct sunlight.

Date: _____	Temperature	Precipitation	Wind
10:00 A.M.			
12:00 NOON			
2:00 P.M.			
4:00 P.M.			

3. Observe the weather four times during the day: 10:00 A.M., 12:00 noon, 2:00 P.M., and 4:00 P.M. Fill in and date your chart during each observation. Include the temperature reading on the thermometer; the type of precipitation if any; and whether the wind is strong, light, or calm (no wind).
4. Repeat Step 3 for two more days. Record your observations on your other two charts.

DRAW CONCLUSIONS

- Did you observe the passing of any fronts?

- If fronts did pass, what kind were they? Explain how you know.

Jane Franklin is a television meteorologist. Each day people see her weather forecast on TV. During weather emergencies, such as tornadoes, Jane gives information that helps people stay safe.

When Jane was growing up, she loved to watch clouds and lightning in the sky. She wanted to know how storms occur and why weather changes each day. After high school, Jane earned a degree in meteorology at college.

Jane could have worked for the National Weather Service, an airline, the military, or a university. However, Jane wanted to do weather forecasts for a TV station.

It takes Jane several hours to prepare for the 6:00 P.M. news.

Jane's TV station has a computer that gets weather data and forecasts from the National Weather Service. They have radar and satellite photos that show approaching storms. Jane uses all of this data to come up with her own forecasts each day. She also uses the data to create weather maps. Jane writes her own script for the TV weather report. If there is severe weather, such as a flood or tornado, she works extra hours.

Critical Thinking

Jane lives in a temperate climate zone. During which season were these readings recorded? Explain your answer.

Jane made this chart of weather data one day. Use it to answer the questions below.

	12:00 NOON	1:00 P.M.	2:00 P.M.	3:00 P.M.	4:00 P.M.
Temperature	80°F	83°F	84°F	82°F	75°F
Precipitation	—	—	Rain	Rain	—

1. At what time was the temperature the highest?
2. At which times was rain recorded?
3. What happened to the temperature after the rain?

Summary
Weather is the day-to-day condition of the atmosphere. Climate is the average weather in a region over many years. Both weather and climate affect people's lives.

Lesson 24.1
Air masses take on the characteristics of the land or water below them. Fronts are formed when two air masses meet. The National Weather Service gathers weather information. Meteorologists use this data to make forecasts.

Lesson 24.2
Severe storms are caused by low air pressure. Winds rush in to low-pressure centers. A cyclone is an area of low pressure. Hurricanes and typhoons are stormy cyclones. Tornadoes extend down from cumulonimbus clouds.

Lesson 24.3
The three main climates are tropical, polar, and temperate. Climate is affected by location, land features, and water.

Vocabulary Review

air mass

climate

front

hurricane

meteorology

tornado

typhoon

weather

Match each definition with a term from the list.

1. The average weather in a region over many years

2. The study of the atmosphere and weather

3. A huge body of air that moves from place to place

4. A stormy cyclone that forms over the Pacific Ocean

5. A stormy cyclone that forms over the Atlantic Ocean

6. Where cold and warm air masses meet

7. The condition of the atmosphere at a certain time and place

8. A cyclone that extends down from a cumulonimbus cloud and forms a funnel-shaped cloud

Chapter Quiz

Write your answers on a separate sheet of paper.

1. Which is more likely to change day to day, climate or weather?

2. How do air masses affect weather?

3. How does a cold front affect the weather?

4. How does an occluded front affect the weather?

5. What kind of weather do cumulonimbus clouds bring?

6. What type of weather would you find in a high-pressure area? What type would you find in a low-pressure area?

7. How are hurricanes and typhoons alike?

8. How do mountains affect weather?

9. Why is there so little precipitation in polar climates?

10. How are tropical and temperate climates different?

Test Tip

Read all of the direction lines before you begin a test. If you do not understand some of them, ask your teacher to explain what you have to do *before* you start to write.

Research Project

Choose an important recent weather event in your area. Find a newspaper or magazine article or an Internet site about how this event affected your community. Then write a report about the event. If possible, interview someone in your community or write to someone at a disaster relief organization. Ask about his or her experiences during the event. Add the person's comments to the report.

Unit 6 **Review**

Choose the letter for the correct answer to each question.

Use the diagram to answer Questions 1 to 3.

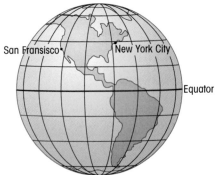

1. Which layer of the Earth does a globe show?

    A. inner core

    B. outer core

    C. crust

    D. mantle

2. What are the north-south lines on a globe called?

    A. equator lines

    B. lines of latitude

    C. lines of longitude

    D. degree lines

3. What happens to time if you go from the Eastern time zone in New York City to the Pacific time zone in San Francisco?

    A. The time does not change.

    B. You gain several hours.

    C. You lose several hours.

    D. You lose one whole day.

4. Which kind of plates form the Earth's crust?

    A. plates of melted rock

    B. plates of solid rock that slowly shift position

    C. plates of solid rock that do not move

    D. plates that hold only the continents

5. Which type of rock forms from particles pressed together?

    A. sedimentary rock

    B. marble rock

    C. igneous rock

    D. metamorphic rock

6. In which layer of the atmosphere can you find the Earth's weather?

    A. thermosphere

    B. mesosphere

    C. stratosphere

    D. troposphere

7. Which front forms when a warm air mass moves into a cold air mass?

    A. a cold front

    B. an occluded front

    C. a hot front

    D. a warm front

Critical Thinking

Which climate is probably easiest to live in: tropical, polar, or temperate? Explain your answer.

Unit 7 ▶ Earth Science: Part II

This valley used to be shallow and narrow. However, a glacier carved it wider and deeper. When the glacier melted, it left the beautiful valley you see. These changes took a very long time.

The Earth has changed often over its long history. Earth scientists study these changes. The chart shows some events that can change the Earth and how long they usually take. Use the chart to answer these questions.

Event	Time It Takes
Lightning striking	A few seconds
Earthquake	A few minutes
Thunderstorm	An hour
Volcanic eruption	Several days
Formation of a layer of soil	10,000 years
Carving of valley by glacier	500,000 years
Formation of a mountain	50 million years

1. Which events take place over a short period of time?

2. Which events take place over long periods of time?

3. Compared to the age of the Earth, do you think a hundred years is a long time? Explain.

Chapter 25 / The Earth's History

The Grand Canyon is a cut in the Earth's surface 1 mile (1.6 kilometers) deep. It is a beautiful sight. It is also a useful tool for scientists. The Grand Canyon provides many clues to the Earth's past. What kinds of clues do you think it provides?

Learning Objectives

- Explain how uplifting and folding affects rock layers.
- Describe how geologists use radioactive dating to tell the age of rocks.
- Explain what fossils can show us about the Earth's history.
- Identify the four geological eras.
- List the main geological events and important forms of life during each geological era.
- LAB ACTIVITY: Identify a geological era by its fossils.
- SCIENCE IN YOUR LIFE: Relate field work by students to the study of fossils.

Words to Know

uplifting and folding	a geological process that bends layers of the Earth's crust and sometimes turns them upside down
radioactive dating	a way to find the age of rocks by measuring the decay, or breaking down, of radioactive elements in them
geological era	a huge period of time in the Earth's history
Precambrian era	the geological era that started 4.5 billion years ago and lasted nearly 4 billion years
Paleozoic era	the geological era that started 570 million years ago and lasted 346 million years
Mesozoic era	the geological era that started 225 million years ago and lasted 160 million years
Cenozoic era	the geological era of today that began 65 million years ago

Words to Know

uplifting and folding	a geological process that bends layers of the Earth's crust and sometimes turns them upside down
radioactive dating	a way to find the age of rocks by measuring the decay, or breaking down, of radioactive elements in them

Dating Rocks

Remember
Fossils are the remains of organisms that lived long ago.

The walls of the Grand Canyon have layers made up of many kinds of rock. Each layer is from a different period in the Earth's history. In a way, the striped walls of the Grand Canyon give a history of the area. Its rocks and fossils tell the story of our planet. Scientists date these rocks to learn about the Earth and its organisms.

Layers of rock are arranged by age. The lowest layer is usually the oldest. The top layer is usually the youngest. However, shifting of the Earth's crust can cause **uplifting and folding**. Uplifting and folding is a very slow geological process that bends layers of the Earth's crust and sometimes turns them upside down. Older rock layers may end up above younger ones.

Remember
Radioactive means "giving off radiation, or harmful rays."

Radioactive dating is a way to find the age of rocks by measuring the decay of radioactive elements in them. As a radioactive element decays, it slowly breaks down into other elements. Each element decays at a certain rate. By comparing the decay rates of certain radioactive elements in rocks, scientists can tell when the rocks formed. These elements act as geological clocks. The radioactive element uranium is often used to find the age of rocks.

✓ **What does the arrangement of rock layers usually tell us about the age of rocks?**

Fossils and the History of Life

Geologists can learn a lot about the Earth's history from fossils. For example, fossils show that the Earth's continents and climates have changed a great deal over time. Fossils of tropical plants have been discovered close to the Arctic Circle. The remains of wooly mammoths have been found in New York State. Wooly mammoths lived in very cold climates.

✓ **What do fossils tell geologists about climate?**

Lesson Review

1. How does uplifting and folding affect rock layers?

2. How does radioactive dating determine the age of rocks?

3. CRITICAL THINKING What would you think if you found a fish fossil in desert rock? Why?

On the Cutting Edge

GREENLAND ICE CORE PROJECT

Geologists can also learn about the past from the Earth's ice sheets. A huge ice sheet more than 1 mile (1.6 kilometers) thick covers Greenland. The ice built up over thousands of years and shows how the climate changed over that time. The ice also contains particles and gases from the ancient air that became trapped. So, each ice layer gives us clues to patterns of precipitation, gases in the air, and past volcanic eruptions.

In 1993, an American team of scientists drilled a core 9,160 feet (2,792 meters) into the ice. Scientists are still studying the core. It contains a record of the Earth's history that goes back more than 110,000 years.

CRITICAL THINKING What might scientists find in an ice core that shows ancient volcanic eruptions?

Scientists drilled holes in Greenland's ice to unlock its secrets.

Words to Know

geological era	a huge period of time in the Earth's history
Precambrian era	the geological era that started 4.5 billion years ago and lasted nearly 4 billion years
Paleozoic era	the geological era that started 570 million years ago and lasted 346 million years
Mesozoic era	the geological era that started 225 million years ago and lasted 160 million years
Cenozoic era	the geological era of today that began 65 million years ago

Scientists divide the history of the Earth into four main time periods. Each time period is called a **geological era.** A geological era is a huge period of time in the Earth's history. Each era has different kinds of fossils. The land and climate changed in each era. At the end of each era, many life forms suddenly became extinct.

Remember
Extinct means "gone forever."

The Precambrian Era

The **Precambrian era** started when the Earth formed. Most scientists think this happened about 4.5 billion years ago. The era lasted nearly 4 billion years. That is most of geological time. Every continent has Precambrian rocks. Some of the granite and marble used in building today is from the Precambrian era.

There are few fossils from this era. However, scientists have found signs of early plant life and bacteria. They have also found fossil mud tunnels made by worms.

✓ **How long did the Precambrian era last?**

The Paleozoic Era

The **Paleozoic era** started about 570 million years ago. It lasted about 346 million years. The Paleozoic era is known as the Age of Invertebrates and Marine Life. There are a lot of fossils from this period. Scientists have found fossils of jellyfish, sponges, snails, seaweed, and ferns.

Remember
An invertebrate is an animal without a backbone.

Many coal beds were formed in the Paleozoic era. Coal is made mostly from the remains of plants. This suggests that many plants grew during this era. The Earth must have been warm and wet. There must have been many swamps filled with giant ferns.

Near the end of the Paleozoic era, many mountain ranges formed. The Appalachian Mountains in the eastern United States are an example. As parts of the Earth's crust rose up from the sea, many swamps dried up. Many of the ferns died out.

✓ **Why do scientists call the Paleozoic era the Age of Invertebrates and Marine Life?**

Fossils show that ferns were common during parts of the Paleozoic era.

The Mesozoic Era

The **Mesozoic era** began about 225 million years ago and lasted about 160 million years. It is known as the Age of Reptiles because there were so many reptiles during this era. Flowering plants replaced the ferns that died out at the end of the Paleozoic era.

The animals known as dinosaurs were reptiles. Many kinds of dinosaurs lived during the Mesozoic era. Some dinosaurs lived in the forests. Some lived in swamps. Others lived on the open plains. Some dinosaurs were as small as chickens. Others were as large as houses. Some dinosaurs ate only meat. Others ate just plants. Some dinosaurs traveled in herds, and most were able to move fast.

The Earth was very dry at the beginning of the Mesozoic era. There were many volcanoes erupting. Later in the era, the Sierra Nevada mountains and the Coast Ranges of California were pushed up. There were fruit trees, willow trees, grasses, and grains. Dinosaurs became extinct by the end of the Mesozoic era.

✓ **What large group of reptiles became extinct by the end of the Mesozoic era?**

Figure 25-1 *Huge dinosaurs, such as the plant-eating* Apatosaurus, *lived during the Mesozoic era.*

The Cenozoic Era

The **Cenozoic era** is the geological era of today. It began about 65 million years ago. This era is known as the Age of Mammals and Birds.

There have been several ice ages in the Cenozoic era. During each one, huge glaciers spread south from the Arctic Circle. The glaciers covered the northern parts of Europe, Asia, and North America. The ice was almost one mile (1.6 kilometers) thick in places. The last ice age ended about 12,000 years ago.

Humans first appeared late in the Cenozoic era. There is evidence of species with human features that dates back several million years. But these pre-humans were not as tall as humans today. Their brains were smaller. Their skulls were not as rounded as ours. They also did not walk as erect, or upright.

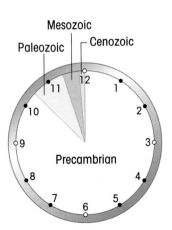

Figure 25-2 *Suppose all the Earth's history was squeezed into 12 hours. This clock shows how much time each geological era would last.*

The earliest fossil evidence of our species, called *Homo sapiens*, is between 100,000 and 120,000 years old. These early humans lived in Africa. By 40,000 years ago, *Homo sapiens* looked very much like humans do today. They had spread as far as Europe and Southeast Asia by that time.

✓ **According to the fossil evidence, when did humans first appear?**

The Future

No one knows for sure what will happen with the geology of the Earth in the future. Some scientists think that the Earth will have another ice age. Others think that pollution will cause the atmosphere to heat up and melt the polar caps. One thing is certain. Things will not stay the way they are today.

For sure, the sun will eventually use up its fuel and die out. All stars do. Without the sun, there can be no life on Earth. Fortunately, there is no danger of the sun dying out in your lifetime or the lifetime of your children or grandchildren. In fact, it will probably be billions of years before the sun dies out.

✓ **What do scientists think will happen to the Earth in the future?**

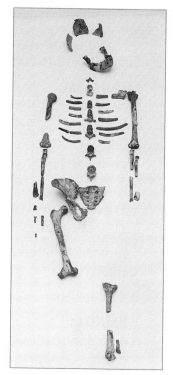

Scientists think this incomplete skeleton, nicknamed Lucy, is an early ancestor of modern humans.

Lesson Review

1. Which geological era started when the Earth formed?

2. During what era did most of the coal found today form?

3. What kinds of animals were found in great numbers during the Mesozoic era?

4. **CRITICAL THINKING** How would our knowledge of the Earth's history be different without fossils?

LAB ACTIVITY
Identifying Fossils From Rock Layers

BACKGROUND
Different types of plants and animals lived during each geological era. As a result, different types of fossils from each era were left behind.

PURPOSE
You will decide which geological era each fossil in the diagram comes from and if the fossils are arranged by age.

MATERIALS
paper, pencil

WHAT TO DO
1. Write the numbers *1*, *2*, and *3* on a sheet of paper.
2. Identify the fossils in the diagram. Look at the first layer. Decide which animal or plant formed each fossil shown there. Write the name next to the number on your paper.
3. Use information from this chapter to decide in which geological era each animal or plant lived. Write the name of the era next to the layer's number on your paper.
4. Repeat Steps 2 and 3 for the next two layers.

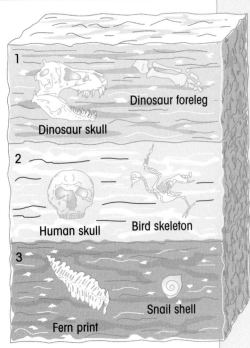

This diagram shows different fossils in different rock layers.

Labels in diagram: 1, Dinosaur foreleg, Dinosaur skull, 2, Human skull, Bird skeleton, 3, Snail shell, Fern print

DRAW CONCLUSIONS
- Notice the order of the layers. Are they correct from bottom to top? Explain your answer.
- Do you think any of these layers were folded and overturned? Explain your answer.
- What can you now say about identifying fossils from where they are found?

People who are interested in dinosaurs can go on digs with *paleontologists*. Paleontologists are scientists who use fossils to learn about life from the past, such as dinosaurs. Paleontologists explain to people on the dig how dinosaurs lived and how fossils formed. They teach the people how to look carefully for fossils. Then groups go out to the site and start digging as the paleontologists supervise their work.

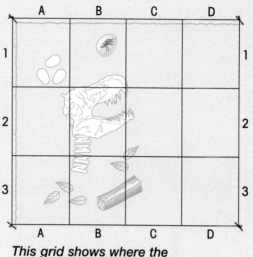

This grid shows where the teenagers found fossils.

A group of teenagers on a dig drew the grid to the right. It shows the area where they found fossils. The teens had to use drills to remove large pieces of rock that covered the fossils. Then they used small chisels, hammers, dental tools for scraping, and brushes to uncover the fossils.

Use the grid to answer these questions.

1. In which square did the teens find a dinosaur skull?

2. In which square should the teens dig to find the rest of the dinosaur—A2 or D1? Explain your answer.

3. In which square did the teens find an insect in hardened tree sap?

4. What objects do you think were found in square A1?

Critical Thinking

Why is it more likely that the dinosaur shown in the grid lived in a forest rather than in a desert?

Chapter

25 Review

Summary

Geologists study rocks to determine their age. The Earth's history is divided into huge periods of time called eras. Scientists use rocks and fossils to learn about each era.

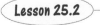

Lesson 25.1

Radioactive dating can determine the age of rocks. Scientists measure the rate of decay of radioactive elements in the rocks. This tells them how old certain rocks are. Fossils also provide scientists with clues to the Earth's history.

Lesson 25.2

Geologists divide the Earth's history into four eras. The Precambrian era is the longest era. Only the simplest life forms existed in this era. In the Paleozoic era, invertebrates and marine life were plentiful. Reptiles such as dinosaurs were common in the Mesozoic era. Humans appeared during the current era, the Cenozoic era.

Vocabulary Review

Write *true* or *false* for each sentence. If the sentence is false, replace the underlined term with another term to make the sentence true.

1. The geological era we live in is the <u>Cenozoic</u> era.

2. The <u>Paleozoic</u> era is known as the Age of Reptiles.

3. A process that sometimes turns layers of the Earth's crust upside down is called <u>uplifting and folding</u>.

4. A geological era is a <u>small</u> period of time in the Earth's history.

5. Dinosaurs lived during the <u>Mesozoic</u> era.

6. <u>Radioactive dating</u> is a way to find the age of rocks by measuring the decay of certain elements in them.

7. The Precambrian era lasted about 4 <u>million</u> years.

Chapter Quiz

Write your answers on a separate sheet of paper.

1. Why are the upper layers of rock in a canyon not always the youngest?

2. What happens to radioactive elements in rocks?

3. What is one important fact that fossils show geologists about the Earth's history?

4. Which are the four geological eras from earliest to most recent?

5. What major geological event started the Precambrian era?

6. In which era were dinosaurs common?

7. What happened to the Earth during the ice ages?

8. What kinds of animals became common in the era in which we live now?

9. According to fossil evidence, about how many years ago did *Homo sapiens* first appear?

10. What can you say for sure about the geology of the Earth in the future?

Test Tip

To practice for a test, make up questions for yourself as you read the chapter. When you finish your reading, try to answer the questions on your list.

Research Project

Research the work of a famous paleontologist such as Robert Bakker, Stephen Jay Gould, Jack Horner, Donald Johanson, Cathy Forster, or Paul Sereno. Find out what the scientist discovered and how it helped to build our knowledge of the Earth's history. Write a short report to present to the class. Include photos, maps, and drawings in your presentation.

Each day the ocean rises and falls along the coast. At low tide, the ocean pulls back from the coast. What was once underwater is exposed. What do you see in the picture that you would not see at high tide?

Learning Objectives

- Identify how much of the Earth's surface is covered by water.
- Compare surface currents and density currents.
- Identify four features of the ocean floor.
- Explain the causes and movements of waves and tides.
- Identify important ocean resources.
- Explain why the ocean is important to life on Earth.
- LAB ACTIVITY: Discover how temperature affects the movement of water in the ocean.
- ON-THE-JOB SCIENCE: Explore what an underwater photographer does.

Words to Know

oceanography	the study of the ocean
salinity	the measure of how much salt is in something
ocean current	a mass of water that flows like a river through an ocean
density current	a current caused by cold, salty water, which is very dense and sinks below warmer water
mid-ocean ridge	a huge mountain range that runs down the middle of some oceans
continental shelf	the gentle slope from the shore out to sea
continental slope	the steep cliff between the continental shelf and the bottom of the ocean
ocean basin	the bottom of the ocean floor
undertow	the backward movement of ocean water near the shore
seismic sea wave	a giant wave caused by an earthquake on the ocean floor
tide	the rise and fall of the oceans, caused by the sun's and moon's pull of gravity

Words to Know

oceanography	the study of the ocean
salinity	the measure of how much salt is in something
ocean current	a mass of water that flows like a river through an ocean
density current	a current caused by cold, salty water, which is very dense and sinks below warmer water
mid-ocean ridge	a huge mountain range that runs down the middle of some oceans
continental shelf	the gentle slope from the shore out to sea
continental slope	the steep cliff between the continental shelf and the bottom of the ocean
ocean basin	the bottom of the ocean floor

Remember
There are four oceans: the Arctic, the Atlantic, the Indian, and the Pacific. All the oceans are connected.

People usually think of land as making up most of the Earth. Yet 70 percent of the Earth is covered by water. Most of the Earth's organisms live in the ocean. The oceans, also called seas, are frontiers. A frontier is a place that has not been carefully explored. Scientists began only recently to study the oceans. The study of the oceans is called **oceanography**.

What Is Ocean Water Made Of?

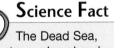

Science Fact
The Dead Sea, between Israel and Jordan, is 23 percent salt. Few plants and no fish live in it. The salinity level is too high.

If you ever got ocean water in your mouth when you were swimming, you know it contains salt. Ocean water also contains chemical elements such as chlorine, sodium, magnesium, and calcium.

Salinity is a measure of how much salt is in something. The salinity of ocean water is usually between 3.3 percent and 3.7 percent.

Salts are carried from the land to the oceans. First, weathering and erosion break down rocks containing sodium chloride (table salt) and other salts. This releases the salts into the soil. Then rainwater flows over and through the soil. This dissolves the salts. Rivers carry the salts to the ocean.

✓ **Where does the salt in ocean water come from?**

Ocean Currents

An **ocean current** is a mass of water that flows like a river through an ocean. Most currents are caused by winds that blow steadily in the same direction. These winds push water along with them. The rotation of the Earth also affects the direction of currents. It causes them to move in circular patterns.

The Gulf Stream System

A current of warm water flows through the Atlantic Ocean. This current is 30 miles (48 kilometers) wide. It is a different color than the ocean water around it. It is also warmer because it flows from the Gulf of Mexico, near the equator. This river of water is the Gulf Stream.

The Gulf Stream current sweeps north along the eastern coast of the United States to Newfoundland. There it meets the North Atlantic Current, which moves east across the Atlantic Ocean toward Europe.

Science Fact

Ships in the Atlantic Ocean going from North America to Europe try to stay in the Gulf Stream system. It helps them go faster. They avoid it coming back because it slows them down.

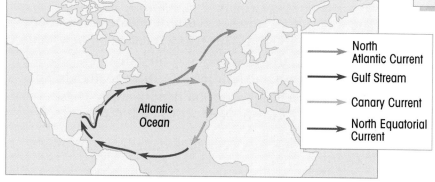

Figure 26-1 *Together the Gulf Stream and the North Atlantic Current make up the Gulf Stream system.*

Density Currents

Currents that are formed by winds are all surface currents. They flow near the surface of the oceans. Another kind of current is an undersea current. This current flows below the surface current. An undersea current is caused by a difference in the densities of ocean water.

A **density current** is caused by cold, salty water sinking below warmer water. Cold water is denser than warm water. Salt water is denser than fresh water. Water that is cold and salty is very dense and sinks. Warmer, less salty water rises.

Huge undersea currents occur between the North and South poles and the equator. Water near the poles is much saltier and colder than water near the equator. This dense water sinks and moves along the ocean bottom toward the equator. In warmer places, such as near the equator, the water rises. It takes the place of warm surface water that flows toward the poles.

Because of this process, every current has a countercurrent. A countercurrent flows either above or below the main current in the opposite direction. For example, the Gulf Stream has a colder undersea countercurrent flowing beneath its warmer surface. The undersea currents flowing from the poles have warmer surface currents flowing above them that come from the equator.

Science Fact

When ocean water near the poles freezes, the salt in the water does not freeze. The salt stays in the water. This makes water near the poles saltier than water near the equator.

The water of an undersea current usually rises when it gets close to land. This rising is called an *upwelling*. Upwellings carry minerals and the remains of sea life toward the surface. Fish feed on these materials. So, areas of upwellings are good fishing areas. These include the coasts of Peru, Chile, and California.

✓ **What are the two main types of ocean currents?**

The Ocean Floor

There are many of the same formations on the ocean floor as there are on land.

A **mid-ocean ridge** is a huge mountain range that runs down the middle of some oceans. Scientists think that new crust is made in these underwater mountain ranges. Hot magma pushes up through openings in the ridges. The magma then cools and hardens into rock on either side of the ridge. This causes *sea floor spreading*, which is the slow but steady pushing of the sea floor crust away from the ridge. Most underwater earthquakes occur along the mid-ocean ridge.

Remember
According to the theory of plate tectonics, the Earth's crust is broken into several major plates. These plates all float on the mantle. Landmasses and oceans ride on top of the plates.

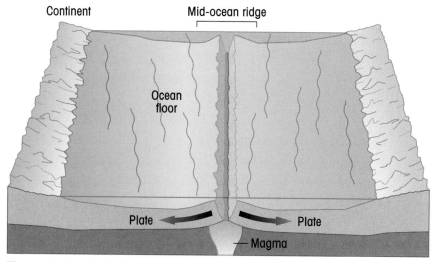

Figure 26-2 *As ocean plates move apart, magma rises to fill the space between them. This forms a mid-ocean ridge.*

Even though the ocean floor is spreading, this does not mean that the Earth's surface is getting bigger. Remember the theory of plate tectonics. Sometimes one plate slips under another plate. The lower plate melts, and the magma returns to the mantle. This happens in oceans as well as on land. Deep trenches form in the ocean where one plate slips under another plate.

The edges of the continents drop gradually to the bottom of the ocean. The gentle slope from the shore is called the **continental shelf.** The ocean floor drops off at the edge of the continental shelf. This steep cliff between the continental shelf and the bottom of the ocean is the **continental slope.** The continental slope leads to the **ocean basin,** the bottom of the ocean floor. Mid-ocean ridges and ocean trenches are found in the ocean basin.

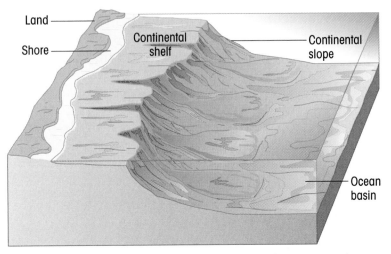

Figure 26-3 *Although we cannot see them, features such as mountains, valleys, and plains can be found on the ocean floor.*

✓ **What parts of the ocean floor are found from the coast to a mid-ocean ridge? Name them in order.**

Lesson Review

1. What substance makes up 3.3 percent to 3.7 percent of ocean water?

2. What is the Gulf Stream?

3. What happens during sea-floor spreading?

4. CRITICAL THINKING Why is most of the ocean still not explored?

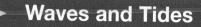

26·2 Waves and Tides

Words to Know

undertow   the backward movement of ocean water near the shore

seismic sea wave   a giant wave caused by an earthquake on the ocean floor

tide   the rise and fall of the oceans, caused by the sun's and moon's pull of gravity

Wind and Waves

Surfers can ride waves for fun.

Local winds cause most ocean waves. Underwater earthquakes and volcanoes can cause waves, too.

If you watch a bird resting on the ocean surface, you will see it rise and fall with the waves. The water under the bird seems to move forward, but the bird does not. This is because it is the wave's *energy* that moves forward. The water itself only moves up and down.

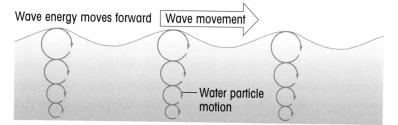
Wave energy moves forward | Wave movement |
Water particle motion

Figure 26-4 *The energy in waves moves forward. The water itself only moves in circles.*

You have probably seen waves, called *breakers*, hit the shore. These form because the lower part of the wave "drags" on the shallow bottom near the shore. So, the wave top spills forward, or breaks. After a wave breaks, water returns to the ocean under the breakers. The backward movement of this water near the shore is called **undertow**.

✓ **What causes most ocean waves?**

Seismic Sea Waves

Once in a while, a giant wave reaches the shore. Scientists call this giant wave a **seismic sea wave.** It is caused by an earthquake on the ocean floor. The word *seismic* means "having to do with earthquakes."

Ships at sea often do not notice seismic sea waves passing. In deep water, the waves are only about 1 or 2 yards (1 or 2 meters) high. However, as they reach the shore, these waves can be over 100 feet (30 meters) high. Seismic sea waves can travel more than 350 miles (560 kilometers) per hour and do a lot of damage when they crash into the shoreline.

✓ **What causes a seismic sea wave?**

A Closer Look

SEISMIC SEA WAVES

Seismic sea waves, or tsunamis, do not happen often. However, they can be destructive. They can race across the sea at hundreds of miles per hour. In the past, they have often struck without warning and have destroyed coastal areas. Many people have been swept out to sea by seismic sea waves.

A seismic sea wave almost 50 feet (15 meters) high hit Japan in 1993. It did great damage.

Today, the Tsunami Warning Center in Hawaii can save many people from harmful seismic sea waves. The center keeps track of earthquakes in the Pacific Ocean basin. That is where most seismic sea waves happen. The center also tracks the height and movement of waves. If a seismic sea wave forms, the center knows within an hour. It then warns coastal communities that a wave is on the way.

CRITICAL THINKING Why is it helpful to know a seismic sea wave is coming?

Tides

Ocean waters rise and fall on the shoreline twice a day. This rise and fall of the oceans is called a **tide.** Tides are caused by the sun's and moon's pull of gravity on the Earth.

The sun's and moon's gravity actually pulls the water back and forth as the Earth spins on its axis. The sun is much farther away from the Earth than the moon is. Therefore, the sun's pull on the Earth is not as strong as that of the moon's pull on the Earth.

During *high tide*, the water is as high as it gets on the shore. During *low tide*, the water is as low as it gets on the shore.

Twice a month the sun and moon lie in a straight line with the Earth. The combined gravity of both of these bodies makes their pull especially strong. So, high tides are very high. Low tides are very low. These tides are called *spring tides*.

Twice a month, the sun and moon form a right angle with the Earth. At these times, the sun's pull works against the moon's pull. That means the tides are neither very high nor very low. These are called *neap tides*.

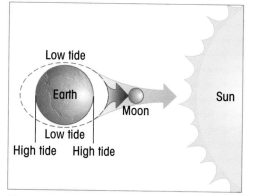

Figure 26-5 *Spring tides are very high and very low tides.*

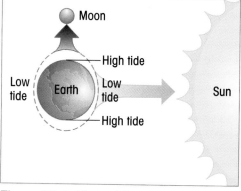

Figure 26-6 *Neap tides are neither very high nor very low.*

✓ **What causes tides?**

Lesson Review

1. Why do breakers form?

2. How do seismic sea waves cause damage?

3. What is the difference between a spring tide and a neap tide?

4. CRITICAL THINKING Why would an undertow be dangerous for swimmers?

On the Cutting Edge

EXPLORING THE OCEAN FLOOR

The ocean floor is totally dark and freezing cold. People cannot live in the high water pressure at the bottom of the ocean. For many years, it remained unexplored. Then scientists invented underwater research vessels called *submersibles*. These vessels can withstand great pressure. They have equipment for exploring the ocean floor, such as cameras, water testers, thermometers, and sonar.

New life forms, such as these 6-foot (2 meter) tube worms, were found near ocean vents.

In 1977, scientists using a submersible came upon cracks, or *vents*, in the ocean floor. Hot, cloudy water was shooting out of these vents. Even more surprising was the variety of new species living around the vents. These included giant tube worms, mussels, clams as large as dinner plates, and many species of bacteria. Scientists wondered how these organisms could live without sunlight.

Scientists found that the bacteria use sulfur chemicals from the vents to make their own food. Animals around the vents feed on the bacteria. The vents are a source of life on the cold, dark ocean floor.

CRITICAL THINKING Some fish live near the ocean floor far from vents. How do you think they get their food?

26·3 ▶ Ocean Resources

People use some ocean resources for food.

The ocean is full of riches. For thousands of years, people have fished the oceans for food. Ocean algae, such as seaweed, is used in cosmetics and ice cream. Algae are also used in some paints, dyes, and papers.

The ocean floor is also rich in oil, natural gas, and important metals. Salt and chlorine are both taken from the sea. In some places, people remove the salt from the ocean to make drinking water. The tides in the seas may one day be a source of energy.

Ocean Resources	
Foods	Fish, seaweed, shellfish
Energy	Natural gas, oil
Minerals	Cobalt, copper, manganese, nickel
Medicines	Blood thinners from algae; muscle relaxers from sea snails
Jewelry	Coral, pearl, shell

Remember
Algae are plantlike protists. A protist is a one-celled organism.

Ocean algae make about 90 percent of the food produced by living organisms on Earth. They are the first step in many food chains. Many organisms would not have food if it were not for algae. Algae also produce up to 90 percent of all the oxygen in the air we breathe.

✓ **What are three ocean resources?**

Lesson Review

1. What is the importance of algae to life on Earth?

2. What metals are found in the ocean?

3. CRITICAL THINKING Why would people in some places need to remove salt from ocean water to make drinking water?

LAB ACTIVITY
Making a Cold-Water Current

BACKGROUND
Cold water is dense. It sinks. Warm water is not as dense. It rises. These differences in temperatures help create density currents in the ocean.

PURPOSE
You will use differences in water temperature to create a current.

MATERIALS
large wide-mouth glass jar, ice cube tray, water, blue food coloring, eyedropper, spoon, freezer, paper, pencil

WHAT TO DO
1. Fill the jar with water. Stir in several drops of blue food coloring.
2. Fill the ice cube tray with the blue water. Put the tray in the freezer for a few hours.
3. Fill the glass jar with clear water. Let it stand for an hour to reach room temperature.
4. Remove the blue ice from the tray. Float one of the ice cubes on the surface of the water in the jar.
5. Observe what happens in the jar. On a sheet of paper, sketch what you see.

DRAW CONCLUSIONS
- What happens to the frozen blue water? Explain why this happens.
- What happens in the jar that is similar to what happens with density currents in the ocean?

ON-THE-JOB SCIENCE
Underwater Photographer

You have probably seen photos of underwater shipwrecks, coral reefs, and strange sea life. Underwater photographers take these photos.

Susan is an underwater photographer. She became one because it combined two things that she loves: taking photographs and scuba diving.

After high school, Susan earned a diving certificate. The algebra and physics she took in high school were helpful. Knowing how to swim helped, too. Diving school taught her how to use and repair diving equipment. She learned how to dive safely and how to handle medical emergencies underwater. She also studied oceanography and underwater photography in college.

Susan enjoys being a diving photographer. She travels a lot. She spends a lot of time in beautiful underwater environments. Susan also enjoys seeing her photographs in magazines and newspapers.

In one of Susan's textbooks, she found the chart shown to the right. Answer these questions about the chart.

1. Which animal can go the deepest in the ocean?

2. Which animals could avoid Susan by diving below her?

Susan takes a picture of a fish called a grouper.

Animal	Deepest It Goes
Human scuba diver	500 feet
Sperm whale	3,700 feet
Northern elephant seal	5,000 feet
Octopus	16,000 feet

Critical Thinking

Why do you think so many sea creatures can dive deeper than people?

Summary Water covers 70 percent of the Earth's surface. Water moves in currents, waves, and tides.

Lesson 26.1 Ocean currents flow through the ocean like rivers. Wind drives surface currents. There are also undersea currents called density currents. The ocean floor has mountain ranges, volcanoes, and deep trenches.

Lesson 26.2 Winds cause most ocean waves. Underwater earthquakes cause seismic sea waves. The tide is the regular rise and fall of ocean water near the coast. The pull of gravity of the moon and sun causes tides.

Lesson 26.3 The ocean contains resources such as algae, fish, oil, and minerals. Algae also produce most of the oxygen in the Earth's atmosphere.

Vocabulary Review

continental shelf

salinity

ocean current

density current

mid-ocean ridge

ocean basin

seismic sea wave

tide

Match each definition with a term from the list.

1. Mountain range that runs down the middle of an ocean

2. Ocean movement caused by the pull of gravity

3. The bottom of the ocean floor

4. The measure of how much salt is in something

5. A current caused by cold, salty water that sinks below warmer water

6. Water that flows like a river through an ocean

7. A giant wave caused by an underwater earthquake

8. The gentle slope from the shore out to sea

Chapter Quiz

Write your answers on a separate sheet of paper.

1. How much of the Earth's surface is covered by water?

2. What causes surface ocean currents?

3. What causes undersea ocean currents?

4. How does temperature affect ocean currents?

5. Where do most underwater earthquakes occur?

6. What is the difference between the continental shelf, continental slope, and ocean basin?

7. What causes most waves?

8. What causes tides?

9. What is the difference between high tide and low tide?

10. What are three important ocean resources, and how do we use them?

Test Tip

To prepare for a test, practice writing each of the important vocabulary words in a sentence.

Research Project

Do research to find out about seaweeds. Make a poster that shows and compares a few different kinds of seaweeds. On your poster, include a chart that lists some of the uses for seaweeds. Be sure to include seaweed products, such as algin, agar, and carrageenin, which are added to certain foods. Write a brief report to go with your poster.

Chapter 27

Exploring Space

Saturn looks very different than Earth. There are no large areas of land and water. Thick clouds surround the planet. What else do you see in the photo that makes Saturn unusual?

Learning Objectives

- Describe the Milky Way.
- Describe the sun and its characteristics.
- Identify the nine planets in the solar system.
- Compare and contrast the inner and outer planets.
- Compare asteroids, comets, and meteoroids.
- Describe important events in the history of space exploration.
- LAB ACTIVITY: Observe the moon's phases.
- SCIENCE IN YOUR LIFE: Identify types of artificial satellites.

Words to Know

astronomy	the study of the stars, planets, and all of space
Milky Way	the galaxy that contains the Earth and the rest of the solar system
sunspot	a dark area that forms on the surface of the sun
satellite	an object that orbits a planet
asteroid	a small, rocky object that orbits the sun
comet	a ball of ice and dust that orbits the sun
meteoroid	a piece of rock or dust in space
meteor	a bright streak of light caused by a meteoroid burning up in the Earth's atmosphere
meteorite	a meteoroid that does not burn up completely in the Earth's atmosphere and falls to the Earth

27·1 ▶ The Last Frontier

Words to Know

astronomy	the study of the stars, planets, and all of space
Milky Way	the galaxy that contains the Earth and the rest of the solar system

The Study of Space

People have walked on the moon. They have sent spacecraft to several other planets. They have used telescopes to study distant galaxies. However, space is so vast that most of it will probably never be explored. The study of stars, the planets, and all of space is called **astronomy**. A scientist who studies space and all of the objects in it is an astronomer.

✓ **What do astronomers study?**

The Milky Way

The Earth and the rest of the solar system are part of the **Milky Way** galaxy. Remember that a galaxy is a large group of stars that travel together through space. Astronomers group galaxies by shape. The Milky Way is a spiral galaxy. It has arms that spin around its center like a giant pinwheel. Other types of galaxies are elliptical, or oval-shaped, and irregular, which have no clear shape.

There are more than 100 billion stars in the Milky Way galaxy. There may be about 100 billion galaxies in the universe.

✓ **In which galaxy is the Earth located?**

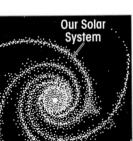

Our Solar System

Figure 27-1 *The Earth is in the outer part of one of the Milky Way's arms.*

Lesson Review

1. How do astronomers group galaxies?

2. What type of galaxy is the Milky Way?

3. **CRITICAL THINKING** Why is it harder for astronomers to study their subject than it is for meteorologists to study theirs?

A Closer Look

A TELESCOPE IN SPACE

Telescopes can be very powerful. However, there are many objects in space they cannot see from the Earth because the Earth's atmosphere gets in the way. In 1990, the National Aeronautics and Space Administration (NASA) put the Hubble Space Telescope into Earth orbit. Radio signals from the Earth control the telescope. The telescope also beams its data back to the Earth by radio signals.

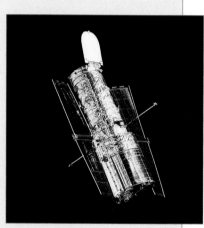

The Hubble Space Telescope is in orbit 380 miles (610 kilometers) above the Earth.

The Hubble has helped astronomers see objects in space in greater detail. It can detect objects a billion times dimmer than the sun as well as galaxies at the edge of the known universe. It has studied supernovae and black holes. A *supernova* is the sudden explosion of a huge star. A *black hole* is a collapsed star whose gravity is so strong that even light cannot escape from it.

Many galaxies contain huge clouds of gas and dust called *nebulae*. Some nebulae formed from stars that exploded. Others are places where new stars are forming. The Hubble has also helped us learn more about nebulae and how stars form.

CRITICAL THINKING How do you think people can repair the Hubble Space Telescope while it is in orbit?

Words to Know

sunspot	a dark area that forms on the surface of the sun
satellite	an object that orbits a planet
asteroid	a small, rocky object that orbits the sun
comet	a ball of ice and dust that orbits the sun
meteoroid	a piece of rock or dust in space
meteor	a bright streak of light caused by a meteoroid burning up in the Earth's atmosphere
meteorite	a meteoroid that does not burn up completely in the Earth's atmosphere and falls to the Earth

The Sun

The sun is a star. Like all stars, it is a giant ball of hot, glowing gases. The sun's core is made up of hydrogen atoms that fuse together to form helium atoms. This gives off energy as light and heat.

The sun is an average-sized star. It looks big to us because it is much closer to the Earth than any other star is. Even though the sun is only average in size, it is still huge. Its mass is 700 times greater than that of all the planets put together. Because it is so big, the sun's gravity is very strong. The sun's gravity keeps the nine planets and other objects of the solar system in orbit around the sun.

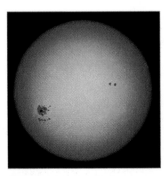

Sunspots are dark areas on the sun's surface.

A **sunspot** is a dark area that forms on the sun's surface. Sunspots are cooler than the rest of the surface. They can last a few hours or several months. Some sunspots are much larger than the Earth.

✔ **What type of object is the sun?**

Planets in the Solar System

The nine planets are among the biggest objects in the solar system. Each planet orbits the sun and spins on its axis. The planet orbits are shaped like ellipses. This means that a planet is closer to the sun at some times than at other times.

Each planet takes a different amount of time to orbit the sun. The Earth takes $365\frac{1}{4}$ days to orbit the sun once. That time period is called one year. Pluto takes 248 Earth years to circle the sun. It takes Mercury only 88 Earth days. As it orbits, a planet also spins. A planet's day is the time it takes to make one turn on its axis.

You can see several planets without a telescope. Planets do not twinkle, like stars. They have no light of their own. They seem to shine with a steady light.

The planets nearest the sun are the *inner planets*. These small, rocky planets are Mercury, Venus, Earth, and Mars. The planets farthest from the sun are the *outer planets*. The outer planets are Jupiter, Saturn, Uranus, Neptune, and Pluto. All of the outer planets, except Pluto, are much larger than the inner planets. These larger planets are made mostly of gases. They have rings and many moons.

Remember
An orbit is a closed, curved path. An axis is an imaginary line running through a planet from pole to pole. An ellipse is shaped like an oval.

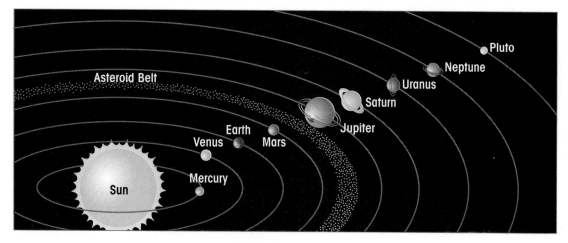

Figure 27-2 *The solar system has nine planets.*

Huge dents called impact craters cover Mercury's surface.

Mercury

Mercury is the planet closest to the sun. The side of Mercury facing the sun is very hot. It has temperatures high enough to melt lead. The side facing away from the sun is freezing cold. Mercury has almost no atmosphere. Life as we know it could not exist on Mercury.

Venus

Venus is the second planet from the sun. It has a thick atmosphere made up mostly of carbon dioxide. The heavy atmosphere traps the sun's heat around Venus. This makes Venus very hot. Venus is even hotter than Mercury, though it is farther from the sun.

Thick clouds hide the surface of Venus.

Earth

The Earth is the third planet from the sun. It is about the same size as Venus. The Earth is the only planet that is mostly covered with water. Its atmosphere is mainly nitrogen and oxygen. So far, the Earth is the only planet in the solar system known to have life.

A **satellite** is an object that orbits a planet. Natural satellites are called moons. Our moon makes one orbit around the Earth every $27\frac{1}{3}$ days.

The Earth's moon

Mars

Mars is the fourth planet from the sun. It has two tiny moons. The atmosphere is made up mostly of carbon dioxide. There is no liquid water on the surface of Mars and almost no water vapor in its atmosphere.

Mars is colder than the coldest places on Earth. The soil on the surface of Mars is reddish. That is why Mars is often called the "red planet."

Spacecraft have landed on parts of Mars and explored it.

Jupiter

Jupiter, the fifth planet from the sun, is the largest planet. Its diameter is about 11 times that of the Earth's. Jupiter has a rocky core. But most of the planet is a large ball of ice and liquid wrapped in gas clouds. Jupiter has 16 moons and a thin set of rings. There are violent electrical storms in Jupiter's atmosphere. Jupiter's Great Red Spot is a large hurricane-like storm.

Saturn

Saturn is the sixth planet from the sun. Like Jupiter, Saturn is a huge planet with no solid surface. It has a rocky core surrounded by liquid hydrogen and helium and thick clouds. Saturn has seven main rings. The rings are made of particles of ice and dust. Jupiter, Uranus, and Neptune also have rings, but they are much thinner. Saturn has 18 known moons.

Jupiter's Great Red Spot (arrow) is a storm larger than the Earth.

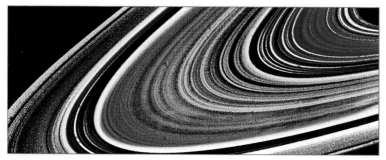

Saturn's rings

Uranus

Uranus is the seventh planet from the sun. It is made up of ice and liquid hydrogen around a solid core. Uranus is unusual because its axis runs sideways rather than up and down. As a result, Uranus seems to roll around on its side in orbit. Uranus has 18 known moons and a set of rings.

Uranus has hydrogen and methane in its atmosphere.

Neptune

Neptune is usually the eighth planet from the sun. But sometimes its path crosses the path of Pluto. Then, for a few years, it becomes the ninth planet. Neptune's thick gas clouds surround a liquid layer and a rocky, icy core. The planet has eight known moons and several rings.

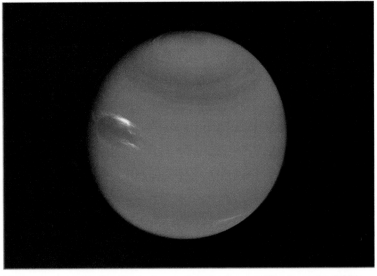

Voyager 2 took the first close-up photos of Neptune in 1989.

Pluto

Pluto is usually the planet farthest from the sun. Its surface is icy, and it is always dark there. Some astronomers think that Pluto may be an escaped moon of Neptune. Pluto has one moon.

Pluto is so far away that even powerful telescopes show little about its surface and its moon.

✓ **How are the inner and outer planets different?**

Asteroids, Comets, and Meteoroids

An **asteroid** is a small, rocky object that orbits the sun. Most asteroids are found between Mars and Jupiter. Asteroids are rich in minerals that people may mine someday. Astronomers are not sure where asteroids came from. They might be the remains of a planet that broke up. Asteroids also may be left over from when the solar system formed.

A **comet** is a ball of ice and dust that orbits the sun. When comets pass near the sun, some of the ice evaporates. The gas streams away from the sun, forming a glowing tail. Most comets are only about 10 miles (16 kilometers) across. However, their tails can extend for 100 million miles (160 million kilometers).

A **meteoroid** is a piece of rock or dust in space. Most meteoroids come from asteroids or comets. When a meteoroid enters the Earth's atmosphere, friction makes it burn and produce a bright streak of light called a **meteor.**

A large meteoroid may not burn up completely as it passes through the Earth's atmosphere. The part of the meteoroid that does not burn and falls to the Earth is called a **meteorite.** A few hundred meteorites fall to the Earth each year. Many are the size of baseballs. Most meteorites are heavy for their size because they contain a lot of iron.

Comets are balls of gas and dust.

A huge meteorite made this hole, called Meteor Crater, in Arizona thousands of years ago.

✓ **How are asteroids different from comets?**

Lesson Review

1. What is the sun made of?

2. Which are the solar system's inner planets? Which are its outer planets?

3. CRITICAL THINKING What do asteroids, comets, and meteoroids all have in common?

Space Exploration

Early Space Flights

Space Firsts
1957: Soviet Union's *Sputnik 1* is first satellite to orbit the Earth.
1958: *Explorer 1* is first U.S. satellite.
1961: Soviet Union's Yuri Gagarin is first person in orbit.
1962: John Glenn is first American in orbit.
1969: Neil Armstrong from *Apollo II* is first person on the moon.
1973: *Pioneer 10* probe flies by Jupiter—first close-up pictures of an outer planet.
1976: *Viking 1* and *Viking 2* send photos from the surface of Mars.
1979: *Pioneer 11* transmits first photos of Saturn and its rings.
1981: First space shuttle flight takes place.
1983: Sally Ride is first American woman in space.
1986: *Voyager 1* transmits first pictures of Uranus and its moons.
1997: *Mars Pathfinder* sends images and data from Mars.

The age of space exploration began in 1957. That is when the Soviet Union (today's Russia and many of its surrounding countries) launched *Sputnik 1*, the first artificial satellite. Over the next 12 years, the United States and the Soviet Union sent space probes to the moon, Venus, and Mars. A space probe is a spacecraft sent into space without people to gather information. These two countries also raced to put the first person on the moon.

In 1961, Alan Shepard became the first American to fly in space. This was just a few weeks after the Soviet Union sent Yuri Gagarin into space. In 1962, John Glenn became the first American to orbit the Earth. Several *Gemini* missions followed. *Gemini* astronauts tested equipment and techniques needed to reach the moon. This included walking in space, joining spacecraft in space, and testing the effects of space on people.

NASA's *Apollo* program began in the late 1960s. In 1968, astronauts flew around the moon for the first time. On July 20, 1969, *Apollo* astronauts landed on the moon. They photographed the surface, did experiments, set up instruments, and collected moon rocks.

✓ **Which two countries competed in space in the 1960s?**

Exploring Space Today

In the 1980s, the space shuttle became the main spacecraft of the American space program. It now carries satellites and probes into space and returns. It is the first reusable spacecraft.

The shuttle does not leave the Earth's orbit. It lifts off like a rocket, then glides back to the Earth like an airplane. Shuttle crews conduct experiments. The shuttle is also being used to help build the International Space Station.

Today, several countries launch satellites and space probes. These include France, Germany, Russia, Japan, China, and India. NASA is hoping to send astronauts to Mars in the not too distant future.

✓ **How is the space shuttle different from past spacecraft?**

The space shuttle is the first reusable spacecraft.

Lesson Review

1. What was the purpose of the *Gemini* and *Apollo* programs?

2. What are two future NASA space projects?

3. **CRITICAL THINKING** What big space project do you think people should try in the future? Explain your answer.

Modern Leaders In Science

MAE JEMISON

On September 12, 1992, Dr. Mae Jemison became the first African-American woman to travel in space. Dr. Jemison is a medical doctor. During her eight-day flight aboard the space shuttle *Endeavor*, she ran experiments on motion sickness. She also studied bone cell growth. In 1993, Dr. Jemison left NASA to work in health care and education.

CRITICAL THINKING Why is it important to study the effects of space on the human body?

Dr. Mae Jemison was the first African-American woman in space.

LAB ACTIVITY
Observing the Phases of the Moon

BACKGROUND

The moon seems to have a different shape at different times of the month. These shapes are its phases. The moon goes through a cycle of phases every $29\frac{1}{2}$ days.

PURPOSE

You will observe some of the moon's phases and predict what the next phase will be.

MATERIALS

paper, pencil

WHAT TO DO

1. Draw seven boxes side by side to represent a week on a calendar.
2. Observe the moon each night for seven days. Draw its shape each night on your calendar.
3. Compare each shape on your calendar with the pictures of the phases of the moon in the chart above. Label the moon phases for each drawing on your calendar.
4. Use your observations to predict the next phase of the moon after the last one on your calendar. Keep in mind how many phases there are, the order of the phases, and how long each phase lasts.

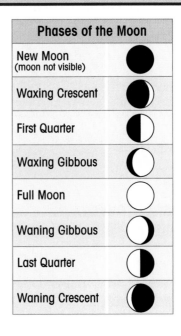

Phases of the Moon	
New Moon (moon not visible)	●
Waxing Crescent	◗
First Quarter	◑
Waxing Gibbous	◗
Full Moon	○
Waning Gibbous	◖
Last Quarter	◐
Waning Crescent	◖

DRAW CONCLUSIONS

• How many of the phases did you observe?

• About how long does each phase last?

• What was the last phase you observed during this period? Predict which phase will come next and why.

SCIENCE IN YOUR LIFE
Artificial Satellites

When you think of space travel, you might think of astronauts landing on the moon. You might also think of space probes flying to Jupiter or Saturn. But the most common type of space traveler in our solar system is the artificial satellite.

There are more than 2,000 artificial satellites orbiting the Earth. They do many jobs that affect your life. Communications satellites broadcast TV shows. They connect long-distance phone calls. Weather satellites help meteorologists forecast the weather. Navigation satellites allow airplanes and ships to track their movements. Earth observation satellites locate minerals and other resources. They also produce data that scientists use to study the effects of pollution on forests and water.

Satellites orbit other bodies in space besides the Earth. Satellites have circled the moon, Mercury, Venus, Mars, the sun, and comets. Satellites have taken photos and sent back data. These data have helped us learn more about other bodies in space.

The chart to the right shows a few of the things that satellites have done during the past few decades. Answer the questions, using the chart.

1. What was the name of the first successful weather satellite?

2. Which satellite orbited and studied the sun?

3. Which two satellites studied the Earth?

Many satellites orbit the Earth.

Name of Satellite	Purpose	Went Into Orbit
Tiros 1	First successful weather satellite	1960
Telstar 1	Sent first TV pictures across Atlantic	1962
MAGSAT	Mapped the Earth's magnetic field	1979
LAGEOS 1	Measured movement in the Earth's crust	1976
SOHO	Orbited and studied the sun	1995

Critical Thinking

Why are satellites important to scientists?

Summary

The solar system contains the sun, planets, moon, and other objects. Many countries have sent spacecraft to explore objects in the solar system.

Lesson 27.1

The Earth is part of a galaxy called the Milky Way. There may be more than 100 billion galaxies in the universe.

Lesson 27.2

The inner planets of our solar system are small and rocky. Most of the outer planets are large balls of liquid and gas. The solar system also contains asteroids, comets, and meteoroids.

Lesson 27.3

The United States landed the first person on the moon. Many countries have sent probes and satellites into space. More missions are planned.

Vocabulary Review

Write *true* or *false* for each sentence. If the sentence is false, replace the underlined term to make the sentence true.

1. The Earth is part of the <u>Milky Way</u> galaxy.

2. <u>An asteroid</u> is a piece of rock or dust in space.

3. A <u>comet</u> is a piece of rock from space that has fallen to the Earth.

4. <u>Geology</u> is the study of the stars, planets, and all of space.

5. A <u>sunspot</u> is a dark area on the sun's surface.

6. A ball of ice and dust orbiting the sun is a <u>meteor</u>.

7. A meteoroid burning up in the Earth's atmosphere causes a streak of light known as a <u>meteorite</u>.

Chapter Quiz

Write your answers on a separate sheet of paper.

1. In what galaxy are the sun and our solar system found?

2. What is the sun, and what is it made of?

3. What kinds of bodies in space make up the solar system?

4. What are the solar system's nine planets in order, beginning from closest to the sun?

5. Which planets are fairly small and solid?

6. Which planets have rings?

7. What are two theories that scientists have about how asteroids were formed?

8. What is the tail of a comet made of?

9. What happens to a meteoroid that enters the atmosphere?

10. What are three important events in the history of space exploration?

Test Tip
To prepare for a test, find key words in the chapter. Be sure you know what they mean.

Research Project

Research NASA's plans to send astronauts to Mars someday. Work with a small group. Choose one part of the story to tell, such as what Mars is like, difficulties in getting to Mars, the type of spacecraft that might go, or when the project will get started. Write a report on what you learn. Make a poster showing some part of the journey.

Unit 7 Review

Choose the letter for the correct answer to each question.

Use the timeline to answer Questions 1 to 3.

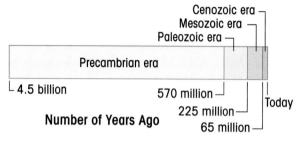

Cenozoic era
Mesozoic era
Paleozoic era

Precambrian era

4.5 billion

570 million

225 million

Today

65 million

Number of Years Ago

1. How many years ago did dinosaurs become extinct?

   A. 65 million years ago

   B. 225 million years ago

   C. 570 million years ago

   D. 4.5 billion years ago

2. According to the timeline, how old is the Earth?

   A. 65 million years old

   B. 225 million years old

   C. 570 million years old

   D. 4.5 billion years old

3. The earliest human-like species appeared in Africa during which era?

   A. Cenozoic era

   B. Mesozoic era

   C. Paleozoic era

   D. Precambrian era

4. Which of the following is true of the Gulf Stream?

   A. It is a cold surface current.

   B. It is a density current.

   C. It is a warm surface current.

   D. It is an upwelling.

5. Together, the sun's and moon's gravity causes which of the following?

   A. trenches

   B. currents

   C. tides

   D. waves

6. What keeps the planets and other objects in the solar system in orbit?

   A. the gravity of the sun

   B. the Milky Way

   C. the sun's burning gases

   D. the gravity of the largest planets

7. Which of the following is a feature of inner planets such as the Earth?

   A. made of frozen gases

   B. many moons

   C. rocky surfaces

   D. very large compared to outer planets

Critical Thinking

Why would astronauts be more likely to explore Mars than Jupiter?

Glossary

air mass a huge body of air that moves from place to place

air pressure the weight of the gases pressing down on the Earth

alga a plantlike protist (plural, *algae*)

amphibian a cold-blooded vertebrate with wet, slippery skin and two pairs of legs; able to live on both land and in water

amplitude the height of a wave

appendage a part that extends out from the body, such as a wing, a leg, an arm, or a claw

area the number of square units that is needed to cover a surface

artery a blood vessel that carries blood away from the heart

arthropod an animal with an outer skeleton, jointed appendages, and a body divided into separate parts, called segments

asteroid a small, rocky object that orbits the sun

astronomy the study of the stars, planets, and all of space

atmosphere the air that surrounds the Earth or another body in space

atom the smallest part of a substance that can still be recognized as that substance

axis an imaginary line that runs from one pole, through the center of the Earth, to the other pole

bacterium a tiny one-celled moneran seen only through a microscope (plural, *bacteria*)

barometer an instrument that measures air pressure

battery a device that changes chemical energy into electrical energy

biologist a scientist who studies the behavior and characteristics of living things

biology the study of all organisms on Earth, including plants and animals

blood vessel a tube that carries blood around the body

botany the study of plant life

bronchi two small tubes that branch off from the trachea and enter the lungs

calcium a mineral found in teeth and bone

capillary a tiny blood vessel that connects an artery to a vein

carbohydrate a sugary or starchy food that gives people energy

cell the smallest, most basic unit of life

cell membrane the thin covering that holds a cell together

cell wall   the thick covering around a plant cell membrane

cellular respiration   the process cells use to release energy from food molecules

Cenozoic era   the geological era of today that began 65 million years ago

centripetal force   a force that causes objects in motion to move in a curved path

characteristic   a quality or feature of a person or thing

chemical bond   a force that holds atoms together

chemical energy   energy stored in molecules

chemistry   the scientific study of what matter is made of and how it reacts when it comes into contact with other matter

chlorophyll   the green material inside chloroplasts that absorbs sunlight so plants can make their own food

chloroplast   a plant cell part that stores a green material called chlorophyll

cholesterol   a substance found in some fats and also in the body, which is needed in small amounts

chromosome   a threadlike structure in a cell nucleus that holds thousands of bits of information about an organism's traits

circuit   an unbroken, circular path that an electrical current flows through; includes a source of energy, such as a battery

circulation   the process of moving blood around the body

cirrus cloud   a high-altitude cloud made of ice crystals

classification   the grouping of organisms by their type

climate   the average weather in a region over many years

cold-blooded   having a body temperature that changes with the environment

comet   a ball of ice and dust that orbits the sun

community   a group of different populations living in the same place and interacting with each other

compound   a substance that is formed when the atoms of two or more elements join together chemically

condensation   the process by which a gas changes to a liquid

conduction   the passing of heat by molecules of matter bumping into one another

conservation   the wise and careful use of natural resources

consumer   an organism that eats other organisms

continent   a large landmass

continental shelf the gentle slope from the shore out to sea

continental slope the steep cliff between the continental shelf and the bottom of the ocean

convection the transfer of heat within a gas or a liquid by the movement of warmer particles

core the layer at the center of the Earth

crossbreeding the matching of parents with different traits to produce offspring with new traits

crust the outer layer of the Earth

crustacean an arthropod with two body segments and five pairs of legs

cumulonimbus cloud a tall, thick, white cumulus cloud that is dark at the bottom; also known as a thunderhead

cumulus cloud a big, puffy, low-altitude cloud that usually signals good weather

cyclone an area of low air pressure with circling winds

cytoplasm the watery substance in a cell

decomposer an organism that breaks down and absorbs nutrients from dead matter

defense a way your body fights off harmful organisms

density the measure of how much mass something has for its size

density current a current caused by cold, salty water, which is very dense and sinks below warmer water

dew point the temperature at which water vapor turns into liquid water

digestion the process of breaking down food into molecules the cells can absorb

discharge the throwing off of static electricity

disease a kind of illness or sickness, often caused by tiny organisms such as bacteria

DNA a molecule in the nuclei of cells that controls many of the characteristics of living things

dominant describes a trait that will show its effect no matter the effect of its partner trait

earth science the study of the Earth, including its rocks, oceans, air, and weather; also the study of the sun, moon, planets, and stars

earthquake a sudden, violent shaking of the Earth

ecology the study of interactions between organisms and their environment

ecosystem a community and all the nonliving things that the community interacts with

effort force a force that is applied when doing work

egg cell a female sex cell

electrical conductor a material that electricity travels through easily

electrical energy energy in the form of electrons moving through a substance

electrical insulator a material that electricity does not travel through easily

electricity a form of energy caused by the movement of electrons

electron a part of an atom that has a negative electrical charge and is found outside the atom's nucleus

element matter that is made of only one kind of atom

energy the ability of something or someone to do work or produce heat

environment everything that surrounds you

enzyme a body chemical; in digestion, it helps break down food

equator an imaginary line that circles the Earth halfway between the North and South poles

erosion the wearing away of rock and soil

esophagus a long tube leading from the throat to the stomach

evaporation the process by which a liquid changes to a gas

evolution the process of change in a species over time, usually over thousands or millions of years

experiment a kind of test that scientists use to discover or prove something

extinct no longer existing on Earth

fat a nutrient in foods that supplies the body with energy

fertilization the process of a sperm cell and an egg cell joining

fetus an unborn baby that develops in a woman's uterus

food chain the path of food through a community

food web a group of food chains that are linked to each other

force any push or pull on an object

fossil the remains of an organism that lived long ago

fossil fuel a fuel made of organisms that died millions of years ago

frequency the number of wave cycles that pass through a point in one second

friction a force that slows motion or prevents it

front the place where two air masses of different temperatures meet

fruit the part of a plant that holds the seeds

fulcrum the support on which a lever turns

fungus an organism that gets its food by breaking down dead matter and absorbing useful elements from it (plural, *fungi*)

fuse a weak link in an electrical circuit; made of metal wire that has a low melting point

galaxy a very large group of stars that travel together through space

gas matter that has no definite shape or volume

gene a bit of information in a chromosome

generator a machine that changes some other kind of energy into electrical energy

genetics the study of how living things pass along certain features of themselves to their offspring

geological era a huge period of time in the Earth's history

geologist a scientist who studies rocks to learn about the history and structure of the Earth

geothermal energy the heat contained in rock deep inside the Earth

germination the process by which a tiny new plant breaks through the hard seed coat that is protecting it

geyser a hot spring that shoots steam and hot water into the air

glacier a large, slow-moving field of ice

globe a sphere, or ball, that has a map of the Earth on its surface

gram the basic metric unit of mass

gravity the force of attraction between any two objects that have mass

habitat the place where an organism lives

heat energy energy in the form of moving molecules

heredity the passing down of traits from parents to offspring

hormone a substance made by organs called glands

host a living thing that supports a parasite

humidity the amount of water vapor in the air at any given time

hurricane a stormy cyclone with high winds that forms over the Atlantic Ocean

hybrid the offspring of parents that have been crossbred

hydroelectric energy the electrical energy from moving water

hypothesis a possible answer to a problem

igneous rock a type of rock formed from magma

inclined plane a slanted surface used for raising objects from one level to another

inertia the tendency of an object to stay at rest or in motion unless it is acted upon by a force

insulator material that does not conduct heat easily

invertebrate an animal that does not have a backbone

ionosphere the fourth layer in the atmosphere, where there are many electrically charged particles

joint a place where two bones meet

kinetic energy energy that comes from movement

kingdom one of the five main groups in biological classification

laboratory a place with equipment that people use to do science

larynx a box-shaped structure below the throat

laser a device that produces a narrow, strong beam of light

lava magma that has reached the Earth's surface

leaf the food-making part of the plant

lever a simple machine made of a bar or rod that turns on a support

life science the study of living things and how they behave

life span the amount of time an organism is likely to live

light energy energy in the form of moving waves of light

line of latitude a line that circles a globe; runs east to west

line of longitude a line that circles a globe; runs north to south

liquid matter that has a definite volume but no definite shape

liter a metric unit used to measure volume of a liquid or gas

load an object to be moved

lubricant a substance that reduces friction between the moving parts of machines

machine a tool or device that makes work easier to do

magma melted rock formed in the Earth's mantle

magnet a solid substance that attracts iron or steel

magnetic field the area around a magnet in which a magnetic force is active

mammal a warm-blooded vertebrate that has hair on its body; the mother's body makes milk to feed its young

mantle the middle layer of the Earth

mass the amount of matter in something

matter anything that takes up space

measurement the size or the amount of something

mechanical advantage a measure of how helpful a machine is

mechanical energy energy in the form of parts moving in a machine

menstruation the monthly flow of blood from the uterus of a woman who is not having a baby

mesosphere the third layer in the atmosphere

Mesozoic era the geological era that started 225 million years ago and lasted 160 million years

metamorphic rock a type of rock formed when igneous or sedimentary rock changes under very high temperatures or pressure

meteor a bright streak of light caused by a meteoroid burning up in the Earth's atmosphere

meteorite a meteoroid that does not burn up completely in the Earth's atmosphere and falls to the Earth

meteoroid a piece of rock or dust in space

meteorology the scientific study of the Earth's atmosphere and weather

meter the metric unit of length

metric unit a unit of measurement that is based on the number ten and multiples of ten

microbiology the study of organisms too small to be seen with the eye alone

microscope an instrument used to study very small objects; it makes them appear much larger

mid-ocean ridge a huge mountain range that runs down the middle of some oceans

migrate to move long distances each year to reach warm areas and better feeding grounds

Milky Way the galaxy that contains the Earth and the rest of the solar system

mineral an inorganic substance found in water and some foods; tiny amounts of some minerals are needed by the body to stay healthy

mitochondrion a cell part that helps the cell store and use energy (plural, *mitochondria*)

mixture a substance made of two or more elements or compounds that are mixed together but not chemically joined

molecule two or more atoms that are joined by chemical bonds

mollusk an animal with a soft body that is not divided into segments

moneran a tiny organism that has DNA but no true nucleus (plural, *monera*)

motion a change in the position or place of an object

mutation a change in the genetic code of an organism

natural resource a substance found in nature that is useful to humans

natural selection   the way organisms that are best suited to their environment survive and pass on their helpful traits to offspring

naturalist   a scientist who studies living things in nature

neutron   a part of an atom that has no electrical charge and is found inside the atom's nucleus

nuclear energy   energy stored in the nucleus of an atom

nuclear fission   the breakup of the nucleus of an atom

nuclear fusion   the joining together of two or more atomic nuclei

nuclear reactor   a device that splits atoms to release energy

nucleus   the part of a cell that controls all the other parts (plural, *nuclei*)

nutrient   a substance usually found in food that body cells need to stay healthy and grow

nutrition   the study of food and eating right to stay healthy

observation   the careful study of something

occluded front   the front that forms when a cold front overtakes a warm front

ocean basin   the bottom of the ocean floor

ocean current   a mass of water that flows like a river through an ocean

oceanography   the study of the ocean

offspring   a new organism that results from reproduction

orbit   a closed, curved path

organ   a body part made up of one or more kinds of tissue

organism   any living thing or once-living thing

ovaries   the female organs where egg cells are stored

ozone   a thin layer of gas found in the stratosphere that filters out much of the harmful radiation from the sun

paleontology   the scientific study of fossils

Paleozoic era   the geological era that started 570 million years ago and lasted 346 million years

parasite   an organism that lives on or in another organism, called a host, and causes harm to that organism

petal   one of the colorful outer parts of a flower; it attracts insects

photosynthesis   the process that plants use to make food in the form of sugar

phylum   the largest of the groupings of organisms below kingdom (plural, *phyla*)

physical science   the study of matter and energy

physics   the scientific study of what energy is and how it interacts with matter

pistil the female part of a flower

plasma the liquid part of blood

plate tectonics the scientific theory that the Earth's crust is made up of plates that slowly shift position

platelet a part of the blood that helps stop injuries from bleeding

pollen the light, powdery dust in stamens that contains the male sex cells

pollination the process of transferring pollen from the stamen of a flower to the pistil of the same or a different flower

population all the members of a species living in the same place

potential energy energy that is stored in matter

Precambrian era the geological era that started 4.5 billion years ago and lasted nearly 4 billion years

precipitation any form of water that falls from the air

prime meridian the 0-degree line of longitude

prism a triangular-shaped, three-dimensional object made of clear glass that breaks up white light into its different colors

procedure a plan that is used to complete a task

producer an organism that makes its own food

property a way to describe matter, such as color, shape, odor, and hardness

protein a nutrient in foods that builds and repairs body tissues

protist a tiny one-celled organism that is neither plant nor animal but may have characteristics of both

proton a part of an atom that has a positive electrical charge and is found inside the atom's nucleus

protozoan an animal-like protist (plural, *protozoa*)

puberty the time in life when the reproductive organs develop

pulley a wheel with grooves in its rim through which a rope or chain can run

radiation energy that travels in waves

radioactive giving off radiation, or harmful rays

radioactive dating a way to find the age of rocks by measuring the decay, or breaking down, of radioactive elements in them

recessive describes a trait that will be masked by a dominant partner trait

recycling reusing a substance over and over again

red blood cell a blood cell that carries oxygen and carbon dioxide throughout the circulatory system

reflection the bouncing of light off an object

refraction the bending of light rays as they pass from one substance into another

reproduce to make more of one's own kind of organism

reptile a cold-blooded land vertebrate, usually with four legs and clawed toes

research to study a subject, usually using books and doing experiments

resistance force a force that must be overcome when doing work

respiration the process that gets oxygen to the body's cells and removes waste gases

root the part of a plant below the surface of the soil; used to hold the plant in place, store extra food, and soak up water and minerals from the soil

salinity the measure of how much salt is in something

satellite an object that orbits a planet

science the study of nature and the universe

scientific method a step-by-step procedure that scientists use to do experiments and make new discoveries

screw an inclined plane that is wrapped around a nail

sedimentary rock a type of rock formed by the pressing together of smaller particles of rock or the remains of living things

seed that part of a seed plant from which a new plant can grow

seismic sea wave a giant wave caused by an earthquake on the ocean floor

skeleton the bones that support, allow movement, and protect the organs of an animal with a backbone

soil rocks on the Earth's surface broken down by weathering to very tiny pieces that mix with the nutrients from living and once-living things

solar collector a device with a dark surface that absorbs sunlight and changes it into heat energy

solar energy energy from the sun

solar system the sun and all the planets and other objects that circle around it

solid matter that has a definite shape and volume

solution a kind of mixture in which one substance dissolves, or seems to disappear, into another substance

species organisms that can reproduce together and have offspring that can also reproduce

spectrum the band of colors that make up white light

sperm cell a male sex cell

stamen the male part of a flower

static electricity the electricity caused when objects with opposite charges are attracted to each other

stem the upright part of a plant; used to carry food and water and hold a plant up so its leaves can get sunlight

stratosphere the second layer in the atmosphere

stratus cloud a low-lying gray cloud that covers a wide area

sunspot a dark area that forms on the surface of the sun

system a group of organs working together to do a job

technology science discoveries and skills that are put to use

tendon a tough band of tissue that attaches muscle to bone

testes the male organs where sperm cells are made

theory an explanation about something that is supported by data

thermosphere the outermost layer in the atmosphere

tide the rise and fall of the oceans, caused by the sun's and moon's pull of gravity

tissue a group of similar cells that work together to do a job

tornado a cyclone that extends down from a cumulonimbus cloud and forms a funnel-shaped cloud

trachea a long tube leading from the larynx to smaller branching tubes that go to the lungs; also called the windpipe

trait a characteristic that can be inherited from parents; it identifies an organism as an individual

trench a deep, long valley in the ocean floor

troposphere the layer nearest the Earth in the atmosphere, where we live and where most weather takes place

turbine a machine with blades that can be turned; used to start an electric generator

typhoon a stormy cyclone with high winds that forms over the Pacific Ocean

undertow the backward movement of ocean water near the shore

unit an amount that is used by everyone when measuring a particular thing

universe all that exists, including the planets, sun, stars, and space

uplifting and folding a geological process that bends layers of the Earth's crust and sometimes turns them upside down

uterus the female organ in which a fertilized egg develops into a baby

vacuole an enclosed space in a cell that stores food molecules, water, and waste

vacuum any place where there is no matter

vein a blood vessel that returns blood to the heart

vertebrate an animal with a backbone

virus a very small disease-causing particle

vitamin a nutrient found in tiny amounts in many plant and animal foods; it is needed by the body to stay healthy

volcano an opening in the Earth's surface that releases magma from the mantle

volume the number of cubic units that is needed to fill a space

warm-blooded having a body temperature that stays fairly constant

waste the part of food that an organism does not need after it uses the food for energy

wavelength the distance from the crest, or top, of one wave to the crest of the next wave

weather the condition of the atmosphere at a certain time and place

weathering a process that breaks down rocks and minerals

wedge a simple machine made of two inclined planes, back to back

weight the measure of the force of gravity on an object

wheel and axle a wheel attached to a rod called an axle; as the axle turns, the wheel also turns

white blood cell a blood cell that fights off bacteria and sickness in the body

work what happens when a force moves something through a distance

zoology the study of animal life

Appendix A: First Aid

You can avoid most accidents by following the lab rules given in Chapter 2 of this book. However, accidents can still happen, in a lab or almost anywhere. Therefore, it is a good idea to be prepared for them.

First aid is emergency medical care given to someone who has just been injured or become very sick. Different emergencies need different kinds of first aid. Here are some rules to follow for any emergency.

- Stay calm so that you can think clearly.
- Call 911 or 0 to reach Emergency Medical Services (EMS). Or ask someone nearby to call.
- Do not move the person unless he or she is drowning or in danger of being burned in a fire.

- Check for signs of breathing and pulse.
- Check for any emergency medical ID tag or bracelet.
- Never do more than you know how to do. Find help if the injury seems serious, if you do not see breathing or do not get a pulse, if bleeding continues, or if the pain is very sharp.

The following chart provides some basic guidelines. However, the best way to learn first aid is to take a course that teaches first-aid techniques such as CPR and the Heimlich maneuver. First-aid courses are available through libraries, fire departments, hospitals, the Red Cross, and other organizations in your community.

Type of Injury	First Aid Treatment
Choking	• If the person cannot talk, cough, or breathe, perform the Heimlich maneuver.
Stopped heartbeat	• Use cardiopulmonary resuscitation (CPR)
Cuts	• Cover and apply direct pressure to the wound. Use a sterile or clean bandage.
Bruises	• Apply ice or cold compresses to reduce swelling.
Poisoning	• Find the container it came in and read the label instructions. Contact your local poison control center.
Fainting	• Make sure the person is lying flat with feet up. • Use cool water on the face. • Loosen any tight clothing.
Insect stings	• Scrape the stinger away; do not pull it straight out. • Rinse the skin with cool water. If the person is allergic, take to an emergency room immediately.
Sprains	• Raise the sprained body part. • Help reduce swelling with ice or a cold pack.
Objects in the eye	• Flush the eye with water, move from the inner to the outer eye corners.
Nosebleeds	• Make sure the person is leaning forward while breathing through the mouth. • Keep pressure on the nostril for ten minutes. Use a cold cloth. • Do not block the airway.
Most burns	• Apply cool water. • Place clean, dry bandage loosely over the burn. • Do not apply ointments or sprays. See a doctor if it looks bad.

Appendix B: The Periodic Table of Elements

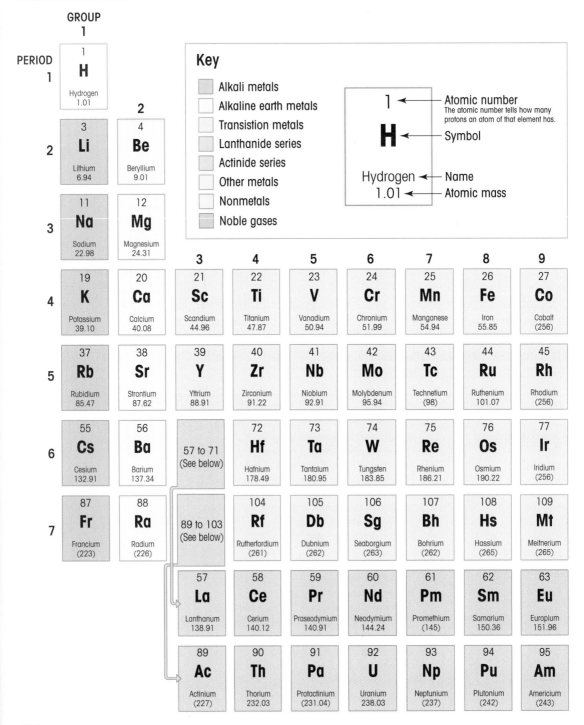

GROUP

Key

- Alkali metals
- Alkaline earth metals
- Transistion metals
- Lanthanide series
- Actinide series
- Other metals
- Nonmetals
- Noble gases

1 ←	Atomic number The atomic number tells how many protons an atom of that element has.
H ←	Symbol
Hydrogen ←	Name
1.01 ←	Atomic mass

PERIOD	1								
1	1 **H** Hydrogen 1.01								

	1	2
2	3 **Li** Lithium 6.94	4 **Be** Beryllium 9.01
3	11 **Na** Sodium 22.98	12 **Mg** Magnesium 24.31

			3	4	5	6	7	8	9
4	19 **K** Potassium 39.10	20 **Ca** Calcium 40.08	21 **Sc** Scandium 44.96	22 **Ti** Titanium 47.87	23 **V** Vanadium 50.94	24 **Cr** Chromium 51.99	25 **Mn** Manganese 54.94	26 **Fe** Iron 55.85	27 **Co** Cobalt (256)
5	37 **Rb** Rubidium 85.47	38 **Sr** Strontium 87.62	39 **Y** Yttrium 88.91	40 **Zr** Zirconium 91.22	41 **Nb** Niobium 92.91	42 **Mo** Molybdenum 95.94	43 **Tc** Technetium (98)	44 **Ru** Ruthenium 101.07	45 **Rh** Rhodium (256)
6	55 **Cs** Cesium 132.91	56 **Ba** Barium 137.34	57 to 71 (See below)	72 **Hf** Hafnium 178.49	73 **Ta** Tantalum 180.95	74 **W** Tungsten 183.85	75 **Re** Rhenium 186.21	76 **Os** Osmium 190.22	77 **Ir** Iridium (256)
7	87 **Fr** Francium (223)	88 **Ra** Radium (226)	89 to 103 (See below)	104 **Rf** Rutherfordium (261)	105 **Db** Dubnium (262)	106 **Sg** Seaborgium (263)	107 **Bh** Bohrium (262)	108 **Hs** Hassium (265)	109 **Mt** Meitnerium (265)

57 **La** Lanthanum 138.91	58 **Ce** Cerium 140.12	59 **Pr** Praseodymium 140.91	60 **Nd** Neodymium 144.24	61 **Pm** Promethium (145)	62 **Sm** Samarium 150.36	63 **Eu** Europium 151.96
89 **Ac** Actinium (227)	90 **Th** Thorium 232.03	91 **Pa** Protactinium (231.04)	92 **U** Uranium 238.03	93 **Np** Neptunium (237)	94 **Pu** Plutonium (242)	95 **Am** Americium (243)

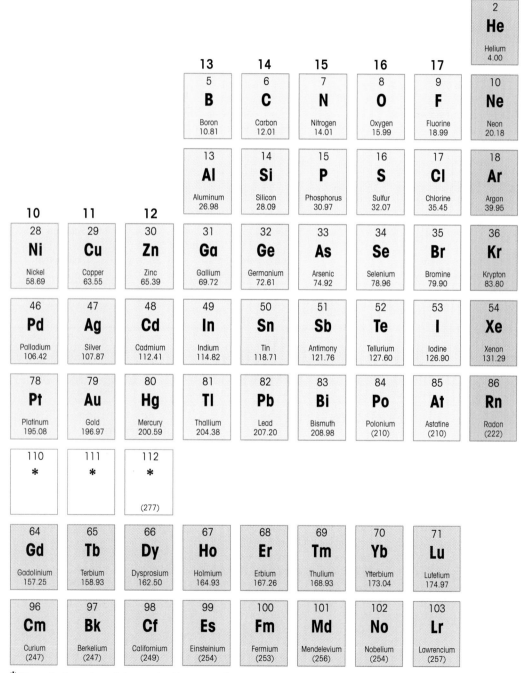

			18
			2 **He** Helium 4.00

13	14	15	16	17	18
5 **B** Boron 10.81	6 **C** Carbon 12.01	7 **N** Nitrogen 14.01	8 **O** Oxygen 15.99	9 **F** Fluorine 18.99	10 **Ne** Neon 20.18
13 **Al** Aluminum 26.98	14 **Si** Silicon 28.09	15 **P** Phosphorus 30.97	16 **S** Sulfur 32.07	17 **Cl** Chlorine 35.45	18 **Ar** Argon 39.95

10	11	12	13	14	15	16	17	18
28 **Ni** Nickel 58.69	29 **Cu** Copper 63.55	30 **Zn** Zinc 65.39	31 **Ga** Gallium 69.72	32 **Ge** Germanium 72.61	33 **As** Arsenic 74.92	34 **Se** Selenium 78.96	35 **Br** Bromine 79.90	36 **Kr** Krypton 83.80
46 **Pd** Palladium 106.42	47 **Ag** Silver 107.87	48 **Cd** Cadmium 112.41	49 **In** Indium 114.82	50 **Sn** Tin 118.71	51 **Sb** Antimony 121.76	52 **Te** Tellurium 127.60	53 **I** Iodine 126.90	54 **Xe** Xenon 131.29
78 **Pt** Platinum 195.08	79 **Au** Gold 196.97	80 **Hg** Mercury 200.59	81 **Tl** Thallium 204.38	82 **Pb** Lead 207.20	83 **Bi** Bismuth 208.98	84 **Po** Polonium (210)	85 **At** Astatine (210)	86 **Rn** Radon (222)
110 *	111 *	112 * (277)						

64 **Gd** Gadolinium 157.25	65 **Tb** Terbium 158.93	66 **Dy** Dysprosium 162.50	67 **Ho** Holmium 164.93	68 **Er** Erbium 167.26	69 **Tm** Thulium 168.93	70 **Yb** Ytterbium 173.04	71 **Lu** Lutetium 174.97
96 **Cm** Curium (247)	97 **Bk** Berkelium (247)	98 **Cf** Californium (249)	99 **Es** Einsteinium (254)	100 **Fm** Fermium (253)	101 **Md** Mendelevium (256)	102 **No** Nobelium (254)	103 **Lr** Lawrencium (257)

* Names for these elements have not yet been agreed upon.

Appendix C: Weights and Measures

Metric Conversion Tables

	When You Know	Multiply by	To Find This OR When You Know This	Multiply by	To Find
Length	inches (in.)	2.540	centimeters (cm)	0.394	inches
	feet (ft)	0.3048	meters (m)	3.281	feet
	yards (yd)	0.914	meters (m)	1.0936	yards
	miles (mi)	1.609	kilometers (km)	0.621	miles
	feet (ft)	30.480	centimeters (cm)	0.0328	feet
Area	square inches (in.^{2})	6.542	square centimeters (cm^2)	0.155	square inches
	square feet (ft^2)	0.093	square meters (m^2)	10.76	square feet
	square yards (yd^2)	0.836	square meters (m^2)	1.196	square yards
	acres (a)	0.405	hectares (ha)	2.471	acres
	square miles (mi^2)	2.590	square kilometers (km^2)	0.386	square miles
Capacity and Volume	fluid ounces (fl oz)	29.574	milliliters (mL)	0.034	fluid ounces
	pints (pt)	0.473	liters (L)	2.113	pints
	quarts (qt)	0.946	liters (L)	1.057	quarts
	gallons (gal)	3.785	liters (L)	0.264	gallons
	cubic inches (in.^{3})	16.387	cubic centimeters (cm^3)	0.061	cubic inches
	cubic feet (ft^3)	0.028	cubic meters (m^3)	35.315	cubic feet
	cubic yards (yd^3)	0.765	cubic meters (m^3)	1.310	cubic yards
Weight and Mass	ounces (oz)	28.350	grams (g)	0.035	ounces
	pounds (lb)	0.454	kilograms (kg)	2.205	pounds
	short tons (t)	0.907	metric tons (t)	1.102	short tons

Temperature	When You Know	Then	To Find
	degrees Fahrenheit (°F)	subtract 32; then divide by 1.8	degrees Celsius (°C)
	degrees Celsius (°C)	multiply by 1.8; then add 32	degrees Fahrenheit (°F)

Metric Equivalents

Unit	Equivalents
kilometer	1 km = 1,000 m
meter	1 m = 100 cm
centimeter	1 cm = 10 mm
liter	1 L = 1,000 mL
milliliter	1 mL = 0.001 L
tonne	1 t = 1,000 kg
kilogram	1 kg = 1,000 g
gram	1 g = 1,000 mg
centigram	1 cg = 10 mg
milligram	1 mg = 0.001 g

English Equivalents

Unit	Equivalents
foot	1 ft = 12 in.
yard	1 yd = 3 ft
mile	1 mi = 5,280 ft
square foot	1 sq ft = 144 in.^{2}
square yard	1 sq yd = 9 ft^2
square mile	1 sq mi = 640 a
cubic foot	1 cu ft = 1,728 in.^{3}
cubic yard	1 cu yd = 27 ft^3
pint	1 pt = 16 oz
quart	1 qt = 2 pt
gallon	1 gal = 4 qt
pound	1 lb = 16 oz
short ton	1 short ton = 2,000 lb

Common Metric Prefixes

Prefix	Meaning
micro-	0.000001, or 1/1,000,000
milli-	0.001, or 1/1,000
centi-	0.01, or 1/100
deci-	0.1, or 1/10
deka-	10
hecto-	100
kilo-	1,000
mega-	1,000,000

Appendix D: Vitamins

Vitamins Used by the Body

Vitamin	Used For	Main Sources	Recommended Dietary Allowance (RDA) per Day for Teenagers	
			Females	Males
A	Normal sight; healthy bones, teeth, and skin; maintaining lining of lungs and intestines	Eggs; liver; yellow, orange, red, and dark green vegetables; orange and red fruits	800 micrograms	1,000 micrograms
B$_1$ (thiamin)	Releasing energy from foods; breaking down carbohydrates; healthy heart and nervous system	Pork, grains, beans, nuts, yeast	1.1 mg	1.5 mg
B$_2$ (riboflavin)	Helping cells use oxygen; repairing tissue; healthy skin	Dairy products, eggs, green vegetables, enriched grains, liver	1.3 mg	1.8 mg
B$_3$ (niacin)	Releasing energy; healthy skin; helping cells function	Lean meat; liver; dairy products; peas, beans, and lentils; grains; fish; leafy, green vegetables; yeast	15 mg	20 mg
B$_6$ (pyrodoxine)	Breaking down proteins, fats, and carbohydrates	Pork, poultry, fish, bananas, grains	1.5 mg	2.0 mg
B$_{12}$	Healthy nervous system; forming red blood cells	Meats, clams and oysters, eggs, fermented cheeses, liver	2.0 micrograms	2.0 micrograms
Biotin	Releasing energy; healthy skin	Liver; meats; fish; eggs; peas, beans, and lentils; bananas; melons	25 micrograms*	25 micrograms*
Folic acid	Forming red blood cells; healthy skin	Many vegetables; fortified cereals and breads; peas, beans, and lentils; citrus fruits	180 micrograms	200 micrograms
Pantothenic acid	Releasing energy	Liver; meats; fish; shellfish; eggs; chicken; grains; sweet potatoes; mushrooms; peas, beans, and lentils	5 mg*	5 mg*
C	Bone, tooth, and tissue growth; healing wounds	Citrus fruits; berries; melons; mangoes; tomatoes; potatoes; green peppers; green, leafy vegetables	60 mg	60 mg
D	Bone repair and growth; helping the body use calcium and phosphorus	Fortified dairy products, fatty fish	5 micrograms*	5 micrograms*
E	Healthy cell membranes; preventing the formation of cell-damaging substances	Vegetable and seed oils, sunflower seeds, nuts, grains, wheat germ	8 mg	10 mg
K	Blood clotting	Dark green vegetables; kiwi fruit; cabbage; liver; soybean, canola, and olive oils; liver; fermented soy foods	55 micrograms	65 micrograms

*Estimated Safe and Adequate Dietary Intake or Estimated Minimum Requirement. RDAs for these vitamins are not established.

Appendix E: Minerals

Important Minerals Used by the Body

Mineral	Used For	Main Sources	Recommended Dietary Allowance (RDA) per Day for Teenagers	
			Females	Males
Calcium	Bone and tooth growth; blood clotting	Dairy products	1,300 mg[1]	1,300 mg[1]
Copper	Healthy red blood cells	Nuts; shellfish; liver; peas, beans, and lentils; grains; cocoa	1.5–3.0 mg[1]	1.5–3.0 mg[1]
Fluorine	Tooth strength; preventing tooth decay	Fluoridated drinking water, fluoridated toothpaste	2.9 mg[1]	3.2 mg[1]
Iodine	Controlling speed of energy use in body	Iodized salt	150 micrograms	150 micrograms
Iron	Forming red blood cells and tissues	Grains; meats; poultry; fish; vegetables; peas, beans, and lentils; nuts; soy	15 mg	12 mg
Magnesium	Nerve, immune system, and muscle functions; releasing energy	Peas, beans, and lentils; grains; nuts; dark green vegetables; cocoa	360 mg[1]	410 mg[1]
Phosphorus	Healthy teeth and bones; nerve and muscle functions	Dairy products; meats; eggs; peas, beans, and lentils; eggs	1,250 mg	1,250 mg
Potassium	Nerve and muscle functions; fluid balance in and around cells	Green, leafy vegetables; bananas; oranges; tomatoes; meats; grains	2,000 mg[1]	2,000 mg[1]
Selenium	Preventing the formation of cell-damaging substances	Meats, fish, grains, Brazil nuts	50 micrograms	50 micrograms
Sodium	Maintaining water balance between cells, healthy blood pressure, and proper chemical balance in body; healthy nerve function	Processed foods, table salt	2,400 mg	2,400 mg
Zinc	Normal senses of taste and smell; healing wounds	Meats, shellfish	12 mg	15 mg

[1]Estimated Safe and Adequate Dietary Intake, Dietary Reference Intake, or Estimated Minimum Requirement. RDAs for these minerals are not established.

Index

A

Abdomen, 82
Acquired immune deficiency syndrome (AIDS), 173
Activity Pyramid, 165
Adaptation, 79
Addiction, 178
Age of Invertebrates and Marine Life, 383
Age of Reptiles, 383
AIDS (acquired immune deficiency syndrome), 11, 173
Air. See also *Atmosphere*
   on the move, 362–364
   properties of, 349–351
   and water, 353–355
Air mass, 361, 362–364
Air pressure, 345, 349
Air sacs, 159
Alchemists, 206
Algae, 63, 67, 191, 401
Alligators, 87
Amphibians, 75, 85–86
Amplitude, 263, 269, 270
Animal Kingdom
   invertebrates, 75, 79–83, 91
   lab activity, 90
   special cells and their jobs, 77–78
   vertebrates, 75, 84–89, 91
Animals, 76
   breeding, 116
   cells of, 55, 76–78
   cloning, 117
   description and examples, 65
Antennae, 82, 83
Anti-A serum, 29
Anti-B serum, 29
Antibacterial agents, 71
Anus, 80, 81, 157
Appalachian Mountains, 383
Appendage, 75, 82
Area, 17, 22, 438
Aristotle, 6, 66
Armstrong, Neil, 416
Artery, 155, 161

Arthropod, 75, 82–83
Artificial skin, 20
Asexual reproduction, 41
Asteroid, 407, 414–415
Astronomy, 407, 408
Atmosphere, 345, 346–348. See also *Air*
Atomic clock, 24
Atoms, 3, 5, 51–52
   and electricity, 282–283
   and elements, 51
   structure of, 206–207
Atria, 160
Axis, 313, 319
Axle. See *Wheel and axle*

B

Babies, 148–149
Bacterium, 55, 63, 68, 71
   causing disease, 71, 83, 170
   in discovery of penicillin, 27
   new kingdom for, 64
   in producing insulin, 114
   size of, 55
   skin protecting against, 143
   using electricity to kill, 179
   white blood cells fighting, 162, 171
   in your home, 71
Banneker, Benjamin, 371
Bar codes, 277
Barometer, 345, 349
Bats, 34, 126
Battery, 281, 286–287
Beams, 270
Bees, 102
Bicycles, 221, 254
Biologist, 63, 64
Biology, 35, 36. See also *Life science*
Birds, 88
Black Death, 170
Blackpoll warbler, 88
Blind, system of reading for, 9
Blood, 161, 162
Blood typing, 29

Acknowledgments

Illustration: MacArt Design. **Photo Research:** Nicholas Communications, Inc. **Photography:** H. Bluestein, Photo Researchers, Inc. 1; Telegraph Colour Library, FPG International 2; Clark University Archives/Goddard Library 7; Index Stock Photography, Inc. 8; Photo Researchers, Inc. 9; National Science Foundation 10; Tom Tracy, The Stock Market 16; courtesy of Organogenisis, Inc. 20; Dennie Cody, FPG International 22; Geoffrey Wheeler, National Institute of Standards 24; Andrew Fleming, Corbis 27; Index Stock Photography, Inc. 29; John Warden, Tony Stone Images 33; Merlin Tuttle, courtesy of Bat Conservation International 34; Tony Hallas/Science Photo Library, Photo Researchers, Inc. 38; Jack Grove, PhotoEdit 39; Kevin Schafer, Tony Stone Images 42; Patti Murray, Animals Animals/Earth Scenes 45; Breck P. Kent, Earth Scenes 48; courtesy of W. L. Gore & Associates 52; Livermore Laboratories 56; Andrew J. Martinez, Photo Researchers, Inc. 57; David Young-Wolff, PhotoEdit 59 (T); Parviz M. Pour, Photo Researchers, Inc. 59 (C); Parviz M. Pour, Photo Researchers, Inc. 59 (B); Tom McHugh/Steinhart Aquarium, Photo Researchers, Inc. 62; Museo Nazionale Napoli, Art Resource 66 (T); Jonathon Scott, Masterfile 66 (B); Eric Gravé, Photo Researchers, Inc. 67; Planet Earth Pictures, FPG International 69; P. Parks, Animals Animals/Earth Scenes 70; Gerard Lacz, Animals Animals/Earth Scenes 74; Eric Gravé, Photo Researchers, Inc. 77 (TL); Quest/Science Photo Library, Photo Researchers, Inc. 77 (TR); Biophoto Associates, Photo Researchers, Inc. 77 (B); Jim Zipp, Photo Researchers, Inc. 78; Andrew J. Martinez, Photo Researchers, Inc. 80; Fred Winner, Photo Researchers, Inc. 81; Scott Camazine, Photo Researchers, Inc. 83; Herbert Schwind, Photo Researchers, Inc. 85 (T); James P. Rowan 85; Marian Bacon, Animals Animals/Earth Scenes 86; Joe McDonald, Animals Animals/Earth Scenes 87; Breck P. Kent, Animals Animals/Earth Scenes 88; Tom McHugh, Photo Researchers, Inc. 89; Aaron Haupt, Photo Researchers, Inc. 91; P. Dayanandan, Photo Researchers, Inc. 94; Andrew Syred/Science Photo Library, Photo Researchers, Inc. 99; Joel Sartore 100; Earl Roberge, Photo Researchers, Inc. 105; American Images, Inc., FPG International 108; Corbis 111; Phil Cantor, SuperStock 114; David M. Phillips/Science Source, Photo Researchers, Inc. 115; AP/Wide World Photos 117; Jerry Cooke, Animals Animals 119; Tom McHugh, Photo Researchers, Inc. 122; Ramey, Unicorn Stock Photos 124; Breck P. Kent, Earth Scenes 125; Julia Cameron, Corbis 128; Scott W. Smith, Earth Scenes 131; Tony Freeman, PhotoEdit 133; Witte/Mahaney, Tony Stone Images 137; V. Palmisano, Tony Stone Images 138; Corbis Digital Stock 149; VCG, FPG International 151; David Young-Wolff, PhotoEdit 154; AP/Wide World Photos 163; David Young-Wolff, PhotoEdit 168; Dr. Kari Lounatmaa/Science Photo Library, Photo Researchers, Inc. 171; Biozentrum, University of Basel/Science Photo Library, Photo Researchers, Inc. 172; American Cancer Society 178 (L, R); Titan Scan 179; Planet Earth Pictures, FPG International 184; Patti Murray, Earth Scenes 189; courtesy of Acura 195; Chris Mooney, FPG International 201; Smithsonian Institution 202; courtesy of IBM Corporation, Research Division, Almaden Research Center 207; David R. Frazier Photolibrary; John M. Roberts, The Stock Market 216; Zefa, The Stock Market 221(T); Jeff Greenberg, PhotoEdit 221 (B); Mark C. Burnett, Photo Researchers, Inc. 222; courtesy of DuPont Fluroproducts 225; Tony Freeman, PhotoEdit 227 (T); David Young-Wolff, PhotoEdit 227 (B); Gerard Vandystadt, Photo Researchers, Inc. 230; David Young-Wolff, PhotoEdit 235 (T); Gerard Vandystadt, Photo Researchers, Inc. 235 (B); Bill Aron, PhotoEdit 236; Sheila Terry, Photo Researchers, Inc. 238 (C); BMW of North America, Inc. 238 (B); courtesy of Univeral Studios 239; Larry Grant, FPG International 241; Tony Freeman, PhotoEdit 244; Smithsonian Institution 248; Telegraph Colour Library, FPG International 253; Davis Barber, PhotoEdit 254; Tom Tracy, Tony Stone Images 255; Christian Michaels, FPG International 261; Bill Aron, PhotoEdit 262; National Geographic Society 275; Jeff Zaruba, Tony Stone Images 277; Telegraph Colour Library, FPG International 280; Corbis 285; Joel Benard, Masterfile 286; PhotoDisc, Inc. 289; Adrienne Hart-Davis/Science Photo Library, Photo Researchers, Inc. 290; Index Stock Imagery 293; Glen Allison, Tony Stone Images 296; courtesy of GM Media Archive 299; Telegraph Colour Library, FPG International 302; Calvin Larsen, Photo Researchers, Inc. 303; Lester Lefkowitz, The Stock Market 304; Warren Gretz, Photo Researchers, Inc. 305; Mark Richards, PhotoEdit 307; Earth Satellite Corporation 311; NASA/K. Horgan, Tony Stone Images 312; Grand Canyon Railway 323; David Weintraub, Photo Researchers, Inc. 328; James Balog, Tony Stone Images 333; Alinari, Art Resource 335; Marilyn "Angel" Wynn 336; Junebug Clark, Photo Researchers, Inc. 337 (T); Blaine Harrington III, The Stock Market 337 (B); Ben Johnson/Science Photo Library, Photo Researchers, Inc. 338 (TL); Geoff Tompkinson/Science Photo Library, Photo Researchers, Inc. 338 (TR); E. R. Degginger, Earth Scenes 338 (BL); E. R. Degginger, Earth Scenes 338 (BR); C. C. Lockwood, Earth Scenes 339; Bob Daemmrich Photo, Inc. 341; Planet Earth Pictures, FPG International 344; Eastcott/ Momatiuk, Tony Stone Images 354 (L); Fred Whitehead, Earth Scenes 354 (R); Michael Giannechini, Photo Researchers, Inc. 355 (T); National Center for Atmospheric Research 355 (B); Paul & Lindamarie Ambrose, FPG International 360; Eliot Cohen 364; Ed Collacott, Tony Stone Images 365; Photo Researchers, Inc. 367; David J. Sams, Tony Stone Images 368; Corbis/Bettman-UPI 371; Bob Daemmrich Photo, Inc. 373; Jon Eisberg, FPG International 377; Donovan Reese, Tony Stone Images 378; Mark S. Twickler, Glacier Research Group 381; David Dennis, Earth Scenes 383; Kenneth Fink, Photo Researchers, Inc. 384; John Reader/Science Photo Library, Photo Researchers, Inc. 385; Anne Wertheim, Earth Scenes 390; Steve Fitzpatrick, Masterfile 397; National Oceanic and Atmospheric Administration 398; J. Frederick Grassle, Wood's Hole Oceanographic Institute 400; Shane Moore, Earth Scenes 401; Chris/Donna McLaughlin, The Stock Market 403; NASA 406; NASA 409; NASA/Mark Martan, Photo Researchers, Inc. 410; NASA 412 (T); A. S. P./ Science Source, Photo Researchers, Inc. 412 (C); NASA 412 (B); NASA 413 (T); NASA 413 (C); NASA 413 (B); NASA 414 (T); NASA 414 (C); NASA 414 (B); Pekka Parviainen/Science Photo Library, Photo Researchers, Inc. 415 (T); Breck P. Kent, Earth Scenes 415 (B); PhotoDisc 417 (T); NASA 417 (B); NASA 419. **Cover:** Wave: The Stock Market; Moon: Jake Rajs, Photonica; Butterfly: Lee F. Snyder/Photo Researchers, Inc.; Roller Coaster: Charles V. Angelo/Photo Researchers, Inc.; Microscope: Artville; Fern: Charles Krebs, Tony Stone.